Annie Maria Barnes

Children of the Kalahari, A Story of Africa

A Story of Africa

Annie Maria Barnes

Children of the Kalahari, A Story of Africa
A Story of Africa

ISBN/EAN: 9783744756587

Printed in Europe, USA, Canada, Australia, Japan

Cover: Foto ©Andreas Hilbeck / pixelio.de

More available books at **www.hansebooks.com**

An Anxious Conference. Page 34.

OF

THE KALAHARI:

A STORY OF AFRICA.

BY
ANNIE MARIA BARNES.

———•———

PHILADELPHIA:
PRESBYTERIAN BOARD OF PUBLICATION
AND SABBATH-SCHOOL WORK,
No. 1334 CHESTNUT STREET.

PREFACE.

No country has been so much written about, especially of late years, as Africa, yet no country, perhaps, is so little known as it really appears. Beyond the missionary journals of Robert Moffat, David Livingstone, the Rev. Mr. Wilson, Bishop Taylor and a few others, and the personal narratives of Captains Grant and Speke, Messrs. John Charles Anderson and Henry M. Stanley, very little has been written that deals accurately with the inner life of the people—their domestic, social and moral condition, their superstitious practices, their present religious status under the fast-spreading influence of the gospel; or of the country itself—its wonderful phenomena, its physical changes, its varied and beautiful flora, its trees, birds and animals.

In the present volume there is scarcely an incident, a description or an adventure that has not its counterpart in the writings of Moffat, Livingstone, Anderson or some other reliable author; indeed, in a few instances their identical words have been used. At the same time, such liberties have been taken as are warranted by an author's natural right. For example, the cave "Lepelole," which was at Dr. Livingstone's old mission-station of Kolobeng in Sechele's country, is placed more than two hundred miles farther north in the Bamangwato country, and the name is also bestowed upon that station where our children of the Kalahari are first introduced. With the exception of giving the mountains to the north and east of the mission-station the name of Mashona—simply because a tribe of that name lived in that direction, and because no other name appeared on the map—the other geographical situations are as accurate as a close study of Dr. Livingstone's map could make them.

CHILDREN OF THE KALAHARI.

CHAPTER I.

"The earth is the Lord's."

IT is early morning at the mission-station of Lepelole, country of the Bamangwato, Southern Africa. The village itself occupies the broad and somewhat level summit of a hill, at the base of which winds the Shashane River, one of the many branches of the vigorous Limpopo. Tall, stately trees, that grow in rich clusters here and there, throw their grateful shade about the doors of the quaint dome-shaped huts arranged in regular lines across the brow of the hill, with a broad, cleanly-kept street directly through the centre and other shorter and narrower ones intersecting it at intervals.

Around each hut there is a small patch of garden, in which are growing yams, maize, pumpkins, sweet potatoes, squashes, even beans and peas, and all in a pleasing state of cultivation. These little gardens are fenced in by palisades formed of stout upright poles interwoven with wisps of the strong and durable tiger-grass. In the corners of the enclosures an occasional castor-oil plant rears its not unattractive head, while every now and then close to the walls of a hut a tall, beautiful banana-shrub shoots its slender, delicate crest high in air.

Some of these huts—that is, the more pretentious of them, those of the chief, his family, and of the head-men of the village—are built of boards rudely sawn from the forest; but the majority of them are of poles closely and ingeniously covered over with thick grass. Those built of boards have square walls and circular roofs, but all the others preserve their dome-shaped form throughout.

In the centre of the village and fronting on two sides of the broad street, which here makes a curve around it, is the kotla, or place of public assembly, a somewhat imposing structure fully seventy-five feet square, and built upon upright posts with cross-beams closely thatched with straw. At each corner grows a magnificent banian tree, which makes a pleasant shade all about it.

Near the kotla and facing one of the side streets stand the church and school-house of the station, and some one hundred and fifty or two hundred yards farther on, and higher up the slope of the hill, is the residence of the missionary.

As the deep gray mists of coming dawn have begun to wrap themselves like fitful curtains about the still sleeping station there is no sight nor sound of life. Not even a stray dog is seen wandering through the streets nor an early hunter eager to be away after the tempting game. But as the first beams of the rising sun begin to color with a rich warm crimson the far-away summits of the Mashona Mountains, and a little later to tinge them with a purple royal in its splendor, there are the stir and pulse of awakening life all about the brow of the hill that sweeps so serenely down to meet the flow of the noiselessly moving river. Directly the mist-curtains have all disappeared, except in the valleys and along the river's line, and over the tops of the dome-shaped huts and down into the yards, where the glad vegetation lifts itself in joyous salutation, come the dancing sunbeams, and along the broad streets, where the tall cocoa-palms nod gracefully to and fro.

One by one forms appear in the open doorways. Children are seen here and there under the trees. A row of figures with stone pitchers upon their heads are betaking themselves along the broad street to the public well or to the spring as their inclinations direct. Others, again, in rear of the huts are stooping above mounds not unlike ant-hills in shape. Soon there is about each the bright glow of fire and the sound of simmering in an oven set back into the mound. Next a blaze is kindled between some upright stones near at hand, over which a rude pot, that emits a savory smell as the contents become more and more under the influence of the fire beneath, is set to boil.

In the midst of these proceedings the loud blast of a horn, followed by the furious beating of a drum in the direction of the kotla, gives the crowning impetus to the bustling activity of the scene. Tall forms start up here and there, children come scampering from every direction, old men move slowly along, younger ones shove each other in their haste, all seeming to have the same purpose in view—to reach the rear of the huts in the quickest possible time.

With these movements alone to guide him, outside the appetizing odors now arising from all parts of the station, it would not take long for even the most careless observer to understand that the blare of the horn and the roll of the drum were the Lepelole summons to breakfast.

The men are served first, from both the oven and the pot, in wooden bowls, in each of which is a rudely-carved wooden spoon. The children patiently or impatiently await their turn, according as their dispositions may be or as their home manners have received attention.

The breakfast consists of rhinoceros meat, which the industrious hunters of the day before have provided, a porridge of Indian meal into which the gravy has been mixed, and potatoes roasted in the ashes. But in whatever manner each little black pickaninny awaits his breakfast, they are all careful to receive it in identically the same fashion; that is, with but one hand outstretched. To receive the bowl with two would be altogether the very worst evidence of bad manners and not at all in keeping with the strict forms laid down in the Lepelole code of juvenile training. That they may eat it afterward either with one hand or two plunged into the gravy-stirred porridge, and serving as the mode of conveyance to the mouth, matters not, so that only one hand is outstretched in receiving.

Three-quarters of an hour later another blare of the horn and deep roll of the drum summon to prayers all the Lepelole Bamangwatos, large and small.

The morning services are held at the kotla, toward which structure men, women and children are now seen hurrying, until soon nearly all the straw mats near the centre are well covered with squatting figures. The missionary's voice is deep and earnest as he reads the lesson from the Psalms:

"The earth is the Lord's, and the fullness thereof, the world and they that dwell therein."

The psalm is rendered in the native language, as is also the short exhortation that follows; then clear and strong the words of the morning hymn ring forth, sung by full three hundred voices:

> "Eternal Wisdom! thee we praise;
> Thee let creation sing."

While the breakfast-scene of the camp is at its height a young girl is coming slowly across a grassy "veldt" some two miles away, riding a donkey. The girl is apparently about fifteen years of age, with a slender yet strongly knit figure. At present, however, she seems quite to have lost herself, and is sitting very loosely and carelessly, with her shoulders bent forward and her eyes upon the ground. The reins have dropped from her fingers and are lying loosely upon the neck of the donkey—a circumstance that, if he were not the most conscientious and self-respecting of donkeys, would permit of his easily following the bent of his own sweet will. But there is that in his eyes which if you could see would actually shame you for having such suspicions of him. It says very plainly that he wishes it understood that he is far too gentlemanly a donkey to take the least advantage of loose reins or of an absent-minded girl, although the grass of the "veldt" *is* most tempting.

The sudden sharp crack of a rifle some little distance in advance startles the girl at once into an attitude of attention, but altogether fails to have a like effect upon the grave and dignified donkey, who has evidently been on the lookout for something of the kind all along. If it *had* aroused him into a sudden exhibition of heels, the young girl in her loose and careless pose would certainly have gone flying over his head.

"That must be Captain Murray on a morning hunt," she says half aloud as she raises her head and glances about her.

It is not what could be called a pretty face that is thus exposed to view, but it certainly is a most interesting and attractive one, and its many good points would not fail to grow upon the observer. A large, high forehead—almost too large and high, some might think, for the other delicately outlined features—and very dark and thoughtful brown eyes arched by soft but strongly-drawn lashes, are the more prominent characteristics of the face. The mouth is rather large, but not unbeautiful, for the lips are deep scarlet and the teeth white, and, though irregular in shape, are yet faultlessly kept. The nose has a decided tendency to turn up, giving to the face an archness and piquancy sometimes quite at variance with its thoughtful expression. The hair is a dark brown and inclined to curl, especially about the forehead, where it now lies in disordered rings.

Having satisfied herself that there is nothing in the crack of the rifle to alarm her, and that it is indeed but a morning salute to the birds on the part of her uncle's hunter-friend, Captain Murray, and after calling the donkey a dear old fellow and urging him forward—an altogether unnecessary proceeding, he thinks, and one he feels strongly tempted to resent—Hope Blandford once more falls into her musing attitude.

Perhaps ten minutes more are passed in this way, when she is again aroused from her reverie, this time by the sudden stopping of the donkey. For the last few minutes donkey and rider have been gradually bearing toward the cup-shaped hill previously referred to, until now they are directly at its base and facing a well-worn path that leads to its summit.

"What is the matter, now, Chumah?" the young girl asks quickly of the donkey as she shakes the lines playfully about his neck. "What has gone wrong with Your Lordship?"

At the words he turns his head slowly and gives her what approaches as near to an indignant glance as his mild eyes are capable of bestowing. It says as plainly as donkey language can express it, "Well, if you don't know and can't see, it isn't for me to tell you."

As though she reads every word of this in the wide, deep eyes, Hope quickly raises her head and glances about her.

"The Wizard's Cup!" she cries, preparing to dismount, "and I wasn't even thinking of it! Oh, you dear, knowing old darling!" throwing her arms about the donkey's neck, for she is now standing on the ground, "to remember so well how much I enjoy the climb to the top and the glorious view from there! To think that in my abstraction I would have passed it by! Rogue, give me hold of your nose and let me have a kiss, for of all the donkeys in the world I do believe you are the most knowing."

Chumah raises his muzzle as though he understands every word, and permits her to fondle it, still with the same grave and dignified bearing; but there is a look in his eyes which says plainly that His Lordship, Chumah, is well pleased indeed.

"And now come along. You know that I like best to climb up the hill for sake of the exercise, but that is no reason why you shouldn't come too, is it, you rogue? Do you know now," shaking her finger very slowly and gravely at him, "that I somehow think you rather enjoy more than is necessary this part of our morning frolic, my going up the hill and leading you after me? It looks very much as if the order of things was being reversed, and that I am carrying you instead of you carrying me, does it not? Oh, you needn't flap those great ears of yours and blink your eyes so innocently, for I know very well it is so."

A few minutes of steady climbing and the summit is reached. Between two trees a rude seat is placed, and, the greater part of the brush covering this portion of the hill having been cleared away, there is an almost unobstructed view in every direction. The sun is now a full hour's journey in the heavens, and, though a few trailing skirts of mist still stir along the lower valleys, the summits of the neighboring hills are all aglow with radiance. Below are the gleaming waters of the river winding in and out among the glittering green tangles of bush and fern. On each side stretch the grassy "veldts," their waving expanses gemmed with brilliant wild flowers and here and there stirred into vigorous life by the cattle that graze upon them. In the direction of the mission-station, and lying in a valley that here follows the trend of the river, are the tobacco and sugar-cane plantations of the natives. To the right there are dense patches of lofty forest that seem to ring in the rich and undulating grass-lands and to serve as a barrier to the farther wanderings of the more restless of the animals. Here and there between the dense portions of the forest and the fertile stretches of the "veldt" are dotted clusters of stately palms, their long fronds stirring gracefully in the morning breeze. Far away against the horizon the bold crests of the Moshana Mountains seem piercing the very blue of heaven, their bases in part still enwrapped by the morning mists that scatter to right and left before the resolute advances of the sun. The summits, having already caught the full effulgence of the rays, are glowing like living pyramids of light.

"Oh!" exclaims the young girl reverently as she pushes back the broad straw hat from her brow and stands with clasped hands and a rapt expression upon her face, "how good is God! and how beautiful the world he has made!"

"Do you really think that, Miss Hope?" a voice near her asks suddenly.

"Oh, Captain Murray," she says as she turns and beholds the brown bearded face of her uncle's hunter-friend, "how can you put such a question to me?"

The next moment she blushes deeply at her own earnestness.

"It came quite naturally," he replies. " This bit of God's world is beautiful enough to call forth enthusiasm, I will admit. But you spoke of the world in general. If you could see some of the ugly spots I have seen, you would not think it on a whole so beautiful."

"That is all in God's wise plan," she says slowly. " If he had made it too beautiful, too attractive throughout, we should not want to leave it for the other beyond."

"And do you believe the other beyond is even more beautiful than this?" with a sweep of the hand that takes in all the fair, sweet scene.

"Infinitely more so," she answers promptly. "Oh, Captain Murray, the eyes of earth have never seen anything to equal the beauties of that wondrous city."

A silence falls between them. Captain Murray's fine brown eyes take on a softer light. Perhaps it is a reflection from the serene radiance of the sky, or it may be, after all, that it is Hope's words that have brought the change.

"Do you come here often, Miss Hope?" he questions, at length, as he follows the movement she has made toward the plank seat between the trees.

"Oh yes, almost every morning when the weather is fine. I usually go for a ride of two or three miles across the veldt before breakfast, and stop here on my return. Chumah has so learned my ways that this morning, when in a fit of abstraction I was about to pass it by, he suddenly recalled me to myself by a decided stand in front of the path leading to the summit."

"Chumah is the name of the donkey, then?" Captain Murray asks with a look in Chumah's direction. "I had noticed that you and your cousin had donkeys very much alike, but I did not know the name of either."

"I call mine Chumah, and Ellie calls hers Susi. They are named for the two noble fellows who headed the expedition that bore the body of Dr. Livingstone half across Africa."

"That was truly a peerless deed," Captain Murray comments, "and I do not wonder at your enthusiasm. I hope the donkeys do credit to the names."

"Indeed they do! You could not find steadier or more dignified creatures anywhere, and they are both knowing and precious old darlings. Why, do you know that I sometimes think Chumah can actually talk. At least, he talks with his eyes just as plainly as I do with my lips. There! he is saying now, 'I think this conference has lasted long enough, and we had better be going, or we sha'n't get a bit of breakfast.'"

At these words and the look directed toward him Chumah gives his great eyes a blink and his long ears a twitch.

"They are both fine fellows, to be sure," Captain Murray says again in allusion to the donkeys as he walks beside Hope down the hill. "I have noticed before that they were unusually fine animals for this part of the country, and have often wondered where your uncle obtained them."

"They were presented to Uncle Clement by Sechele, chief of the Bakwains. Sechele was a great favorite with Dr. Livingstone, who was the first missionary to his people, and through whom Sechele was converted. Livingstone lived for many years with him at his old village of Kolobeng. One of the doctor's little children is buried there, and I have heard my uncle say that Livingstone always had a peculiar tenderness for the spot and an unusually warm regard for Sechele. On the doctor's second return from England he left two fine donkeys at the Cape for Sechele, and these are of the same stock."

"Are you not afraid, Miss Hope, even with so faithful and sagacious a companion as Chumah, to take these early morning rides alone?" Captain Murray questions as at the foot of the hill he stops to assist her to mount.

"Oh no, not at all," is the quick reply. "Why should I be? But I do not always take them alone, as you seem to think. Sometimes both Ellie and Retta come with me, and again one of the boys. However, since my aunt's death, a year ago," her voice dropping into a tone of peculiar sadness, "poor Ellie has so much to see after about the house and elsewhere, besides taking care of the baby Louise, that she has had almost entirely to give up her rides of late, except in the afternoons. Last evening the boys went away with some of the men of the village on a hunting-expedition, Retta was not feeling well, and so I had to come alone. But, Captain Murray, suppose I do ride by myself what danger could there be when I have been here for six years and every native for ten miles around knows me by sight? If it is the wild beasts you fear, why they have all been frightened away from the vicinity of the village by this time."

"Oh, no danger from them, certainly, nor from the natives of the neighborhood, either, I feel assured," Captain Murray rejoins quickly. "But you forget the threatening attitude the Matabele have assumed of late. Those grim Zulus know no mercy when once they start upon the war-path. Then on the other side of us are the Boers. They are even worse than the Matabele, for they seem to have neither a sense of justice nor a principle of honor, while you occasionally will find a Zulu with both, our grim and upright old Inkoosi, for instance, and your uncle's faithful Mazika. If the Boers and the Matabele did nothing more than make you a captive just to harass your uncle, it surely would be a most unpleasant state of affairs. You know what threatening messages both have been sending him of late?"

"Yes, Mosilikatse, the Matabele chief, hates Bubi, and the Boers hate my uncle, and between the two of them, though they are really each other's enemy at heart, they will unite in any mean thing not only to torment the chief and uncle, but to injure them as well. In short, I don't believe they would hesitate an instant to sweep the whole mission-station of Lepelole out of existence; that is, if they could get the opportunity. The Boers are great cowards, as you know, and I don't believe they will openly molest my uncle, for fear of the indignation it will arouse abroad and the almost certain retaliation. As to the Matabele, they stand too much in awe of Bubi and the cannon he has planted upon the hill. Bubi has been a great fighter in his day, and has before completely routed the Matabele in an attack made upon him. They know well what he is when aroused."

"Well, he is a fine old warrior, to be sure, and looks every inch a soldier in that brass-buttoned scarlet coat the officers from the Cape have sent him; and his men are nearly all bold, high-spirited fellows, who wouldn't hesitate a moment, I feel sure, to charge the most formidable line of Zulus that could be formed, though they do seem so quiet and peaceful in every-day life."

"And to think that twelve years ago they were dirty, ignorant creatures, so debased in many things that they were scarce raised above the beasts of the forest!"

"A striking illustration, truly, of the power of the gospel of Christ Jesus when proclaimed by one earnest, consistent man," Captain Murray says with fervor.

They have now reached the main entrance of the mission-station, and as his eyes take in the somewhat imposing appearance of the church and school-house, the neat, well-arranged huts, the blooming gardens, the broad, clean-swept streets—further, as he notes the air of prosperity and happiness everywhere visible—words of appreciation escape Captain Murray's lips, followed the next moment by an unconscious sigh, as though of some dim foreboding.

"This is indeed a pleasant picture to look upon," he exclaims with deep feeling, "and it would be terrible to think of its being swept out of existence by the fierce Matabele or yet by the more cowardly and treacherous Boers. Yet I really do not think that either the Matabele or the Boers will dare put their threats in execution," he says by way of assurance as he notes the girl's troubled face. "Still, I feel that I would like to stay some weeks longer, at least until it can be definitely ascertained just what the situation is."

"And can you not?" she says somewhat entreatingly.

"I am afraid not, Miss Hope. My friend Cumming and I have long promised Captains Osgood and Saunders of the Cape to join them in a hunting-expedition to the Zambesi. They will be along next week, with their Makololo guide and company of Kaffirs. Cumming, Inkoosi, the Hottentot Chaka and I will join them here."

"Are you not afraid to go so far into the wilds? I have heard that some of the natives between this and the Zambezi are hostile and treacherous."

"So they are, Miss Hope, in many respects. But do you know that ever since Livingstone journeyed and preached among them, teaching them the peace on earth and good-will to men of the Christian religion, as well as exemplifying in his own blameless life the beauties of an honest and generous manhood, none of us hunters, who intend being perfectly straightforward with the natives, fear to go among them, especially when we use the name of Livingstone. It is indeed a magic word and has many times saved from death. A friend of mine, who has just been up in the Makonde country, told me of a very critical position in which the quick use of the name of this matchless man snatched him and his comrades from instant death. A fierce chief and his band had rushed upon them when, having come from a bath in the river, they were without weapon of any kind. The axes of the savages were raised to slay, when my friend noticed the right shoulder and sleeve and part of the skirt of a white man's coat adorning the body of the chief.

"'Hold!' cried my friend—'a white man's coat!

Where did you get it? It surely must be Livingstone's, for no other white man has ever been in these parts.'

"At the word 'Livingstone' the chief instantly lowered his axe, and his men followed his example.

"'Yes, the good man Livingstone,' the chief quickly replied—'a short man with a bushy moustache and a kind, piercing eye—a man who treated all men as brothers. Did you know him?'

"'Yes,' my friend answered truthfully, 'I knew him once, but I do not know him now. He is dead. He is up there,' pointing to the sky above them. 'He sees us now while we talk, and he is very, very angry to know that you are not treating us as he taught you to treat all men—as brothers.'

"The chief, at once thoroughly overcome, fell upon his knees and besought their forgiveness."*

"What a grand and noble man Dr. Livingstone really was!" Hope says, with her fine eyes glowing, "and how his influence is growing from year to year! We have at the station now a Londa-man, by the name of Intemese, who once acted as a guide for Livingstone, I believe, in his famous march from sea to sea. He fairly worships the name. When the news of the great missionary's death came it was hard at first to convince Intemese.

"'Oh no, missie! oh no!' he kept persistently reiterating. 'Such men never die. He is but gone

* This scene actually occurred.

away upon a journey, as he so often used to go. He will come back again—he will come back.'"

They have by this time come in sight of the kotla. Hope's face falls as she notes its almost deserted appearance.

"It is even later than I thought it was," she says regretfully. "They have not only had breakfast, but prayers are over as well. I fear uncle will be vexed with me, as he does not like us to miss the morning services. It sets a bad example, he says, to the more carelessly inclined of the natives."

"I somehow feel that he will forgive you this time," Captain Murray says reassuringly, "especially when he comes to know that you have been worshiping in another and far more beautiful temple."

A few yards farther on they come in sight of the mission-house.

CHAPTER II.

"Many are they that rise up against me."

THE mission-house at Lepelole faces the same side-street as that upon which the church and school-house stand. It is about two hundred yards beyond and somewhat more elevated, as the brow of the hill here gives a gently-sloping rise. The walls of the house are formed of rudely-pressed, sun-baked brick. It has a high-raised, pointed roof of thick, strong boards carefully thatched with straw, and small, evenly-set glass windows, the frames of which, though rude, are yet light and strong. The glass has been brought from the Cape, the frames are the work of native carpenters. It is one story in height, and has broad verandas all around it, about many points of which vines have been trained to clamber.

In the rear there is a smaller building of similar construction, though more open, which serves as a kitchen. Underneath the dwelling-house there is a cellar used for storing away supplies in order to keep them fresh and cool. Behind the kitchen there is a large and beautifully kept vegetable garden, and still farther beyond this an orchard of many kinds of fruit trees, both native and imported. Some of these are just in bloom; others, again, are laden with a tempting array of ripened fruit. At one side of the house a small grove of carefully tended orange trees is growing, and at the other about the same number of lemon and lime trees. Both are in full fruit, and both present a highly attractive appearance.

The house, garden and orchard are all enclosed by a high palisade of upright poles stoutly woven together with strong withes of tough bark. Along the four sides of this palisade is a dense hedge of quince-bushes, too thick to be at all productive, and evidently serving principally as a means of further protection against marauding man and beast.

A little beyond the house, just where the side of the hill slopes down somewhat gently to meet the almost dry bed of a water-course that has once been an important feeder of the Shashane, there is an immense wall of banian trees that quite shuts off the view in this direction.

The country on this side, which may properly be called the rear of the mission-station, presents an altogether different appearance from that on the front and to the left and right. Only a few hundred yards beyond the almost dry bed of the stream rise immense masses of black basalt, some of them nearly a thousand feet above the plain, and one or two of them quite overtopping the modest hill upon which the mission-station is planted. From base to summit they are scarred and split by innumerable chinks and cavities which give plain evidence of some mighty volcanic eruption. Further proof of this is found in the immense beds of lava that lie heaped upon the plain surrounding the bases of these hills. Strange to say, however, they do not appear to detract from the fertility of the soil, but rather to add to it, for upon these very beds the foliage seems to grow all the more luxuriantly. Innumerable broken masses, having rolled downward from the summits of the hills, have caught and hang piled against each other, forming wild yet safe nooks of retreat in times of danger. Indeed, Bamangwato tradition has it that the natives of the village have more than once been saved from complete extermination at the hands of cruel foes by fleeing to these rocks for protection.

The small yard in front of the mission-house slopes somewhat like a terrace. In it are growing many of the native wild flowers, which in a state of cultivation present a decidedly more attractive appearance. Among these are several varieties of lilies and a few specimens of the more prepossessing of the prickly-pear cactus. There are also a number of small, sturdy trees of the guava, and several of the avocado, or alligator pear as the natives call it.

Water is brought up to these gardens and orchards, as well as to those of the natives, by means of pipes set along the hills and worked by ingeniously contrived pumps, nearly every part of which is the production of home mechanics. But the planning and successful carrying out of this somewhat rude yet quite satisfactory system of water-works is due to the Rev. Mr. Lillington, who in fitting himself for the work before him recognized that he would be called upon to do other things besides leading lost souls to Christ. Thus he can handle a carpenter's plane, a blacksmith's hammer or a surgeon's scalpel with equal success, as well as pray with all the fervor of his honest heart for a dying soul or exhort others to repentance.

As Captain Murray and Hope come in sight of the mission-house the latter suddenly exclaims,

"Why, there are uncle and your friend Mr. Cumming on the front veranda! They seem to have been on the lookout for us, and now they are coming with haste to meet us. What can the matter be?"

"I was uneasy about you, Hope," her uncle says as he reaches her side, and then leads the donkey within the palisades, where he assists her to dismount with old-time chivalrous courtesy. "Where have you been all this time, my dear?"

"Across the veldt, uncle, for two or three miles, and then up on the Wizard's Cup for the view. I assure you that I did not intend to linger so, but my thoughts have been so abstracted all the morning I scarce noted how the time was slipping by."

"Well, you must never go again without your

brother or Pierce, not even with Ellie and Henrietta," Mr. Lillington says positively and with a shadow upon his brow.

"Why, uncle," Hope returns with some astonishment, "what has caused you to take this sudden decision? You know you have several times consented to my going a short distance alone, when neither Ellie nor the boys could go with me."

"The truth is, Miss Hope," Mr. Cumming here interposes as he notices the perplexed look upon her face and the somewhat abstracted air of Mr. Lillington, "your uncle is very much worried over some news that has just been brought him by the Kaffir boy Jim. The latter was out this morning before sunrise hunting for some stray cattle, and reports to have seen, about five miles to the northward of this, a band of suspicious-looking Zulus. They seemed to be reconnoitring, and Jim considers it lucky they did not see him, and took care to continue crouching in the bush until they were out of sight. He says they were coming in this direction."

"Do you really think, uncle, they mean any harm?" Hope turns to ask of him anxiously.

"I do not know what to think, my dear. Maybe they do and maybe they do not. Mosilikatse has been threatening us for some time; though he has threatened us before, for that matter—not, however, so determinedly as now. Still, it is best to be cautious. Perhaps I would not have been so uneasy at your protracted absence but for the news

Jim brought. I knew Captain Murray was out that way and would likely chance upon you."

"Yes," returns Captain Murray, "I met Miss Hope at her favorite resort, the Wizard's Cup, and most glorious indeed I found the view from its summit. Perhaps it is a little my fault that she is so late, as I detained her in conversation."

"Oh no, Captain Murray, you must not take any of the blame," Hope says quickly. "When once I get to the summit of the Wizard's Cup, I scarce know when to come away."

As these words are passing between Captain Murray and Hope, Mr. Lillington seems scarcely conscious of what they are saying, but stands gazing away into space with the troubled look upon his face deepening every moment.

The missionary is perhaps fifty years of age. His frame is tall and spare—in truth, very much inclined to boniness. But when he walks he carries himself so well and his finely-shaped head is set so firmly between his broad shoulders that he has quite a commanding air. His hair is of a dark brown, almost black, and plentifully sprinkled with gray. It is cropped short, as is also the thick moustache. Of beard there is no further sign, the remainder being closely shaven away. The face is rather lean and deeply furrowed, with a slightly perceptible hollowness about the cheeks, the whole being thoroughly well tanned by the African sun. The most persistent expression of the face is that of inflexible resolution, especially that given by the firm setting together of the lips that show plainly beneath the closely-trimmed moustache. It speaks of an habitual self-command, of a constant keeping on guard. It is well, considering the good missionary's desire to win the love and the confidence of his people, that the kind, bright eyes may have so decided a tendency to soften all the sterner expressions.

By this time Captain Murray and Hope have reached the stone steps leading to the front veranda.

"Is it really you, Hope?" an anxious voice asks as a young girl, some two years older than herself, meets her at the top of the steps. "We were all getting so uneasy about you. I suppose father has told you the news Kaffir Jim brought?"

"Yes, Ellie, and I am sorry to have caused even a little distress," Hope says regretfully, laying her hand affectionately upon her cousin's shoulder as she speaks. "I will try to be more thoughtful in the future."

Though older by two years and some months than her cousin, Ellie Lillington is yet not so tall, neither is her figure so compactly built. It is, indeed, like her father's, decidedly inclined to spareness, but, like her father, she carries herself well, with her head finely poised between firm, upright shoulders. She has fair, delicate skin, which even the sun of this torrid climate has failed to tan into any degree of roughness, soft light-brown hair worn in a simple coil low on her neck, and very kind and gentle eyes of a changeable gray. The other features of her face are in accord with the fairness of the skin, being very delicately outlined, with the exception of the nose, which is rather large, though well shaped. But the principal charms about Ellie are her low, beautifully modulated voice, which is never raised into harshness even under the most provoking circumstances, and her warm, loving and loyal heart.

"Come right along and get your breakfast, both you and Captain Murray," Ellie says as she pushes Hope gently toward the apartment that serves as both sitting-room and dining-room: "I know you must be hungry."

"Oh, Ellie, I hope you haven't worried about keeping breakfast for us," Hope says with some compunction. "I for one do not deserve it. I know how many duties you have and how precious your time is. It makes me ashamed to think of your being put to extra trouble on my account, and all because of my thoughtlessness. It is time now for your class in the mission-school, is it not?"

"No, not quite, but even if it were you must not let that worry you. Being so anxious about you, and not knowing exactly when you would come, I sent word a short while ago that I might not be there for an hour yet. They can manage very well until then without me. As to keeping breakfast, that has been no trouble. I am only sorry that it is in such a state by now that you will hardly enjoy it.—I do wish, Captain Murray," turning to the latter, " you could have been here to get some of your antelope meat when first cooked. It was delicious: I told Mamochisane she must have tried herself.—And the griddle-cakes, Hope, that you like so much, I know are quite spoiled."

"Please do not worry about it, Miss Ellie," Captain Murray hastens to say. " I feel somewhat, with your cousin, that we laggards do not deserve even such as awaits us."

The room in which they now find themselves is a moderate-sized apartment about twelve feet square, and is very simply and quaintly furnished. The inside of the brick walls, as an extra preventive against heat, are covered with a thick plaster of so rude a manufacture that particles of the coarse straw with which it is mixed show all over its surface. But it is packed tightly and somewhat smoothly against the bricks in spite of its coarse quality, and really looks quite well. There are two small windows, each of which is covered with a thick curtain of spotless cotton cloth. About the floor are arranged mats of straw and of cocoa-fibre, all of native manufacture. An oblong table of some light-colored wood, and also, like the mats, an article of home production, occupies the centre of the floor. From its position, as well as from two or three suggestive appointments, it is easy to surmise that it is upon this table the family of the mission-house is accustomed to take its meals. A smaller table is set in a neighboring corner, and on this are piled a few magazines and papers, none of them, however, of recent date. On the walls are several attractive engravings, all in frames of home construction and all suggestive of refinement and taste. A dozen or two of choice, well-worn books occupy three or four rows of enclosed shelves, in front of which a curtain of bright cloth, partly drawn, is fastened. On two other and smaller shelves to the right and left of the books are two slender earthen jars in which are tastefully arranged native ferns and wild flowers. Above each of these is a group of photographs tacked upon the walls and protected from the flies and other similar marauders by thin coverings of gauze. The other prints are also protected in the same manner. Various stools and chairs of native workmanship, and others, again, that have been brought from the Cape, are arranged about the room.

In a few moments Ellie, assisted by old Mamochisane, who acts in the double capacity of nurse to Baby Louise and cook for the many hungry mouths of the mission-house, has upon the table what is assuredly a most tempting breakfast for a South African mission-station, in spite of the time it has been kept waiting and of Ellie's repeated protestations that she knows that it is altogether spoiled. First there is a delicious stew of antelope meat, then come griddle-cakes of Indian corn-meal, butter, baked yams and a porridge of well-beaten maize. These, together with milk and various kinds of fruits, including the guava and avocado pear, make up a repast that would certainly tempt persons far less hungry than the two who now sit down to it.

"Do you really think there is any danger to be apprehended from the Zulus?" Captain Murray asks of Mr. Lillington as, the missionary's morning work completed, they, together with Mr. Cumming, are sitting upon the veranda in the shade of the vines.

"I scarcely know how to answer that question,' Mr. Lillington replies, with the perplexed look that has not for a moment left his face deepening into one of intense anxiety. "Sometimes I think it is only threatening on their part, and again I am inclined to believe that they will really put their threats into execution this time. The Matabele hate Bubi; they have an old grudge against him which grows more relentless with time. They are bitterly jealous of the present prosperity and successful growth of the village, and hate me as its cause. They would like to see it all wiped out of existence. And yet they are afraid of the fierce chief, for his record in war is well established. As long as the chief lives I am inclined to believe they will not make the attack, unless they could gain the advantage over him in some way. Should anything happen to Bubi, however," he adds anxiously, "and Sebubi succeed him, there is no question as to what they would do then, for, unfortunately, Sebubi has none of the fine traits of his father, but, on the other hand, is not only weak, but, I fear, cowardly."

"Too bad!" Captain Murray exclaims. "But how about the Boers?"

"Ah! there is where I apprehend the real danger. Though the Matabele and the Boers have long been enemies at heart, and the latter have never forgiven the expulsion of their great chief from the Cashan Mountains and the occupancy of them by the Boers, yet they will unite in anything that would be of injury to Bubi and myself. Urged on by the Boers, who are themselves too weak and cowardly to lead the attack, there is no telling what the Zulus may do. The Boers are both unprincipled and revengeful. The seeds of rebellion are fast germinating both over here and in the Cashan Mountains. I wouldn't be surprised at any moment to hear of them rising up in rebellion against England.* As to myself, though I am not an Englishman, they hate me cordially. I am even worse than an Englishman in their eyes; I am a missionary, and the Boers declare that the best way to treat any missionary is to kill him.†

---

* These words were spoken prior to the Boer rebellions of 1880 and 1881.

† A Boer commandant was once heard to use almost identically these words.

"I have taught the people the shame and the sin of the traffic in human flesh," Mr. Lillington goes on in a voice of deep feeling—"the binding out of their weaker brothers as slaves to these cruel taskmasters. I have shown them, too, the advantages of legitimate trade. I have gone farther, and endeavored to establish a line of trade between here and the coast. I have thus closed against the Boers the chief source of their ill-gotten gains, they having formerly obtained even the most valuable of the wares of the Bamangwatos for a few trifling ornaments of beads and brass wire. Bubi has also, at my instigation, cordially welcomed the English traders and hunters to the country. Almost every week they pass across his territory unmolested. They go farther north and west of this, and there purchase the ivory at fair prices. This, perhaps more than anything else, has aroused the Boers, for heretofore they have obtained the tusks at shameful prices."

"It is too bad that the Boers should act so," Mr. Cumming says after a few moments of silence. "Those Cashan-Mountain Boers seem to be the very worst of their class. Over in Cape Colony, now, they are quite different—in fact, are an honest, industrious and reasonable people."

"Yes, the two peoples are altogether different, as you say," returns Mr. Lillington. "The Cashan-Mountain Boers are principally those who have fled from English law on various pretexts, and have been joined by English deserters and every other variety of bad characters."

"And what objection can these Boers have to English law?" questions Captain Murray. "It is certainly liberal and just enough to satisfy any reasonable people."

"Ah! that is just what these Boers are not," says Mr. Lillington—"reasonable. Their great animosity to the English law lies in the fact that it makes no distinction between white men and black. The Boers have never forgiven the freeing of their Hottentot slaves. Thus they seem determined to erect themselves into a 'republic,' in which they may pursue without molestation what they term 'the proper treatment of the blacks.'"

"And anything else but this I dare say it is."

"You are right. The essential element of this 'proper treatment' in the eyes of the Boers is compulsory unpaid labor. When the Boers first took possession of the Cashan Mountains after having driven therefrom the cruel and tyrannical chief, Mosilikatse, the poor Bechuanas rejoiced, for they looked upon the white men in the light of deliverers. But their joy was soon turned into wailing and sorrow, for they found the new-comers even more terrible than their old oppressor, Mosilikatse. The people declared that Mosilikatse, while cruel to his enemies, was yet kind to those he conquered, but that the Boers destroyed their enemies and made slaves of their friends. Before Livingstone came among the Bechuanas the Boers had reduced the greater part of them to such subjection that even those tribes which still retained the semblance of independence were forced to perform all the labor of the fields for these cruel masters, such as manuring the land, weeding, reaping, building, making dams and canals, and at the same time being compelled to support themselves. It was a brave and vigorous war Livingstone waged against these tyrannical oppressors, and that he suffered for it severely the records show. Twice was his house entered and plundered and everything he possessed destroyed. Again and again was his life threatened. But he was too courageous, the purpose of his heart was too pure and steadfast, to be intimidated."

"He certainly taught them many lessons which they did not seem likely soon to forget," comments Mr. Cumming, "and his sojourn near to them has had this good effect: it has made them less bold and self-assured in their efforts to enslave the poor ignorant natives."

"Yet they have by no means ceased the enforcement of their horrible levy upon human flesh. I myself have been an eye-witness—an unwilling and indignant one, you may suppose—of Boers coming to a village and, according to their usual custom, demanding twenty or thirty women to weed their gardens, and have seen these women proceed to the scene of unrequited toil, carrying their own food on their heads, their children on their backs and the instruments of labor on their shoulders. Nor have the Boers any wish to conceal their meanness in thus employing unpaid labor, but, on the other hand, they seem to glory in it, frequently declaring that they make the people work for them in consideration of allowing them to live in their (the Boers') country."

" Horrible! It is a wonder the vengeance of an outraged Heaven does not overtake them."

" It will sooner or later. God does not slumber, neither are his ears deaf to the cry of his tortured people. He will yet avenge their woes.—if not now, then in his own good time. The Boers would long ago have imposed the same shameful levy upon this station but for my presence here. They had done it many times before I came, and the poor frightened people dared not resist them, for they would come with their great roers,* threatening to shoot any one who opposed them. Even Bubi had to submit, brave as he is, for the station had no firearms then, and his people were not what they are at this time. Now that you know how cordially the Boers hate me," Mr. Lillington concludes, " you can easily see what probability there is of an attack. With the help of the Zulus they may be bold enough to attempt it."

" What means of defence have you in case of
* An ungainly gun of immense calibre.

an attack?" Captain Murray asks with much concern.

"Very little outside the cannon Bubi has planted upon the hill," Mr. Lillington returns, with the cloud upon his brow deepening; "and this is what worries me: in case of the attack coming from an unexpected direction the gun would be rendered almost useless. I am, as you know, a man of peace: it is a requirement of my calling. I have therefore made little, if any, preparation for war. There are not more than two dozen muskets in all the station, and these have heretofore been used only in slaying game for meat. Never in all these years have I raised my hand to shed man's blood: the very thought of such a proceeding is revolting to me in the extreme."

"But if the occasion demanded you would not hesitate to strike?" Captain Murray questions anxiously. "If these bloodthirsty savages do put their threats into execution and attack the station, you will be prepared?"

"Yes, I shall begin to-day, this very hour, to make what defence I can, and I thank you cordially," turning to Captain Murray, "for the extra guns you were this morning so kind as to insist on my taking. There is one thing in our favor," he adds, his face brightening wonderfully at the thought of it: "Bubi is a soldier—a great soldier, in fact, though a savage—and it will be hard even for such fighters as the Zulus to overcome him in free and open battle. As to myself, I am no coward, but my soul grows sick at the thought of dyeing my hands in man's blood. However, should the worst come," he adds with a determined fire in his eyes, "then I shall remember my helpless children and strike; and may God forgive me the blood I must spill!"

"Would it not be best to send to the Cape for assistance?" Mr. Cumming inquires.

"No; I do not wish to take this step. It looks too much like premeditated war, and this is the very thing I want to avoid. It might only precipitate matters, whereas, after all, there may be nothing in these threats."

"Well, I do sincerely hope they may prove nothing but threats," Captain Murray says earnestly. "I do wish Cumming, Inkoosi and I could stay with you until this matter is definitely settled. You would find us no mean fighters in case of a Zulu attack."

"I am convinced of that, and deeply regret that you must leave us so soon. But before you go, even to-day, if you will not be otherwise engaged, I want you and Mr. Cumming to give me your advice in regard to some additional defences I purpose erecting. I shall also suggest to Bubi the advisability of putting sentinels on duty during both the day and night.

"Ah! here comes the chief now," Mr. Lillington resumes a moment later. "And Mopane is with him, too! I do wish Bubi would not keep such close company with that sorcerer, or rainmaker, as he is called. It serves only to draw poor Bubi farther and farther back into the net of superstitions from which I have tried to rescue him.—Well, Bubi, what is it now?" Mr. Lillington asks kindly as, having greeted the chief, he motions him to a seat upon the other end of the wooden bench he is occupying. As to Mopane, he has taken up his position some distance away, and stands there glowering upon the party with a most rebellious and discontented scowl upon his forbidding countenance.

"The soul of Bubi is troubled," the chief says in the native language as, slowly rising from the bench, he stands before them, his tall, erect form looking taller and more powerful still in the close-fitting scarlet uniform he wears. "It has known no rest, no sleep, since the message of the good father" (the name by which Mr. Lillington is known throughout the station) "has reached him. It said to Bubi that his old enemies, the Matabele, were again upon his path—that the axes had already been whetted to drink the blood of his people. That is true, my father. They even now creep through the bushes, and from the hills watch the smoke of the fires that burn within Bubi's village. They are dogs, they are snakes; they strike not in the daytime, nor yet when Bubi awaits them with the spears of his people sharpened for battle. They will not come up the hill where the great gun is; they will not seek to enter by the straight entrance where Bubi's people can see them. If they were men and soldiers, and did but give us open fight, neither Bubi nor his bold warriors have aught of fear for the end. But they will come by night when my people lie dreaming in their huts, not knowing of the danger; or, if by day, then when they have the hoe or the plough within their hands, and not the gun or the spear. The dog of an enemy will creep upon them as they are at work in the fields. They will crouch for the spring when the back of my people is bent over the rows of maize and cane. O friend of my heart's full confidence! you know not the treachery of the Matabele, cowards all of them when it comes man to man. I know not how to meet this blow that will be given in the dark. I know not to which point to go and there make ready for the spears of Mosilikatse. If I did, there would be an end to all the trouble that now gnaws like the hyena at Bubi's heart. Then would Bubi prepare for battle strong and jubilant; then would the chief's bold warriors chant the death-song of the Matabele dogs; then would their worthless carcasses be given as food to the vultures of the air. Yes, that would be the end, for Bubi is both a chief and a warrior."

At these words Bubi draws his form still more erect, while his small black eyes flash and his fine open face has an expression which shows plainly that he feels deeply every word he has just uttered.

"O friend of my heart's best love!" he breaks forth again, addressing Mr. Lillington, "hear the plaint of Bubi, and bend to him the ear that will hearken to his cry. There stands Mopane, the rain-maker of Bubi's people. He it is whose mighty magic can bring rain from the clouds; he it is who knows the things that are hidden from the eyes of others; he it is who by his power can reveal to Bubi where the Matabele are to strike. O my father, but speak the word that will let Bubi seek the aid of Mopane in this matter. Say that the magic of Mopane may be wrought before the eyes of Bubi, that he may read therein not only the fate of himself and of his people, but also of the good father, the man who talks to him of the great God on high, and of the good father's children. Only this once, my father, only this once, and Bubi will ask it no more."

"Bubi," Mr. Lillington says kindly as, rising, he places his hand upon the shoulder of the now much-agitated chief, "listen to me, my friend. The arts of Mopane are but as the feather that flies in the air or as the pebbles at the bottom of the rushing river. They are naught—naught but as idle words spoken for their sound, naught but the tricks of vain and sinful jugglery. He can tell you no more of the plans and intentions of the Matabele than can I—nay, not so much. Have nothing to do with him, Bubi, nor with his hurtful magic. Seek help and enlightenment alone from the great God on high, who only can aid you. Come to me this evening, just before services at the kotla, and we will both pray to him together. His wisdom is above all others, and it will direct us."

During all the time that Mr. Lillington has been speaking to Bubi the eyes of Mopane have been upon the missionary's face with a look of the most deadly hate. He is a villainous-looking man, a few years older than Bubi. He is nothing like so tall, and there is a droop in one of his shoulders that gives him a somewhat misshapen appearance. He has little hair upon his head, with the exception of a few tufts near the top. His face sinks in at the nose, which is broad and flat, while his chin and lips project to a considerable distance. Upon his cheeks and forehead there are innumerable seams and scars which add to the villainousness of his looks. He is almost nude, with the exception of the skin of some animal fastened about the waist and which falls nearly to the knees. About his person are a quantity of charms and little sacks of "medicine," while he carries in his hand a whip made of antelopes' tails.

As Mopane goes away with Bubi he turns his head once more to give Mr. Lillington a look that makes even Mr. Cumming, hardened old hunter as he is, shudder.

"What a terrible countenance that fellow has!" he exclaims as the line of palisades shuts off Mopane's retreating figure. "I do not know when I have ever seen a more wicked one. I would hate to be in his power. I may be mistaken," turning to the missionary as he speaks, "but I should say he dislikes you cordially."

"Unfortunately, he does," Mr. Lillington admits, "and, to be candid with you, I deeply regret it. I have tried in every way to appease him and to win him from his superstitious practices, not only for the good of his people, but for his own good as well. But he seems to have no kindly impulses whatever, no generous feelings, no tenderness of heart. He scoffs at all religious services, and tries to oppose me in everything I undertake for the benefit of the village. If I could but reach his stubborn heart in one little impressible spot, I should have some hope of finally bringing him to Christ. But he seems utterly abandoned to his wicked course, and as utterly determined to do all he can to weaken my influence among the natives. In this direction, however, I am glad to say that he has very little success now, though he did have much at first. He has been a great rain-maker and sorcerer in his day, even more looked up to than the chief himself, and his present displacement from the high pedestal he occupied he very properly attributes to me— though if he would but look at it in the right spirit, he would see that I have intended it only for the best—and he hates me accordingly."

"It is too bad," Captain Murray says. "Such a man is apt to breed some discord even among the best inclined natives. What a pity you could not get rid of him! He hates you so that I would not risk him for making his own price with the Zulus. He would as soon pilot them into the village as not, even at the risk of seeing his own people massacred."

"I must warn Bubi against him more strongly than ever," Mr. Lillington says thoughtfully. "At any rate, whatever happens, Mopane must not be put on duty as a sentinel."

CHAPTER III.

"He is our help in time of trouble."

THAT evening, as the members of the family with their two guests are at the early supper that is one of the established features of the mission-station, the two youths, Pierce Lillington and Cunnyngham Blandford, return from their hunting expedition. They are fine, manly lads—one of them almost a young man, in fact—and their pleasant manners and polite bearing speak well for the home-training both have received.

Cunnyngham is the older of the two by three years and a half, and is nearly twenty years of age. He is of a much stouter build than his cousin, has a strong, good face with a high, broad brow, pleasant blue eyes and a kindly smile that wins all hearts. Pierce is smaller and darker, with a brown skin, tanned even browner than is its wont by the hot African suns, and with a pair of very keen and restless dark eyes that seem unwilling to remove their gaze until whatever it rests upon has been thoroughly mastered.

Both boys as they come into the dining-room seem filled with some unusual excitement that it is hard to suppress. Cunnyngham is the first to give the clue to this state of feelings as the room is reached.

"You could never guess, uncle, and all of you," he says between quick, short breaths, "what we have found, and right here almost at home, too."

"A den of young lions, perhaps, or a herd of spring-bok in the almost dried-up channel of the stream," his uncle says at random.

"I know," suddenly exclaims Marvin, Mr. Lillington's remaining son, and a wide-awake, enterprising little fellow of ten: "it is an eagle's nest. I saw the old one flying around the basalt cliff last week, and I just knew it was up there somewhere."

"Wrong," says Pierce, coming to Cunnyngham's aid, for he sees that he is almost too much excited to speak clearly. "It is something that has to do with the basalt rocks, Master Marvin, but it isn't an eagle's nest."

"Then what can it be?" exclaims Miss Henrietta at this point, letting her knife drop in her excitement. "I do wish, Pierce, that you'd hurry up and tell us, and not keep us waiting so long."

"Well, then," answers Pierce promptly, "it is a cave."

"'A cave'?" echo more than one voice.

"Yes, a cave, and just the grandest one you ever saw. It is nearly a mile long and at its narrowest place is over fifty feet wide. And there is no end to the beautiful stalactites.—Oh, Ellie, they would just make your eyes dance to see them; and there is water all through it."

"Why, where can it be?" Hope asks, now as much excited as Henrietta and the boys.

"About three-quarters of a mile from here, just to the right of the taller of the basalt hills, and beneath a ledge that projects from the left-hand cliff in the deepest and wildest part of the gorge."

"And how did you come to find it?" Mr. Lillington questions, now much interested.

"Pierce and I left the men when within a mile of the village," Cunnyngham here speaks up, "and went by the basalt hill, as we were very anxious to procure some of the prettier of the detached fragments in order to make Ellie and Hope the inkstands we had long promised them. While hunting about the lava-beds we suddenly surprised a small herd of elands, and among them several exceedingly fine spring-bok. As it was something of an unusual sight so near the mission-station, we determined to give them chase in order to find out their haunt, if nothing more. They took at once to the almost dry channel of the stream, and headed off up the gorge as fast as their slim legs would carry them. Finally, even with our best running, they soon got out of sight, with the exception of two of the bucks, who suddenly swung to the right and plunged through a seemingly almost impenetrable thicket just beneath an overhanging ledge of rock. We had no idea we could follow them, and hence were much surprised when we found a way around the thicket, and not only that, but an opening in the cliff. We had to wade some distance in the water, however, before we found it. Our surprise increased more and more as we found ourselves in a tunnel-like aperture through which fully ten men could have walked abreast. We felt at once that we were in a cave. Fortunately, we had a box of matches with us, and we explored our find to some extent. We lost sight of the bucks, of course, for we had forgotten all else in the discovery of the cave."

"No one would ever think of there being a cave at that place," says Pierce at this point, "the entrance is so cunningly hidden by the overhanging cliff. If we hadn't waded up the stream as we did, we never would have found it. Why, the bed of the stream is a natural roadway," he concludes after a moment's pause, "and there would be nothing to hinder a big wagon from getting into the cave by a little clearing away of the bushes around its mouth."

A strange expression comes into Mr. Lillington's face at these words. He opens his lips to speak, checks himself, and then adds after a moment's pause, "Well, who knows, boys, but that this cave of yours may yet prove a lucky find? At any rate, we will go to-morrow or next day and see more of it. In the mean time," lowering his voice, "I would advise keeping its discovery a secret even from Mazika and Pitsane."

"You look tired, Miss Ellie," Captain Murray says with much solicitude as, half an hour later, the supper-things having all been cleared away, she is standing by one of the little windows gazing wistfully out to where the tall grass is just beginning to stir gently beneath the line of stately banian trees. "There is a fresh breeze springing up and the evening promises to be delightful, even for this climate. Will you not come for a walk?"

"I would like so much to do so," she says with the wistfulness deepening, "but it will soon be time for the services at the kotla, and I do not like to miss them."

"Never mind the services at the kotla this evening, my child," her father's voice at this moment says near her. "You are tired, I know. There is so much for your willing hands to do. The fresh air will revive you. Go with the captain for a walk. You can return in time for family prayer and to see Baby Louise off to her nest. Until then Mamochisane can attend to her."

Thus adjured, Ellie no longer hesitates, but, throwing a light wool wrap over her head and about her shoulders, goes down the walk beside Captain Murray. Although it is still daylight, the full moon has arisen. Here and there in the deepening blue of the vault above them a star is beginning to show its faint light, and, as it grows bolder and brighter, to twinkle cheerily. The soft wind stirs gently through the long fronds of the palms, giving out from them a faint clicking sound that, despite its monotony, is not altogether unmusical. All the air about them is laden with the perfume of many sweet-growing things.

They pass out into the principal street of the village. Many hurrying forms meet them as they go onward, some in groups, others again singly. All greet them pleasantly, and more than one pair of eyes turn to gaze gratefully after the slender form of the missionary's daughter as she walks beside her tall companion. Men, women and children all alike adore the quiet, gentle girl whose warm heart has a place for the woes of each and every one, whose kindly voice has ever an encouraging word, and whose firm, soft hand has held to the last that of more than one soul going out into the darkness.

"I am sorry to miss the services at the kotla," Ellie says at length, regretfully, "and I fear some of the blacks will not understand it. They seem to gaze after me as though they can scarcely realize that it is I, and going away from the kotla, instead of toward it."

"I do not think that is the reason they gaze after you," Captain Murray begins, then checks himself, for he has read this fine, honest nature sufficiently to be well aware that anything approaching the least bit to flattery will be very distasteful to her. The next moment he adroitly changes the subject to one he knows well she loves to talk upon.

"Your father's whole soul seems wrapped up in this place and this people," he says at length.

"Oh, indeed it is," she cries, her eyes glowing. "Father is at heart a true missionary: I think he was born for the work. I do not believe he would change it for the highest calling on earth; and why should he? Wherever he should be and whatever he should do, he would be a Christian, and as the salvation of men ought to be, and is, the chief aim and desire of every true Christian, what nobler lot, after all, could be his than this?"

"Are you yourself satisfied here?" Captain Murray asks. "Do you not sometimes long for the civilized world and for a few at least of the many pleasant things found there?"

"Oh no," she says vehemently, as though somehow fearing that he may find it a little hard to believe her. "I care nothing for the world of which you speak, nor for the things of that world. I have never for one moment in all my life craved any other life away from this—any other earthly life, I mean," hastily correcting herself. "Why should I, when it is all I have ever known? Sometimes I have thought it would be very pleasant to meet other faces besides these rough black ones I see every day, to hear other and more cultivated voices, and to see a few at least of the many beautiful things of which I have heard. It has often grieved my father deeply that he has not been able to send me back to his old home in the States to be educated, but I have never minded it at all. My mother," her voice breaking here in spite of the brave effort she makes, " has taught me all of the best that I would have learned there. As to the rest, I feel no deprivation in having missed it."

"You are a brave, true girl," Captain Murray says involuntarily, "and you deserve all the happiness Heaven can send you. God grant that there may be no cruel awakening from this quiet, peaceful life into which you seem to have grown so fixedly!"

"You speak like one who has sad forebodings," she says anxiously. "Tell me," turning to place her hand upon his arm in her earnestness : "you really do not think there is any trouble to be apprehended from the Zulus and the Boers? Oh, surely, surely, God will not let such cruel and wicked intentions dwell long in their hearts. But if they do attack us," she concludes after a moment's silent communing, "I feel that God's arm will be about us."

"One can never tell how matters of this kind will turn out," Captain Murray says at length in answer to her anxious questioning. "The Zulus are fierce, the Boers treacherous in the extreme, and both seem determined. But keep your faith strong in the all-powerful Arm, Miss Ellie. I am not a professed Christian, as you know, but I believe firmly in the rulings of an almighty Power and the justness of his decrees, though they may seem at the time far from just to us."

"But, best of all," she adds earnestly, with her eloquent eyes turned full upon him, "he is the God of the trusting and the Father of his children. Oh, Captain Murray," she goes on pleadingly, "do not say that you are not a professed Christian—do not make such an admission. Do not acknowledge merely a belief in God, a firm conviction of his justness and power, but say that you love him—love him because he is God, love him because he first loved you."

"It is indeed hard to resist so eloquent a plea, and from such a source," Captain Murray says in an unsteady voice and with his eyes turned resolutely away from the earnest gray ones that are seeking to read their expression. "But you must make what allowance you can for me, Miss Ellie. Give me time to put to myself the points you have put to me, and perhaps I may then give you a different answer."

Seeing how deeply moved he is, Ellie delicately refrains from speaking further upon the subject, but in her heart there is borne upward with the incense of the night a silent prayer that this splendid man may yet be led to be a bold, brave soldier for Christ.

The daylight has now entirely faded from the

sky, and the moonlight, which in this latitude is always exceedingly bright, is flooding everything with its full deep radiance. Even the crests of the distant mountains stand out distinctly against the sky. Here and there, dotted about upon the brow of the hill, are the glowing eyes of a fire not yet out beneath the ovens at the rear of the huts. In the patch of moonlight between two thick-foliaged Thibet trees a group of little pickaninnies are rolling about upon each other in great delight. An old woman who is watching them is crooning to herself the guttural words of a song that seems to please her very much, to judge by the way she applauds herself between the stanzas.

Guided by the unusually bright glow of an eye of fire that gleams upon them from a small grove of palms, Ellie and Captain Murray leave the main street they are following and come upon a pair of native blacksmiths who are busy with coals, anvil and bellows, and all upon the ground.

"I suppose they find it pleasanter out in the open air than they do in the shop," Ellie says as they draw near the line of fire. "Oh, it is only old Kamati and Botla," she adds as they reach the place—"two harmless, well-meaning fellows who never have been able to get used to the improved methods and tools introduced by my father, but who prefer the old way."

The two blacksmiths are kneeling upon the ground in front of a fire of charcoal that is lying in a little hollow that is scooped out of the earth. One of them is working a most primitive-looking bellows, and the other is pounding a piece of metal upon an anvil equally as rude and primitive as the bellows. The bellows consists of two wooden cylinders about a foot and a half in diameter. These cylinders are hollowed to the depth of five or six inches and covered over with two tanned goatskins. To the skins are attached two handles about two feet long and from a half to three-quarters of an inch in thickness. By a rapid upward and downward movement of these handles a current of air is produced. This has full play upon the charcoal through two hollow wooden tubes which are attached to the cylinders at the bottom and furnished with muzzles of clay.

The anvil is only about a foot and a half in height and from eight to ten inches broad. It is shaped somewhat like a cone with the base upward. The hammer is another cone-shaped instrument, only much slenderer and not quite so long.

"Good-evening, Kamati," Ellie says pleasantly. "Busy at work, I see?"

"Yes, missy. There are a hundred great spikes to be made by morning, and Kamati must do his share."

Leaving the blacksmith, the saunterers return to the main street and pass down the slope of the hill toward the chief entrance. A hushed silence seems now to have settled down upon everything.

Even the voices of the negroes singing at the kotla, the echoes of which now reach them, have a far-away, eerie sound, a mournful cadence that causes Ellie to shiver in spite of herself.

They have now reached the slope of the hill and are walking toward the main entrance. The heavy gate is closed, and on two rude platforms built against the rough stone wall that leads away on either side the same number of sentries are placed, one upon each. They are in a sitting position, while just in front of them are small circular holes some four or five inches in diameter, through which they are constantly peering. Every now and then they raise themselves for an outlook over the top of the wall, but not before they have first cautiously peered through the port-holes.

"I see my father has his people on guard already," Ellie says with an unconscious sigh. "Oh, I do hope there will be no necessity for war; it is so dreadful!"

Captain Murray does not answer right away. He is busily engaged in examining the wall and the gate.

"It seems to me, Miss Ellie," he says after a moment's silence, "that the fastenings of the gate are not such as they should be. It might easily be thrown open by one man, especially if the sentries were off their guard. It is much too light, though it seems so large. If I were your father I would remedy the matter right away: the delay of a day may be dangerous. The walls, too, need strengthening in one or two places. And what can he be about to allow the thorns and bushes to grow so thickly around the mouth of the ditch as completely to hide it from view? Why, enemies, even in strong numbers, might lie concealed therein without his suspecting it, especially if they crept to their places in the darkness of the night."

"Please speak to father about it all, Captain Murray, when you return to the house," Ellie says a little anxiously. "I know he will be glad to receive any suggestions from you, and will act upon them, I feel assured."

When the matter is brought to the knowledge of Mr. Lillington, he expresses himself as very grateful for the warning and suggestions, and says at once, "I shall attend to those things just as soon as we are through with the weak places in the south wall. Somehow, I cannot help thinking," he adds a little apologetically, "that the attack will come from that direction. At any rate, it is the weakest place of all, and I dare not leave it as it is."

"But do not forget that the gate and the ditch are equally as urgent," Captain Murray warns him.

The good missionary's face grows deeply shadowed as he ponders over the many perplexing things that trouble him. It is truly a time of much anxiety and care.

That his heart is sorely troubled and his mind filled with many painful and anxious forebodings his voice and his face give full evidence as in tremulous tones he reads the psalm for the evening:

"Lord, how are they increased that trouble me! Many are they that rise up against me. Many there be which say of my soul, There is no help for him in God. But thou, O Lord, art a shield for me, my glory and the lifter-up of my head."

His voice is too shaken with emotion to lead the evening hymn, so Ellie's clear, sweet voice takes it up instead:

> "Saviour, breathe an evening blessing
> Ere repose our spirits seal;
> Sin and want we come confessing;
> Thou canst save and thou canst heal."

CHAPTER IV.

"His tender mercy is over all his works."

ABOUT four o'clock in the afternoon of the following day Mr. Lillington and the two youths, Cunnyngham and Pierce, make an expedition to the cave in the gorge in order to explore it still farther. They descend the channel of the stream by way of a little footpath that leads along beside the row of banian trees just beyond the mission-station, and thence to the verge of the gorge. At this particular spot the walls of the cañon slope gradually, so that it is no very difficult matter to find a footing all the way to the bottom, especially as innumerable projecting roots and stones serve as resting-places for the feet. On the opposite side, however, as also on this side a little farther up, the cliffs rise sheer and abrupt, with full twenty-five to thirty feet added to their height. Rank-growing vines and tangled vegetation of every description cover nearly every foot of the cliffs from the summit to the bed of the stream, rendering it almost impossible for a descent to be made from that side.

The original bed of the stream is about thirty

feet wide, but succeeding droughts have so dried it up that now it has only a shallow flow of water from three to four feet wide. In some places it is only a few inches in depth, in others only about a foot and a half. The water is quite clear, and at the bottom are innumerable little pebbles and sharp-pointed rocks that would certainly cut the feet did any one attempt to walk over them.

Luckily, however, Mr. Lillington and the boys are not compelled to take any such mode of proceeding, for they easily find footing over the dried bed of the stream along the base of one of the cliffs, where the only drawbacks are the large heaps of drifted sand they sometimes encounter and the innumerable thickets of tangled thorn. As they go onward the scene along the channel of the stream becomes more wildly beautiful. The cliffs now rise to the height of over a hundred feet on either side. Along the summits grow clumps of the silvery-leafed sandal-wood, the delicious perfume of which is filling all the air. In many places upon the walls of the cliffs, especially near the bottom of the cañon, are large clusters of exceedingly beautiful deep-green ferns, with their slender feathery fronds sometimes many feet in length.

As they advance there is a gradual ascent of the bed of the stream, with a barely perceptible increase of water in the channel. The cliffs, too, seem to increase in height, the foliage to grow denser, and the

vines more tangled, while in some places the boughs
of the trees appear almost to meet overhead. Suddenly
at a spot where he is little expecting it the
boys point out to Mr. Lillington the position of the
cave. But for their guidance, however, he would
never have found the entrance, it is so shut in by
the dense-growing bushes and the overhanging
ledge. Still, the opening is of considerable width
—so wide, in fact, as to surprise him after he has
examined it. It can be made wider yet, he discovers,
by clearing away some of the bushy growths
that almost shut it in. The light is very dim, but
it is sufficient to reveal to them a space of some
fifteen or twenty feet beyond the entrance. At
this point they stop and light the lantern Mr.
Lillington has been careful enough to provide.
Considering the situation of the cave, the walls
and floor in many places are remarkably dry. At
two points they find water—in one instance a tiny
thread trickling down from a considerable height
overhead, and in the other a small but bold spring
that bubbles up from the very floor of the little
arched chamber that surrounds it. The main
chamber of the cavern is fully four hundred feet
in extent and about one-third as wide. Beyond
this is a succession of smaller chambers.

"I cannot help but think that this is a most fortunate
find, my boys," Mr. Lillington says at length,
as, having made a satisfactory exploration of the cave,
they are seated upon a small mass of rock just at

its entrance. "These are troublesome times, and there is no telling what may happen. In case of an attack by the Boers or the Zulus, and their successful entrance of the village, you might escape hither with Ellie, Hope and the children."

"But what would become of you, father?" Pierce asks anxiously.

"I shall remain by my people," he says resolutely. "If they fall, I must fall too."

"But, uncle," Cunnyngham exclaims vehemently, his fair face flushing, "you surely would not ask of us anything so cowardly as to fly and leave you at the mercy of the enemy? I at least must stand by you. I am no longer a boy, but nearly a man. If you must face the danger, I beg—nay, I entreat—you to let me face it with you."

"Oh, father," Pierce adds at this point, his voice quivering with emotion, "how can you want us to flee like cowards, as my cousin has suggested, and leave you to face the fierce Zulus or the cruel Boers alone? They will surely kill you, and then think what our feelings will be to know that we have deserted you and willingly left you to the dreadful fate of being murdered by them! No, no! better death with you a hundred times than an escape without you."

"But you must think of your sisters," Mr. Lillington says as resolutely as before—"of Henrietta, of Marvin and of helpless Baby Louise. Think of the deadly axes of the bloodthirsty

Zulus beating out their innocent brains, or, worse still, of your delicate sister and gentle, refined cousin being carried away into a captivity far more dreadful than death. No, no, my boys. I know that it is hard, but you must listen to the voice of judgment and reason. Should the Zulus attack us and gain an entrance to the village, there will be death and destruction on every side. No quarter will be given, not even to the helpless women and children, not even to my own precious bairns. The Zulus are incited by the Boers, and the Boers are cruel as death. Therefore, it is my positive command that at the first sound of an attack, should one really be made, you will remain in the house, or at once seek its shelter, wherever you may be, if that is possible. You will remain there, keeping watch over the girls and the children, until a certain signal from me, hereafter to be agreed upon, when you may know that the town is entered. Then I charge you, as you love me, to escape with the girls and the children as fast as you can to the cave by way of the banian trees and the path we have marked out down the side of the cliff. It may be that we shall conquer even after the enemy has gained an entrance, if such a calamity is indeed to befall us. It may be, again, that some of us may escape though the turn of the battle should prove disastrous, and thus be able unobserved to join you at the cave. I have an idea that this cavern has before served as a refuge in time of war—not, however, within the memory of any of the present members of the tribe, or I should have heard something of it. In the mean time, we will secretly remove hither a stock of provisions and bedding. The atmosphere of the cave is remarkably dry, and there are several articles of food we can bring that will not be injured here even should they remain for months. I cautioned you last night to keep the discovery of the cave a close secret. Upon second thought, however, I think we had better tell Mazika. He is as true as steel and will not betray us, neither will Pitsane. I do not know but that it will be a good plan to tell them both. We shall need all the help we can get."

"But do you not fear, father, that some of the natives may discover us in our frequent trips hither?" Pierce asked as they arose to go.

"I think not. They may see us coming into the gorge, but I do not believe they will guess our intention, especially if we are careful to conceal the nature of our burdens. They will doubtless think we are only on a hunting-expedition. But, to make sure, we had best let all our trips be at night. Most of the natives," he continues, "in spite of the advancement they have made toward enlightenment, still cling stubbornly to many of their old superstitions. This gorge is regarded with much dread by the natives. They have fixed upon it as the abode of revengeful and turbulent beings who try to injure all who dare enter herein. Consequently, they seldom, if ever, venture into the cañon. I believe we shall be absolutely safe from detection, even in the daytime, by coming down by way of the banian trees."

As they return Mr. Lillington notes very clearly the form of the bed of the stream.

"It is a natural roadway," he says at length. "You were right, Pierce: it would be no difficult matter to get a wagon along here by entering below the mission-station, even a wagon drawn by a number of oxen. This has set me to thinking again, my boys. There is nothing like preparing for even unanticipated emergencies. In case the Zulus do overcome my people and enter the village, and you children escape by being safely concealed in the cave, you could not of course remain there always. We must think of a position of this kind and prepare in advance for it. Should the worst happen and I fall with my people, if the means were at hand you might make your way to the village of Sechele, fifteen days' journey south-west of this. Once there, Sechele could help you on down to the Cape, where you could with little difficulty, I doubt not, get passage for the United States. My earnest desire is that, should anything happen to me, my children may escape and make their way to my old home in the States. So I want you to promise me, my dear boys, in the event that I am to fall by fighting with my people, you will sacredly carry out, so far as it lies in your power and with God's help, my wishes in this matter.

"I will," he continues, "to-morrow night, with your aid and with Mazika's and Pitsane's, remove hither the wagon and oxen. The wagon can be driven into the cave and a pen can be made for the oxen. They can be shut in the upper end of the gorge, where there is, I noticed, splendid pasturage."

While Mr. Lillington has been speaking they have entered the main gateway of the village. They are proceeding up the principal street to the side-street on which the mission-house stands, when a somewhat unusual commotion a short distance to the right of them and in rear of the chief's hut attracts their attention. Men are seen running to and fro in various directions; others, again, are standing in little groups talking excitedly; even the women and children are gathered about. Some of the women are wringing their hands in a helpless kind of way that is distressing to see. The majority of them, however, are talking excitedly together, as the men are doing. The children are crying and tugging at their mothers' skirts as though greatly frightened.

As Mr. Lillington and the boys approach they see lying upon the ground in the chief's milking-pen one of the most beautiful and valuable of the cows he owns, and one of which he has been especially proud. The poor creature has just ended her death-struggles, with her glossy throat cut from ear to ear.

"Why, who could have been guilty of a deed so mean as that?" Pierce cries indignantly. "Poor Nameta! such a beautiful creature as she was, and so gentle and so kind! There wasn't another cow in the whole village that gave such rich, sweet milk. What will the chief say?"

"The lips of the chief himself ordered the hand of Mopane to draw the knife across the throat of Nameta," says one of the men, approaching.

"Impossible!" exclaims Mr. Lillington hurriedly, turning so as to face the speaker.

"But the words I have spoken are nevertheless the words of truth, my father. Nameta was in the pen. The chief, Mopane and Sansawe, all three, saw her, while lying down, beat violently upon the ground with her tail. She did beat yet the third time, and then they knew that she was bewitched and was thus calling down death upon the tribe. She was guilty of 'tlolo,' and must be killed, for if she were not killed, then would others have to die. Mopane saw her first, and cried out to the chief that his hand must draw the knife across the throat of Nameta, else would his own life and that of many of his people be required of him. But this the chief would not do. It seemed as if he could not, for she was truly a beautiful creature and the chief valued her so. He tried to reason with Mopane, but the ears of the rain-maker were deaf to all his entreaties. Finally, Mopane said something, we heard not what, that made the chief draw back as though some mighty hand had struck him. Covering his head with his kaross, he called forth at length to Mopane in a trembling voice to slay, and then rushed madly away in the direction of his hut."

"And where is Bubi now?" Mr. Lillington questions.

"He is within his hut, good father."

"Bubi," Mr. Lillington says in a gentle and reproachful voice as he kneels beside the couch of skins where the chief lies with his head still wrapped in his kaross, "what is this I hear? What is it mine own eyes have seen? The gentle and affectionate Nameta, the delight of the chief's eyes and the pride of the whole village, lies with her beautiful glossy sides weltering in blood and her slender throat severed from ear to ear, slain—slain by Mopane's hand and at Bubi's command."

"It was beyond the power of Bubi to stay the hand that struck," the chief says mournfully, and still refusing to let his eyes meet the searching gaze he knows well is fixed upon him. "O friend of my heart's best confidence! do not reproach Bubi. The tongue of Mopane is fierce, the fire of his eyes like the lightning that slays, the force of his words as a mighty hand that presses all down before it. The heart of Bubi at times is weak— weak, my father, in spite of the strength you have tried to put into it—his soul like that of a child's that gropes in the dark. The practices and customs of his people are strong upon him. Even the religion of the great God is sometimes not so strong. The tail of Nameta did beat upon the ground; it beat fiercely, as though she were very, very angry and were calling down death upon us all. I know that already the assegais of the Zulus are raised to strike; therefore was the soul of Bubi sore within him. I stood firm against Mopane until he said he had seen it all in a dream, of how the tail of Nameta was to beat upon the ground, and how Bubi was to refuse to have the knife drawn across her throat, and then how—O my father, it is terrible!—the Matabele were to strike when Bubi least expected it and where he looked not for it, and the blood of his people was to run like the water of the river, while his own head was to be borne aloft on the spear of his old enemy, Mosilikatse."

"Bubi," Mr. Lillington says in a voice rendered husky through repressed emotion, "let us pray, my friend—let us beseech the great God on high to strengthen the weak heart of Bubi and to send light to his troubled soul;" and then and there the good missionary falls upon his knees and pours forth such a petition as must assuredly pierce the innermost sanctuary of the Most High.

"And now, Bubi," Mr. Lillington says in deep and earnest tone as he arises from his knees and bends once more above the recumbent form of the chief, "rouse yourself, my friend, and go forth strong in the strength of Him who is both your God and the God of your people. Have no more to do with Mopane and his wicked superstitions; close your ears to the seductive words of the voice that but seeks to lead you and your people to destruction. Come away from the old ways; look not back upon them, but turn your eyes resolutely toward the new. Believe in Christ Jesus, Bubi, with all your heart, and you shall be saved."

Mr. Lillington cannot at this time tell just what is the effect upon Bubi of his words or of the deep and heartfelt prayer he has offered up in his behalf. The chief seems much overcome—so much so, in fact, as to be unable to converse further— and so Mr. Lillington leaves him, hoping and still praying silently and fervently that he may be completely drawn back from the net that seems outstretched to ensnare him.

It is two days ere he sees him again, and then he appears so much subdued, so thoroughly repentant, so gentle and submissive, that the heart of the good missionary loses much of its solicitude in regard to him, and he feels that all may yet be well with the fine old chief. But alas for these hopes!

CHAPTER IV.

"He shall redeem Israel from all his iniquities."

THE night is a sultry one—exceedingly so even for this climate. All day long the sun has shone with a hot, white glare that has made the eyes smart and burn and the head tingle. Finding the house oppressive, Hope has, after their return from the evening services at the kotla, proposed to Ellie, Pierce and Cunnyngham that they take a walk.

"There is one place I should like to go to so much," says Ellie wistfully, in a voice that is far from being as steady as her tones usually are. "It has been more than a week since I was at—at mother's grave, and if you do not object, Hope, I would like to go there; that is, if father thinks it safe. It is only a little distance outside the walls of the station, as you know, and we might take Mazika with us."

Mr. Lillington finally consents to their going, with the provision that they shall be very careful and look about them constantly, and also that they take both Mazika and the Hottentot Pitsane. "For," says Mr. Lillington, "Pitsane has the ear of a cat and the scent of a dog."

The little cemetery in which the dearly-loved wife and mother has been laid to her last long sleep is at the summit of a gently-sloping knoll to the right of the valley that lies in front of the main entrance. It is but little more than a mound in size, and is only about two hundred yards from the wall that encloses the station. Not far from it, and crowning the slope of a similar mound, only one that is much larger, is the native burial-place. The little plot in which Mrs. Lillington rests with two of her children who have preceded her some years to the land beyond all shadows is about thirty feet square, and is enclosed not only by a strong wall of stone-work, but also by stout palisades fully ten feet high. The graves are carefully kept by tender and loving hands. At the head and foot of each is a neat white board with the names and the dates of birth and death. That of the wife and mother bears a longer inscription that tells of the courage and many virtues of her who has died, nobly doing with all her might that which her hand found to do. Many beautiful shrubs have been trained to grow about the graves, while above all two slender, willowy motsouri keep their mournful vigil.

They linger for perhaps three-quarters of an hour within the enclosure, for there are many things Ellie's loving hands find to do, while outside Mazika and Pitsane keep close and faithful watch.

"No dog of a Matabele about here," Pitsane says confidently as they turn to make their way back to the mission-station—"no vulture of a Boer, either, waiting to pick the bones of the lions the Zulus have threatened to slay. If there were, Pitsane would scent them out; Pitsane's ears would hear the footfalls of the hyenas that prowl through the woods seeking to lap the blood of the brave Bechuana lion." *

"But will they not come, Pitsane? will they not come soon?" Hope pauses beside him to question anxiously.

"Pitsane cannot tell, White Lily. Perhaps they come soon, perhaps they come not at all. The name of Bubi is great, and the heart of the Zulu dog fails him when he thinks of the shining battle-axe of the lion chief."

"Are you not afraid to talk so, Pitsane, when Mazika is so near?" Hope asks in a low voice. "Will he not grow angry to hear his people thus abused?"

"They are not his people, White Lily. The blood of the Zulu, it is true, flows in the veins of the Mazika, but it is not their blood. It is the blood of the Amazulu, of the old brave Amazulu, who scorned to kill an enemy save in open battle, and who were kind to the helpless and whose ear was not deaf to the cries of women and children.

* The Bamangwato are one of the many branches of the fine old Bechuana tribe.

But the blood of these Zulus has been mixed with the blood of the Boers, of the treacherous white-skinned Boers, who are as cruel as death to an enemy and traitorous to their friends. The hands of these Zulus and of the Boers have crossed in deeds that would make even the cheek of a Bakalahari warrior burn with shame. They hate each other at heart, as the lion and elephant hate, yet for the sake of the mean deeds they may do will again join hands."

"Pitsane has spoken as a man speaks," says the grim old Zulu, now taking up the conversation in his deep and musical native tongue, "and the words of Pitsane are wise. The blood of these Zulus has become as the blood of dogs and cowards; therefore will Mazika have none of it. I speak of the Zulus who know too well the Boers—who, as Pitsane has said, have crossed hands in evil and cowardly deeds with the whining jackals that even now possess the mountains from whence their brave fathers were driven. But farther away, beyond the crests of the great mountains, still dwell many of the people Mazika claims as his own. There still wander the bold children of the tribe of the Maquilisini, of the royal blood of the great and mighty king T'Chaka. They are men and warriors, and of them Mazika is not ashamed to say that he is one. They are the men who can die like men and meet face to face in battle the warriors against whom they fight. They are not dogs and jackals who creep upon the prey they are hungry to possess when the backs of those they seek are turned. Oh that Mazika could with this axe draw from his veins every drop of the blood that may be mixed even so little with that of these Zulu dogs, whose fathers once sat with his fathers in the house of the Amazulu!"

As he speaks he brandishes somewhat wildly about his head the great axe he carries, then a moment later drops it and stands gazing away into space as motionless as though carven in stone.

He is a powerful-looking man, fully six feet three or four inches in height, with a pair of shoulders and long, sinewy arms that seem to have in them strength enough to fell an ox at one blow. But, strange to say, his feet and hands are rather small for his size and quite aristocratic-looking in shape, while his face has few of the features of the negro. His nose is high and long, with the thin, dilating nostrils so often seen in those race-horses noted for their powers of endurance. His hair is piled in masses on top of his head, with a brilliantly shining black ring of gum crowning the centre. His mouth is large and his jaws as strong and firmly set as those of a mastiff. But for the keen, brown, restless eyes that light up the face it would have a grimness and severity about it that would render it almost a terror to those not accustomed to the sight of it. But the heart of the Zulu, though stern and brave when the necessity offers, is nevertheless warm and tender, and in many things he is as gentle as a woman.

At the great gate Mazika and Pitsane leave them, while the others take their way on toward the mission-house. As they reach the brow of the hill near the kotla an unusual stir and the hum of many voices about the hut of Mopane, that stands some little distance from the chief's hut, attract their attention.

"I wonder what old Mopane can be about now?" Pierce says quickly. "I don't like the look of that crowd, and the sounds, too, are a little suspicious. Suppose we go by and see what it all means?"

The entrance to the palisades enclosing the hut and its little patch of garden is wide open, as is also the door of the hut. About the latter are congregated many moving forms, which make way at once as the little group from the mission-house draws near. Within the hut and plainly in view are Mopane, Bubi and several of the head-men of the tribe. Something altogether unusual seems to be going on, to judge from the appearance of Mopane, the chief and the others.

Bubi is so dressed that at first sight it would be difficult to associate him with the tall, intelligent-looking chief in civilized dress we have first seen on the veranda of the mission-house. His scarlet uniform has been completely discarded, and in its place he wears a single garment of leopard-skin that is fastened about his neck and falls nearly to his knees, with wide openings at the sides through which his arms, naked to the shoulders, are thrust. Behind, this garment is adorned with innumerable white cow-tails that sweep the floor as he walks. Around his neck are many strings of large glass beads, while his ankles and wrists are bound with broad bands of copper wire from which are pendent many jingling bits of steel, iron and ivory. His head is adorned with innumerable feathers of the eagle and vulture and his face covered with a smearing of red and yellow paint. In his right hand he carried a rungu, or knob-club, and in his left a great shield made of rhinoceros-hide painted in bands of black and white.

Mopane is even more gorgeously arrayed. About his middle is a covering made of white monkey-skins with the tails pendent and striking below the knees. Around his neck is gathered a flowing garment of brilliant red baize, which falls behind in a train and is carefully carried by a small boy. All over his body are fastened innumerable charms and little sacks of "medicine," while two enormous antelope-horns, beautifully polished, are strapped upon his head. In one hand he holds the jaw-bone of some large animal and in the other a dried gourd filled with rattling pebbles.

As Cunnyngham and Pierce first reach the doorway and gaze through it into the hut, Bubi, preceded by Mopane, is passing around in a circle, each muttering the words of some low, weird chant, while at the end of every stanza Mopane wildly throws his arms into the air as though invoking the aid of an unseen spirit. At the same time he rattles violently the pebbles in the gourd. Directly the rain-maker drops upon his knees and dips his head once or twice toward the floor, while Bubi stands near him with a solemn face, and the other men in the hut join hands and circle about them, chanting the words of the same guttural refrain Mopane and the chief have just been singing.

In a little while the chant stops and the men withdraw to the shadow of the walls. Rising to his feet, Mopane now faces the chief, who immediately drops to a recumbent position upon the floor, while Mopane moves nearer. Then Mopane takes from a small basket a beautifully polished ox-horn which is filled with a soft white powder. Some of this powder he spreads out upon the chief's hand, and then begins another weird chant as he bends above it. He next scrapes it carefully from the chief's hand into a small vessel of stoneware, to which he adds other powders obtained from various little sacks upon his body. Last of all, he pours into it a crimson liquid that comes from the covered basket. Then, flourishing the jawbone thrice across it, he raises the vessel in his hand, swings it wildly above his head in a circle, shrieks out some fearful incantation, and the next moment presses it against the chief's lips, bidding him drink. This he obediently does, while the wicked-looking face of Mopane is working with the most horrible contortions. Ere Bubi has drunk quite all the contents of the vessel Mopane's hand again seizes it, and pours what is left down the throat of a cock one of the men is holding. The next instant the head of the terrified bird is completely severed from its body by one swift, dextrous stroke of Mopane's glittering knife. Then, while the headless body is giving convulsive plunges, Mopane smears his face and hands in the warm, spirting blood.

"This is too horrible!" exclaims Ellie, as, covering her face with her hands, her slight frame trembles like that of one shaken by an ague. "Let us go; I can stand no more. Oh, of what can Bubi be thinking?"

Hope too is trembling violently, and as they pass out through the opening in the palisades her brother has to support her.

"It is too dreadful you girls should have seen that," Cunnyngham says in an unsteady voice as they go on toward the kotla. "Had I for a moment dreamed of the nature of that gathering, I would never have encouraged your coming hither. Why, Bubi seems possessed, while as to Mopane— well, he is just too horribly wicked for anything. He seems to have Bubi again completely under his control, and that is one point very clear."

"What did it all mean?" Hope asks, not yet sufficiently recovered from the nervous excitement of the moment to control her voice, so that the question is spoken very little above a whisper.

"Simply one of Mopane's high-and-mighty exhibitions of the old-time sorcery of his people," answers Pierce. "He certainly must have laid his plans very cunningly, or father would have found out something about it. It surprised me to see so many of the head-men there, and taking part too. Poor fellows! this threatened Boer and Zulu attack seems to have completely demoralized some of them."

"Oh what will father say?" Ellie cries as she clasps her hands unconsciously in her emotion, while her eyes are filling with tears. "Poor father! he has counted so much on Bubi's firmness and the genuineness of his conversion."

"Bubi has his weak points like all of us," says Cunnyngham pityingly, "in spite of his many fine qualities. It is hard for him at his age altogether to shake off the longings after the old superstitious practices of his fathers. He is very impressionable and easily worked upon. I doubt not that Mopane has made him fear that some terrible calamity will overtake him and his people if he does not call upon the aid of the many unseen spirits in which the tribe has for generations had full confidence. I feel assured that he has made the poor chief believe that these spirits must be appeased in some way, or else he and all the village will be destroyed when they go into battle."

"But Bubi seemed so far above all this!" Ellie says again. "He appeared so earnest and faithful in his professions—so repentant too after that affair with the poor cow whose throat he let Mopane cut. Oh, how can he act in this way? how can he deceive us so?"

"Do not be too hard upon him, dear cousin," Cunnyngham says again. "Bubi is but a poor weak savage after all, and it is hard at his age, even with the strength of Christ's love in his heart to help him, to quite draw himself away from the old habits and customs of his people, especially in the presence of so wily a tempter as Mopane. It is like seeking to tear up a strong tree that has stood long rooted in one place."

When Mr. Lillington is told of what has transpired at Mopane's hut his heart is heavy within him, though his faith never once falters. One there is, he knows, whose ways are past our finding out, and who in his own good time will doubtless give him to see how out of this very evil good may be wrought.

"God is good," the missionary murmurs to himself. "He has promised, and most steadfast is that promise, that Israel through him shall yet be redeemed from his iniquities."

CHAPTER VI.

"From everlasting to everlasting Thou art God."

"TO-DAY is court-day in Lepelole, Captain Murray," says Pierce gayly, as a morning or two later they are all sitting about the breakfast-table. "Will not you and Mr. Cumming come with us? You will see some sights and hear some arguments from the lawyers on both sides that will well repay you."

"Courts and lawyers?" questions Captain Murray. "Why, isn't this quite progressive for a South-African native village?"

"Oh yes, indeed it is. It was my father's idea. All the graver offences are carried to him and to the chief for adjustment, but the petty affairs he has arranged to have settled by a regular court; and it works beautifully, I can assure you."

The court holds its session in the kotla. The judge is a grave-looking old Bamangwato warrior, who follows with a most serious and attentive expression every point of the various testimonies, and whose charges to the jury often evince a clearness of insight and a power of reasoning that sometimes astonish even Mr. Lillington. The lawyers are all chosen because of their readiness of speech and gift of argument, that makes them the envied of their less fortunate fellows. As to the jury, they are generally very wise and knowing-looking, despite the fact that they are pledged beforehand to have no previous leaning to either side.

One of the cases tried on this occasion amuses Captain Murray very much. Even grave Mr. Cumming smiles more than once over it. It, however, shows them very clearly just how shrewd and intelligent some of these Bamangwato amateur lawyers really are.

The case is against two men who have been caught in the very act of dragging off to eat the carcass of a neighbor's ox. Their defence is that they did not slay the animal, but found it dying of a wound inflicted by another ox, which, according to an old-established custom of the Bamangwatos, made it theirs, especially as they claim to have driven off the infuriated beast that inflicted the wound and rescued the dying animal from the probability of being devoured by hyenas.

When the defence is ended the lawyer for the prosecution arises and begins in true lawyer-fashion to examine the chief witness, whereupon the following colloquy ensues:

Lawyer. "Does an ox-tail grow up or down or sideways?"

Witness. "It grows downward."

L. " Do the horns of an ox grow up or down or sideways ?"

W. " They grow upward."

L. " If an ox gores another ox, does he not lower his head and gore upward?"

W. " He does."

L. " Could the ox whose horns are turned downward gore upward ?"

W. " He could not."

" Just so it is," concludes the wily interrogator as he turns to the jury triumphantly, " and if you will examine the ox found in the possession of the accused you will find that the wound has been given downward, and hence could not have been made by the horn of another ox, as claimed by the defence, but by the stab of some instrument; and as animals are not in the habit of carrying swords or knives around with them in this country, we may well know what to think." *

On making an examination this is found to be the case, and so the offenders are sent to work twenty days on the village streets.

The next day the long-expected hunting-party from the Cape arrives, and the morning following, at daybreak, Captain Murray, Mr. Cumming, Inkoosi and the Hottentot Chaka bid adieu to their friends at the mission-station and set off for Zambezi.

* This cross-examination is given almost literally, though it did not occur in this part of Africa.

The following Thursday afternoon, as Ellie was down in the cellar superintending old Mamochisane and Jim, who were busy cutting up meat to dry, she was given quite a shock by seeing her father appear suddenly at the door with a white, set face and almost speechless from some excitement that had evidently very nearly overcome him.

"Father," she cries, springing at once to his side and clasping her hands together in nervous dread, "what has happened? Why do you look so? Tell me quickly."

"Bubi!" he gasps almost inarticulately—"Bubi has been blown up in an explosion of gunpowder. We know not how badly he may be hurt; he may be dead even now."

"How did it happen?" she asks, trembling so that she can hardly stand.

"Through some wicked experiment of Mopane's. The rain-maker was trying, as he said, to get the 'bewitchment' out of the powder."

"And is Mopane also hurt?"

"Yes, to some extent, but nothing at all like poor Bubi. The chief was bending directly over the powder when Mopane blew the spark into it. I do not like to judge," he says, only for her ears to catch, "but it seems to me to have been premeditated. Mopane certainly knew that the powder would explode."

"Poor, poor Bubi!" Ellie exclaims pitifully. "Will he really die, father?"

"I do not know, my child. I have not made a close examination yet. I came for my medicine-case. Will you not go with me and try to say something that will comfort poor Nyamona? She seems nearly beside herself over this terrible accident to her husband. Indeed, the whole village is so excited that every man and woman seems as a creature demented. It is a wonder you did not hear some of the cries and lamentations."

"I thought I did, father, at one time hear an unusual noise, but I have been down in the cellar nearly all the afternoon."

"Well, leave what you are doing now to Mamochisane and Jim and come with me to the chief's house. In the mean time, dear," in a lowered tone, "give no hint to any one of my suspicions in regard to Mopane. I may judge him unjustly, after all. Did the village but get even so much as an inkling that he had willfully led the chief into danger, I would not answer for his life, rain-maker though he is. This is truly a bad affair," he concludes, "and if the chief dies it will be worse still."

"We must trust in God and hope for the best," Ellie says bravely, unconsciously taking her father's place as comforter.

They find a large crowd around the door of the chief's hut. In truth, so large is it that they have much difficulty in making their way through it; but all press back as best they can to make way for the missionary and his daughter. Sobs and moans are heard on every side, even cries and wailings from strong men, for the chief has been much beloved and this calamity is sudden and grievous. But the lamentations of poor Nyamona, the one faithful wife the chief has retained after his conversion to Christianity, are heartrending to hear. The poor chief lies stretched upon his couch of skins, blind, speechless and almost without life. It is an appealing and a pathetic sight.

It takes all Ellie's powers of persuasion to get Nyamona away from the chief's side long enough for her father to make the examination he desires. With a sad and heavy heart Mr. Lillington soon discovers that for poor Bubi recovery is impossible. He may, however, linger for some days, and the painful knowledge of the chief's real condition he determines to keep to himself, at least for a time. He will doubtless tell the older members of his own family, but no one else.

Bubi in a short while recovers consciousness, but his intense suffering has rendered him so weak that it is with great difficulty he can reply to the good missionary's questionings even in monosyllables. In the mean time, Mr. Lillington has given him something to deaden in part his pain, and applied soothing lotions to his burnt face, chest and shoulders.

After the first burst of passionate weeping, and having been considerably quieted by Ellie's gentle comforting words, Nyamona makes her way back to the chief's side, and remains there calm, tearless and watchful. Cautioning her to let Bubi speak only when absolutely necessary, and giving her careful instructions as to how to administer the medicines he places in her hands, Mr. Lillington with Ellie leaves the hut, promising to return in a short while.

The next morning Mr. Lillington informs the older members of his household of Bubi's true condition, and also tells them sadly that the end may be even nearer than he thinks. His words seem prophetic, for that very afternoon he is summoned to the bedside of the chief. The messenger is no other than Sebubi, the eldest son of the chief and the successor to the chieftainship in case of the latter's death. Weak and vain as he is, Sebubi has nevertheless a tender heart, and his father's terrible condition seems to have made a deep impression upon him, for the tears are rolling down his cheeks as he entreats Mr. Lillington to do all he can to save the chief.

Ellie, Hope, Cunnyngham and Pierce accompany Mr. Lillington to the hut. It is a solemn and impressive scene as they stand grouped about the bed of the dying chief—for dying they can now see plainly that he is—and a scene that not one of them ever forgets. Poor Nyamona, to whom Mr. Lillington has told the sad truth, is sobbing bitterly but noiselessly in a distant corner, for, having been cautioned that an outburst of any kind may prove hurtful to the chief, she bravely controls every paroxysm. Near his father's head Sebubi has taken up his position, and stands there weak, trembling and smitten with terror in the consciousness of the approach of some dread presence, of some impending danger, he knows not what. How truly awful is the march of this fearful shadow of death to him whose groping, darkened soul can grasp no light from the Beyond!

"Come nearer, good father," the chief says faintly. "Put out your hand and touch Bubi, that he may know you are here. Oh, alas is me! The soul of Bubi is undone! O friend of my heart's best love! if I had but hearkened unto the words you spoke!"

"It is not too late yet, Bubi, poor friend," the missionary returns in soothing but resolute tones as he bends nearer and lays his hand upon that of the chief.

"'Not too late'! Oh, say you so, my father? Then, indeed, does the soul of Bubi leap at the words. Tell me, tell me of the great God you serve, and to whom you were ever trying to keep Bubi faithful; is he not very, very angry?"

"I doubt not that he is angry, Bubi," the missionary says firmly, but in the same kind tones, "but he will not long remain so if Bubi will tell him how sorry he is that he has offended him."

"Oh, he must know—he must know how Bubi

hates the strong hard head, the sinful heart, that led him to pay no heed to the good father's entreaty. The words of Mopane were as the blast that rushes through the forests. They drove poor Bubi before them as the leaves are blown hither and thither upon the ground. The words of Mopane were tempting and as the honey that drops from the trees. The words of Mopane were deceitful as the flashing of the lake that is no lake within the desert.* Oh that Bubi had never hearkened thereto! But if it is true, as the good father says, that the great God will forgive, then is Bubi no longer afraid to go to him."

"Yes, Bubi, my friend, he will forgive. The great God of whom I have told you is both patient and long-suffering, and he that cometh unto him repentant and believing he will in no wise cast out."

"And will he open to Bubi the gate of the mighty village where he dwells? or will he leave him without, to wander alone upon the great black hills where the wolves are and where the vultures wait to pick the bones of those the wolves destroy?"

"If Bubi goes believing and repentant and knocks upon the gate, humbly asking admittance in the name of the Lord Jesus Christ, who gave himself to die upon the cross for all such as Bubi, then will the gate be opened. O my friend!"

* The mirage.

goes on the missionary with impassioned fervor as he bends nearer and clasps the hand of the dying chief in his, "cannot you understand that while he hates sin and condemns it, he is yet Love itself? He forgives because he loves to forgive. Lean upon him, Bubi—lean hard, my friend, and trust him to the end, even when your feet are sinking deep within the mire over on the other shore. If all seems dark at first, it will but be a trial of your faith. Oh," he goes on in the same impassioned tones, turning his head as though to address those about him—"oh, *when* will man begin to realize that 'he that committeth sin is the servant of sin,' and that the 'wages of sin is death'? But thank God for the blessed privilege of repentance! Thank God, too, above all else, for the precious 'blood of Jesus Christ that cleanseth from all sin'! Oh the inestimable gift of that eternal life we have through Jesus Christ our Lord!"

"Oh," cries Bubi suddenly, striving to raise himself upon his elbow, "I see a light, a little light!" But it must have been the light breaking upon the other shore, since poor Bubi's sightless eyes will nevermore catch a ray upon earth.

A few moments he lies silent, then as a look of indescribable gladness steals across his poor burnt face, he makes a feeble effort to clasp his hands together, while his lips murmur faintly, "Lord Jesus Christ, I believe in the forgiveness of sins."

He lies quiet after this for perhaps five or ten

minutes. Then rousing himself once more, he asks suddenly for Ellie. She comes tearful and silent to his side, for for the time she is so overcome as to be incapable of speech.

"Bubi wants to touch the hand for the last time and say good-bye to the child of the good father—to the little missy with the brave heart and the steady eyes who has told Bubi and Bubi's people so many beautiful things of the great God who lives on high. Child of the good father, Bubi wants to thank you for the earnest words and for all the gentle ways; he wants to beg you that when he is gone you will still talk to his people, that you will seek to win them from the old evil ways, that you will still tell them of the loving God who smiles when they do what he wishes them to do, and who is very angry when they disobey. And Sebubi—Sebubi, who is to take the place of Bubi when he is gone—will you not say again and again to him the words that will make him a good son to his mother and an upright chief to his people? Will the little missy do what poor Bubi asks?"

"I will try, Bubi—oh, I will try with all my heart," Ellie answers between her sobs.

"And Nyamona? Will the child of the good father be very kind to poor Nyamona, whose soul will be very sore when the soul of Bubi leaves it?"

"I will do everything I can for Nyamona, Bubi."

"Then the great God bless the little missy, and when the message shall come for her own white soul, may it fly as the dove flies straight to the sweet-scented groves in the garden of the King's palace. Oh, there will be no waiting at the gate for little missy. Her white wings will bear her over the wall, and the King's Son himself will guide her to the house of his Father. The child of the good father has spoken very bravely to Bubi and to Bubi's people; with her own mouth she has told them many things that have sunk into their hearts as the seed sinks into the moist earth; therefore will the great God, in whose service she has spoken, reward her. God bless you! God bless you! brave-mouthed, white-souled child of the good father—God bless you!"

After calling his son to him and giving him many words of warning and of wise counsel, and taking a most touching adieu of the grief-stricken Nyamona, Bubi lies silent again for many moments. A little later the same smile they have previously noted gathers about his lips, while he murmurs over and over, "The forgiveness of sins! the forgiveness of sins! Lord Jesus Christ, I believe in the forgiveness of sins."

Ten minutes thereafter he is dead, with the same smile beautifying all his poor burnt face. Although the whole village is willing, nay desirous, that over Bubi's body shall be performed the rites of Christian burial, yet they at the same time claim the privilege of interring him in accordance with the customs of his fathers. He has been a great chief, they declare, one of the greatest the Bamangwatos have ever had, and he must therefore be buried with all the honors and ceremonies befitting his rank. To this Mr. Lillington makes no dissent. It can do no harm, he tells himself, to allow these poor savages to find what solace they can for their grief in burying their chief as his fathers for long ages before him have been buried. So that Bubi's soul has found eternal peace in the land beyond, it cannot matter in what way his body, the mere shell, the husk of life, is given back to the dust from whence it came.

As soon, therefore, as Bubi is dead he is dressed in the full costume of a Bamangwato chief. His club and shield are then laid beside him, and he is placed in a sitting position upon the same couch of skins where he has died. His arms are folded across his breast, his feet drawn up and his head bent forward until his chin touches his knees. A glossy leopard-skin is finally thrown over him, and two vessels half full of water are set, one on either side.

From the time that Bubi is placed in this position until he is borne forth to his interment, which is near sundown on the third day from that on which he has died, there are kept up, at intervals of an hour each, the solemn roll of the drum and the beating of several rude instruments.

On the morning of the first day after the death a great feast is spread under the trees in front of the hut, of which all partake. Late in the afternoon of the third day the body is borne in sad and slow procession to its last resting-place. The grave has been dug by itself not far from the centre of the valley that lies without the mission-station, and is some seventy-five or a hundred yards from the mound where Mrs. Lillington and her children are buried, and between it and the native cemetery. Just above it is a widespreading tree with deep-green foliage. It seems to stand as a lonely sentinel, keeping watch beside the dead in their silent slumbers.

The grave is dug six feet deep and three square, and when finished the interior is rubbed with the large bulbs of a certain kind of wild flower. The bottom is then sprinkled with water from a bowl into which the branches of a tree that bears red berries have previously been trailed. The grave being in readiness, the body of Bubi is placed therein, still in a sitting posture, with the face toward the north. Mr. Lillington's voice is broken with emotion as with uncovered head he reads the deep and impressive words of the Christian burial service:

"I am the Resurrection and the Life: he that believeth in me, though he were dead yet shall he live; and whosoever liveth and believeth in me shall never die. . . .

"Lord, thou hast been our dwelling-place in all generations.

"Before the mountains were brought forth, or ever thou hadst formed the earth and the world, even from everlasting to everlasting thou art God."

As the words of the fervent prayer he offers up at the close of the reading fall from the minister's lips, he steps slowly backward and leaves the people free to carry out whatever may be their will in regard to the further burial-ceremonies of their chief. Two men now approach to place within the hands of the corpse of the chief his club and shield, which during the progress of the body to the grave have lain beside it on the bier. This undertaking, however, is hard to accomplish, as the poor, powerless hands of the corpse again and again refuse to do what is required of them. But finally, after a great deal of propping up and moving of the hands into first one position and then another, it is accomplished. A number of eagle-feathers are now placed within the hair, the whole body being at length covered with a kaross, or skin rug, most beautifully dressed.

This done, four of the men lower themselves into the grave and begin packing tightly and carefully about the body a fine clay previously prepared. This work is kept up until the clay reaches the mouth. The earth is then thrown in by means of bowls in the hands of the women.

All the spaces in the grave being now filled, a number of sprigs of acacia with several long stems of grass are placed directly over the chief's head and packed about with the earth to keep them in position. When the grave is entirely filled the ends of these are left exposed in the centre of the mound. All this being completed, several bowls of water are poured upon the grave by the women, who cry as they do so, "Pula! pula! water! water!" following the cries by a mournful kind of dirge, the refrain of which is "Yo! yo! yo!" All the while they are doing this the spectators clap their hands silently as though applauding. This finished, the people withdraw and leave the grave to poor Nyamona and the chie's daughters, who at once prostrate themselves upon it and give vent to the most distressing lamentations.

On the fifth day after Bubi's burial the mound is enclosed by slabs of stone cemented together. A canopy on stout poles is also raised above it, while innumerable polished stones, bits of colored earthenware and the skulls of various animals are placed about the slabs.

Many and grave apprehensions now fill the waking hours of Mr. Lillington, while his sleep is constantly troubled by torturing dreams. Bubi is dead and Sebubi has succeeded him in the chieftaincy; and well does the good missionary know the effect this intelligence will have upon the Zulus when it reaches them. It may take weeks, however, for them to hear of it, while, on the other hand, they may have already heard of it. This depends upon whether they really have spies and scouts out, as has been apprehended. But all the same, they will hear of it only too soon, the missionary thinks with a sinking heart.

So far, no sign of the Zulus has been seen anywhere near the mission-station, and but for the threatening messages that have continued to come with unpleasant regularity through the various native traders passing back and forth, Mr. Lillington would look upon his anxious fears of the past three weeks as only the tormenting fancies of some fevered dream.

Poor Bubi's tragic death is deeply and universally mourned. Even Mopane seems greatly changed thereby, and Mr. Lillington thinks with some compunction that he may, after all, have misjudged him in regard to the share he has had in the chief's untimely taking off. Doubtless, he reasons, if Mopane had intended the explosion of powder to injure Bubi, he would have been careful himself in keeping farther away from it. His own hands and arms have been severely burned. His horribly tattooed face, too, is rendered still more hideous by several scars that are left upon it when the burnt flesh has healed.

Somehow, in spite of the repentant protestations of Mopane and the deep remorse he seems to feel in regard to being the cause of poor Bubi's death,

Mr. Lillington cannot trust him. There is something in his face and in his manner that does not bear the stamp of sincerity, and although Mr. Lillington does not quite believe that Bubi's death has been intentional on Mopane's part, yet he cannot help but feel that Mopane is not so sorry as he seems. Then, too, some of Mopane's movements of late have grown a little suspicious. Try as hard as he can, Mr. Lillington finds himself unable to get rid of a feeling of vague uneasiness that has taken possession of him in regard to Mopane.

"Is it possible that this man is really a traitor at heart?" the missionary asks himself again and again. "Could he do a thing so mean as to sell his own people into the hands of their enemies?"

Sometimes he feels as though he must speak out and accuse him before the tribe, but when he recalls that he has, after all, nothing with which to accuse him beyond mere suspicion, cooler judgment prevails. The man may really be entirely innocent despite the compromising circumstances that surround him. If this were the case, his accusation would doubtless only result in the bringing about of a state of affairs not at all to be desired.

In the mean time, despite the sad interruption of Bubi's death, Mr. Lillington and the boys, aided by Mazika and Pitsane, have been busy stocking the cave with a view to its future occupancy. They have also made ample provision for a journey of several days across the plains in case such a one should become necessary. The wagon and sixteen of the best salted oxen have already been conveyed thither, with enough provisions to last a party of a dozen or more several weeks. There is also a good supply of bedding, cooking utensils and many other useful articles, including a change of clothing for each member of the family. The oxen, too, are well provided for, not only in the supply of food stored away for them in the cave, but also in the amount of pasturage the upper end of the cañon affords with its many waving and luxuriant grasses.

CHAPTER VII.

"For lo, the wicked bend the bow."

ON the night of the tenth day after Bubi's burial the station is visited by one of those terrible rain- and thunder-storms which seem preeminently to distinguish Africa. But so terrible is the one that now breaks upon the village that all others that have preceded it seem as nothing. It begins just as the evening services at the kotla are concluded, and continues with but little abatement for fully an hour. The night is rendered absolutely dreadful by the terrific peals of thunder and the vivid and startling flashes of lightning, while the rain pours in torrents and the angry winds go shrieking by.

But, though the storm is so terrible, little damage is done by it beyond the blowing down of one or two huts, the partial unroofing of the schoolhouse, and the killing of a few cattle by the lightning. Yet it has a most demoralizing effect upon the poor Bamangwatos. Coming so soon after Bubi's death, they look upon it as the herald of some far worse calamity. In vain Mr. Lillington tries to reason with them, and to assure them that the storm has come only through natural causes. The great God is very angry with them, they tremblingly declare. First he has taken Bubi from them, and now he has caused to break over them the mighty rushing and roaring of his elements, during which the earth has been dressed in fire and the voice of the thunder is more terrible than that of all the wild beasts upon the hills. Next he will send some awful thing that will sweep them all out of existence.

To add further to Mr. Lillington's anxiety, the news is now brought to the village that a large band of Zulus had again been seen the evening before, and not more than four or five miles from the mission-station. It is true they may not be a hostile band, but only a company on their way down to the Cape bent solely on trading purposes. Bands of this kind have passed through Bubi's territory before, and are likely to pass again at almost any time. But these reflections, nevertheless, do not diminish Mr. Lillington's anxiety nor cause him to delay a moment in getting his little garrison in readiness for the attack that may come now at almost any moment.

As the evening closes in he has done all that can be done. The cannon has been cleaned and reloaded, the guns divided, the spears and battle-axes newly polished and sharpened and everything placed in readiness. All along the walls sentinels are mounted, with the number doubled at the weaker points. Mr. Lillington has in the mean time talked with Hope and Ellie upon the same subject previously broached to the two youths in the cave. They know now what is his desire in case the enemy should succeed in entering the station. With the tears streaming down their cheeks they entreat him to require anything else of them but this, declaring, as the youths have done, that they would rather die with him than save their lives by deserting him. It is long ere he can restore them to any degree of calmness or bring them to see that their refusal, instead of benefiting him, will only render his position the more trying; and it is not until he assures them that, after all, there may be chances of escape for him that they consent to do as he wishes, though still sadly against their own feelings.

The signal for them to leave the mission-house for the cave has now been agreed upon, and it is to be three sharp, rapid strokes of the church-bell.

"Must you go out again to-night, father?" Ellie questions of him anxiously, as, having finished supper and having had prayers, he is taking up his hat to leave the room.

"Yes, my child. I have asked every man in the village, except those on guard, to meet me at this hour at the kotla. There are affairs of grave import about which I must talk to them."

"Oh how I wish you did not have to go! I

hope you will not think me weak and childish, father, but somehow I feel as though something were going to happen to-night—something dreadful. I try to tell myself that it is only the result of the nervous strain in which I have been all day, but I can't get rid of the feeling. Please don't call it foolish, but if you just wouldn't go to the kotla I would feel so much better."

"You are excited and nervous, my child, as you suggest. It is not to be wondered at, after all that has been talked over to-day. Try to compose yourself, my dear. We know not, it is true, what a day may bring forth, but there assuredly can be no more danger in my going to the kotla than in remaining here."

As he turns to leave her he notes that her eyes are filling with tears. Obeying a sudden yearning, he opens his arms to her. With a little cry she springs to their embrace; then as her own are clasped about his neck she draws his head down until his lips meet hers.

"Good-bye, father," she says, struggling bravely with her emotion as she kisses him.

"You mean good-night, my dear child?" he says, returning the caress. "But there is no need for either 'good-night' or 'good-bye,' as I shall return before your bed-time."

"I do not think there will be bed-time for any of us to-night, dear father, except the children," she says sadly. "I, for one, cannot go to sleep when danger seems so near, and I have heard my brother and cousins say the same."

"But it may not be so near as we apprehend. We have seen nothing absolutely to warrant this state of feeling. We have no more cause to expect the Zulus to-night than we have had any night since their threats began," he says, trying to reassure her; yet, thinking of the band of prowling Matabele seen only yesterday, he does not himself feel as composed as he would have her believe.

"Where are the boys, Ellie?" he stops to question as he again starts to go out.

"They are in the sitting-room with Hope and the children."

"Well, I wish you would ask Cunnyngham to make a tour of the walls while I am at the kotla, and report to me on my return."

"And if he finds anything amiss, father, shall he not speak to you at once in regard to it?"

"Yes, dear, if it is anything of grave import."

When his uncle's request is made known to him, Cunnyngham goes at once to attend to it.

He has been out of the room barely fifteen minutes when Ellie is much surprised to hear him returning. At sound of his footsteps coming rapidly across the veranda she unconsciously rises to meet him. Cunnyngham is greatly excited, but seems striving to overcome as much of it as he can before speaking.

"Ellie," he questions hurriedly as he comes up beside her, "do you think uncle could have put Mopane on guard at the front gate?"

Ellie starts visibly at the words, while her face pales.

"I am sure he did not," she returns quickly. "I know father's opinion of Mopane too well to believe for a moment that he would have given him any such post of trust."

"Well, he is there, all the same. I saw him with my own eyes not ten minutes since."

"There surely must be some mistake," Ellie says again, her anxiety deepening. "Are you certain, Cunnyngham, that it was Mopane you saw at the gate?"

"'Certain,' cousin? Why, as certain as that I am looking at you now. He was on the platform at the right of the great gate and peering over the wall. What makes me more anxious than anything else is that there seemed to be no sentinel on the other platform. Mopane, so far as I could see, was alone."

"And did he see you?"

"He did not. Somehow, I felt that it would be best for me not to show myself. Even if he were there rightfully, I knew he would resent any inspection on my part, he is so conceited and headstrong."

"Oh, I am sure something is dreadfully wrong," Hope cries at this moment, starting up from her chair and throwing her arms with a sudden movement about Ellie's shoulders. "We all know what uncle thinks of Mopane, and if he is at the gate, rest assured my uncle did not put him there."

"No, I feel satisfied my father did not," Pierce here speaks up, "and he must be informed of it at once."

"Just what I had concluded," Cunnyngham says. "But," after a moment's hesitancy, "will uncle like me to disturb him with such a thing as this?"

"Yes, oh yes he will!" cries Ellie excitedly. "Father must know it, and at once. Do not delay a moment."

As she speaks she pushes him gently toward the door, but at the very moment there comes a sound, or rather a commingling of sounds, that strikes terror to every heart. It is the noise of many hurrying, trampling feet, hoarse wild shouts, blood-curdling shrieks; then the sickening ring of steel, and then the discharge of musketry.

"God help us!" Ellie cries, staggering back against the door. "It is the Zulus, and they are even now within the village."

An agonized shriek bursts from Hope, and for a moment she looks as though she were going to faint. The next instant Cunnyngham's arm is around her and he is holding her tightly against him, while his own heart throbs wildly and his face is pale and set.

At Ellie's cry Mamochisane has attempted to rise from her chair, has fallen back again, and is now rocking aimlessly to and fro, moaning to herself, while the baby, aroused from its light slumber, is sobbing affrightedly against her shoulder. Marvin and Henrietta too are both crying bitterly and clinging to their sister's dress as though its folds at present constitute the only ark of safety left them on earth. It is a pathetic scene.

"Yes, it is the Zulus," says Cunnyngham in a stifled voice. "They are even now at the kotla. Mopane has proved the traitor and let them in. Now I know why he was so intently peering over the wall. The Zulus were even then hiding in the ditch and awaiting his signal to enter. Oh, if my uncle had but heeded Captain Murray's warning about that ditch! My God! those cries are horrible, and many of them are cries of women and children.—Let me go, Hope. I must go to my uncle: I cannot stand here and think of him as being butchered."

At these words an agonized cry breaks from both Ellie and Pierce.

"Oh, my father!" the latter cries wildly as he rushes toward the door; "I must help him or else die with him."

"Yes, go, brother, go," Ellie urges. "We cannot, oh we *cannot* do what he has asked."

As Pierce springs through the doorway Cunnyngham is close beside him. Both are half way across the veranda when suddenly there come the three sharp, distinct strokes of the church-bell.

Cunnyngham stops as though a heavy hand has fallen upon him.

"Oh sister, cousin," he cries, springing back toward them, "I *must* do as my uncle entreated. It is his own hand that has rung the bell, and I must obey. He made me promise him again and again that I would not disobey. It will kill him to know that you are left to the mercy of the savages. Oh, come, I beseech you. There is no time to lose. Come, all you! Quick! let us go!"

But Pierce has not turned back. He has kept straight on. At the head of the short flight of steps leading down into the yard he comes in sudden and violent contact with some one coming up with the same haste that he is going down. It is the Hottentot Pitsane. The little attire that he wears is in wild disorder, while the gleaming black skin of his arms and breast is splashed with blood. Without a word he seizes Pierce and drags him back into the room.

"The good father has sent me to his children," he said as soon as he could command his breath. "The gates of the village have been opened by the traitor dog Mopane, who through his lies gained the places of Sansawe and Motlatsa. Thus the wolves have crept upon the lions as with their backs turned they sat within the kotla. The numbers of the Matabele to the Bamangwatos are as five to one; therefore it will go hard with the Bamangwatos. But the good father is brave, his heart is as the heart of the great rhinoceros, and his people will fight like warriors and men. But the hand of the good father cannot be steady in battle until he knows that those who are dearer to him than the eyes with which he sees or the ears with which he hears are beyond the wolves' fangs. Therefore he has sent Pitsane to see that his children are safe within the cave."

"We must do as my uncle wishes," says Cunnyngham with decision. "There is no use to hesitate longer. If we delay all may be lost.—Pierce, dear cousin, bear yourself like a man and think of your sister!"

The terrible sounds in the direction of the kotla have increased tenfold, though it is not so much the cries and shrieks now as the sickening ring of steel and the deafening volleys of the musketry. It is a hand-to-hand battle, and because of the overwhelming numbers of the enemy and the disadvantage under which the Bamangwatos have been caught, it grows fiercer and more desperate for the latter every moment. It is well that with all they surmise the heartsore little band now creeping noiselessly along within the shadow of the garden-wall are far from suspecting anything like the real state of the case. If they did, it is doubtful if even with all Pitsane's effort they could keep from rushing back.

Never has the way to the cave seemed so long to the two youths, who for the time have manfully suppressed their own emotion for sake of the gentle, suffering girls, whose chief protectors they have so suddenly become. But the cave is reached at last, and they at once set about the kindling of a fire in order to dispel the darkness, which in their present state of mind seems all the more oppressive.

Pitsane stays by them helping, but as soon as he sees that they are as comfortably provided for as they could be under the circumstances, he suddenly raises himself from before the fire, exclaiming,

"Now will Pitsane to the village to see how fare the brave lions the cowardly wolves have attacked."

"If you are going to return to the village, Pitsane," Pierce says with sudden resolution, "then I am going with you. I *must* know something of my father."

"Do not think of such a thing," Cunnyngham interposes. "It will be the height of rashness. Why, by this time the whole village is swarming with Zulus, and wherever you may go you will be certain to be seen and slain."

But it seems useless to reason with Pierce. His heart is sick with anxiety over his father's uncertain fate, and even death in its most dreadful form would be preferable to his present feelings. His sister too, beside herself with grief and solicitude, is urging him to go, not seeming to realize in her distracted state just what it is to which she is sending him. As Pierce goes out behind Pitsane, Cunnyngham's eyes sadly follow him. He expects never to see his cousin again in life.

"Try to be as cautious as you can, Pierce," he urges, "and do not give your life rashly."

He follows them to the entrance to speak these words, with his hand lingering on Pierce's shoulder some minutes after the words are spoken. After watching them as far as he can see them through the dense shadows of the gorge, Cunnyngham returns within, replenishes the fire, speaks to Ellie and Hope a few reassuring words which he is far from feeling, and then glances at the plain little silver watch which has been a present from his dead father.

"It is fifteen minutes after ten," he says to himself—"more than an hour and half since we left the mission-house. What may not have happened in this time!"

CHAPTER VIII.

"The Lord will have mercy upon his afflicted."

IN the mean time, Pierce and Pitsane are steadily making their way back in the direction of the mission-station. As they reach the top of the gorge near the wall of banian trees, they are surprised at the intense stillness that everywhere reigns. At first they think it must be the lull before some renewed outbreak, but as they stand listening for many moments, and there is still no sound save the mournful call of a night-bird and the sighing of the fitful gusts of the wind as it goes sweeping by, their astonishment momentarily increases.

"What can it mean, Pitsane?" Pierce questions in a low voice.

"Pitsane knows not. If the wolves have overcome the lions, then there ought to be lights and loud shouts and the sounds of a great feast. If, on the other hand, the lions have driven away the wolves, then there ought to be at least lights and some sound of the lions. Instead there is darkness everywhere and silence, like the tombs where the dead lie. Hist!"

At that moment the wild yelpings of dogs break upon their ears. The sounds seem to come from the hills without the village.

"The poor brutes are driven nearly out of their senses by what has happened," says Pierce. "Pitsane, I don't like the way they howl. It is too terrible. Oh, what can have happened?"

"Hist!" cautions Pitsane. "Speak not so loud. Let us go on and we shall soon see."

Moving slowly and with great caution toward the house, they are on the point of moving around it to the front yard when a figure crouching upon the steps of the back veranda catches Pitsane's sharp eyes.

"Hist!" he says again to Pierce as he lays a detaining hand upon him; "some one moves upon the steps. Be still, that Pitsane may catch the sounds."

A moment later he is apparently well satisfied with some discovery he has made, for he says to Pierce,

"There is but one of them. Pitsane thought at first there were more. Call, but make your voice low, and see if he will answer."

"Who is there?" Pierce questions in cautious tones.

"Oh, Massa Pierce," cries a quick, glad, guttural voice, "is it really you, Massa Pierce? It's me, the Kaffir, Jim. You no know me?"

"Yes, Jim, I know you now; but how came you here?"

"Me go at sundown to dribe in stray cattle. Cattle wander far. Jim hab bad time gitt'n cattle back. Night him done come good while 'fore Jim reach big hill by village. Dere him hear big noise, big heap o' shoutin', mo' big heap o' hollerin', lots o' big heap o' ring—ring o' de spear. Den Jim him know dat Zulu dog hab come. Jim hear nex' growl o' de big Dutch Boer, en den him know wicked Boer dere too. Den Jim him run wid all him might to he'p brabe lions what Zulu hyena hab sprung 'pon. Jim, massa, dough him skin black, no coward. Jim tink, too, ob de good farder what hab allus treated Jim like him nudder white man, an' o' de good farder's chillern what Jim lub like um brudder an' sister. But while Jim run, him all sudden hear big heap o' tramplin' comin' 'long down by yudder side o' ribber. Him stop an' lissen. Dere 'twas 'gain, mo'n ebber! Soun' like de gallopin' o' many horses. Sogers f'om de Cape, Jim tink to hisse'f—der sogers hab come to he'p de good farder's chillern. Den Jim him break an' run, him run fas' as ebber him could, an' as him run him shout at top o' him voice, 'De sogers! de sogers! De sogers f'om de Cape am comin'!' Den all at onct de Zulus an' de Boers dey hear de tramplin' too, eben troo de big soun's o' de battle, an' dey hear Jim too, what him holler, an' dey t'ink it one o' deir own men, 'cause Jim him holler it in Zulu.* En

---

* The Kaffirs are one branch of the great Zulu tribe.

den, massa, 'fore Jim know 'zactly how it happen, de Zulus an' de Boers dey come tearin' down de big street toward de gate, and when dat reached dey pitch troo like cattle when de wasp git 'mong 'em. An' such shoutin' an' such hollerin' f'om dem Zulu, an' such cussin' f'om dem wicked ole Boer, you nebber heard. It make Jim hair rise to lissen. When onct dey git out'n de gate, you orter see dem how dey cut bee-line for de mountains what lie 'tween here an' Zulu-lan'. An' dat de las' Jim see o' wicked Boer or dog o' Zulu."

"And have the soldiers really come, Jim?" Pierce cries aloud in his excitement.

"No, Massa Pierce, dey hab no come. De tramplin' what Jim hear, an' what scare Zulu dog an' ole Dutch hyena nearly out'n him skin, been made by drove of wild buff'lo what git frighten deysebs at somethin', an' come tearin' by wid noise like mo'n two hundred sogers f'om de Cape."

"And what has happened to our people? and where, oh where, is my father?" Pierce cries again in his freshly-aroused grief.

"Jim no know, massa. Him come hear fus' to see 'bout good farder's chillern, 'cause good farder him make Jim promise dat whatebber happen him, see to him chillern fus'. Dat what him say many, many times ober: 'Jim, when Zulu dog come, he'p my chillern;' an' dat what Jim allus mean to do till bref go out'n him body. So Jim come straight here, an' when him fin' no light, no soun', all gone, den Jim him jus' fall down, all broke up. Him no able for moment to go fudder. Den you come, Massa Pierce, an' po' Jim mos' jump out'n him skin when he hear dat voice."

"Well, let us go to the kotla at once and see what has happened. Oh, this suspense is awful. —But wait, Pitsane, and you, also, Jim, until I get my father's lantern. We cannot manage well without it."

As he goes into the house something starts up suddenly and with low piteous whines begins to rub itself against his legs. It is Henrietta's little poodle, Chitane, who at the time of their sudden and confused flight has been in another part of the house, and who on finding himself the sole occupant has become helpless and frightened.

"Poor Chitane! poor dog!" Pierce says soothingly as he stoops to caress him.

The glad dog leaps and gambols about him as though quite beside himself with joy, and when Pierce, finding the lantern, goes out of the house, the animal keeps close at his heels.

The sight that greets them as the kotla is reached is terrible beyond description. Pierce feels as though he must faint in spite of his bravest efforts as the sickening spectacle of mangled corpses piled one upon another meets his gaze. Bamangwato, Zulu and Boer all lie in one ghastly blood-covered heap, just as they have fallen in the last throes of death, many of them with their arms entwined still in the desperate clutch with which they have gone down, never to rise again. Where, oh where, is his father? Over and over again Pierce asks himself this question. Can it be that he is one of these stark and lifeless objects lying with rigid, blood-stained face and sightless eyes upturned to the pitiless sky? They have been mowed down, many of them, just as they sat within the kotla, little dreaming of the terrible assegais of the bloodthirsty enemy even then raised to strike the deathblow as the stealthy forms came up the hill. Others, again, who have had time to spring to their feet, and even to grasp their guns and battle-axes, which are near at hand, have been hewn down as they sprung, slashed, stabbed, literally hacked to pieces, and then trampled upon until the faces of many of them are beyond recognition.

It is truly a ghastly carnival of death, for all seem dead, not a groan nor a moan from any direction reaching the ears of the little searching-party. This strikes them as strange until they afterward learn that in the sudden flight of the Zulus and the Boers at the sound of the trampling buffaloes, many of the Bamangwatos, including fully two-thirds of the women and children, have escaped the massacre that would otherwise have been complete. Finding that the sounds came from a herd of stampeded buffaloes—for they, remaining behind, have seen what the fleeing Zulus and Boers have failed to see, that the maddened animals go rushing by the village and into the forests beyond—and fearing that at any moment the enemy, finding their mistake, will return to complete the horrible slaughter so successfully begun, they have fled from the village in the direction of Sechele's, carrying their wounded with them.

About the entrance of the kotla that faces the broad street leading up from the main gate, through which the treacherous Mopane had admitted the foe, the fight seems to have been most desperate. Here bodies are piled up four and five deep, Zulu and Bamangwato and Boer, all in one terrible unyielding embrace.

Pierce's trembling knees can scarce sustain his weight as with anguished heart he stoops over first one body and then another, flashing the rays of the lantern into the hacked and distorted faces, expecting yet dreading to find in one of them the well-loved face of his father. Pitsane and Jim, also upon the same painful quest, turn body after body over and disentangle others from the awful piles of ghastly humanity, still with the same disheartening result: there is no trace of Mr. Lillington living or dead.

Suddenly, as they are about to give up in despair, the low whines of the poodle, some little distance away from where they are now standing, attract their attention. As they flash the rays of the lantern in that direction they see him crouched beside a body near a mass of shrubbery just beyond the kotla. Indeed, he is crouched almost upon the body, the face of which he is piteously licking. With a wildly-beating heart Pierce bends over the body, which is lying upon its back, and the next moment lets the rays of the lantern fall full upon the face of his father. Feeling sure that he is dead, for his face and clothing are covered with blood and he lies silent and rigid, Pierce in an agony of grief falls upon his breast. But as he does so he notices that the body is still warm, in spite of its rigid pose. In an instant he has his hand beneath his father's clothing and upon his heart. It is beating faintly.

"Oh, Pitsane! Jim!" he cries in a glad, excited voice, "he is not dead! He may even not be so badly wounded as we think; the blood may be that of others as well as his own. At any rate, we must get him to the cave, and as quickly as we can. Make a litter of boughs, do, my good fellows, while I run to the house for some blankets and a pillow."

The arrangements are soon completed, and at the expiration of only about fifteen or twenty minutes the unconscious form of Mr. Lillington is upon the litter ready to be borne to the cave. As he is lifted from the ground a low moan escapes him, while there is a perceptible movement of the muscles of the face. At intervals as he is borne along he gives vent to the same sound, that is half moan and half sigh.

"We must go by way of the main entrance and into the gorge by the gradual descent," Pierce says. "We could never get him down over the steep path beyond the banian trees. Go softly, Jim, and you, Pitsane, keep your eyes open."

On his return to the house, Pierce has secured his father's medicine-case and a number of strips of soft cloth which he knows will be useful for bandages. They now set off, Pitsane and Jim carrying the litter and Pierce walking beside it with the medicine-case in his hand, while close upon his heels follows the faithful poodle, Chitane.

They are only a few yards or so beyond the kotla when suddenly a towering form uprises from a clump of mimosa-bushes near their path and stands confronting them. This apparition, for they look upon it as nothing else, so startles Pitsane and Jim that but for Pierce's timely intervention they would assuredly have dropped the litter.

"Do you not see," he cries as he springs toward them, "that it is Mazika? But, oh heavens! what a sight!"

And a sight most terrible to behold the tall, powerful Zulu does in truth present. He is wounded in full a dozen places, but, luckily, most of them are assegai thrusts, the full force of which he has warded off by means of his giant battle-axe. Yet though they are merely flesh wounds, they have been given deep enough to make the blood flow freely, staining his great black body from head to foot. Upon the side of his face, however, there seems to be a most desperate wound, for as Pierce covers him with the rays of the lantern the sight of the mangled, bleeding flesh for the moment so sickens him that he staggers as though about to fall.

"Oh, Mazika," he cries, "what has happened to you?"

"The Zulu dogs have given Mazika many tastes of the sharp tongues of their assegais, but it takes more than the assegais of the Matabele dogs to drink the life of Mazika. The arm of Mazika is strong, the heart of Mazika is as that of the great rhinoceros that fears naught, not even the growl of the fierce lion. The axe of Mazika is as deadly as the cobra-bite, and woe unto him who tastes it! Twenty times in a circle did Mazika swing his axe, and as many times did a wolf of a Boer or a Zulu dog bite the dust before it. Ay, and the dog of all dogs, Mopane. I saw him as he stood for one moment overlooking the fight, and as quick as the flash of the wheels of the great sun's chariot did I swing Balala" (his axe: the word means "the killer"), "and lo at my feet lies the traitor whose leprous hand unbarred the gate to the wolves that swept down upon his own people."

It is even as he says: there at his feet lies Mopane with his ghastly, blood-stained face upturned to the sky, the skull split almost in twain. Terrible but just has been the fate that has overtaken him.

"But yourself, Mazika?" Pierce questions again. "You are badly hurt. How did it happen?"

"A dog of a Matabele struck me from behind, but even as he raised the axe to strike, Mazika turned, and thus caught upon Balala a part of the blow, but only a part, for the great blade of the axe fell flat upon Mazika's head and cut down through his cheek. It must have been a blow such as that with which the butcher fells the ox, for it sent Mazika down before it, and there he lay as dead until a little while ago he came to himself to find the Matabele dogs fled from the village and only Mazika left with the spirits of the dead. Then came the son of the good father, with the good father borne before him wounded unto death. Mazika hears the voices, Mazika sees the light, and lo, Mazika is here!"

"And glad enough are we to see you, poor fellow!" Pierce says pityingly, "though so desperately wounded. Do you think you can make the journey to the cave, Mazika? But first let me bandage your head and face. You have already lost too much blood.—Pitsane, Jim, lay the litter down a moment. Gently, my good fellows, and come and help me."

In a short while Pierce, who has before done such things under his father's careful directions, has the Zulu's wounds very skillfully bandaged. The grim old warrior is quite weak from the loss of blood and faint with the pain of the desperate wounds upon his head and cheek, but his courage and resolution are equal to the effort that is necessary to carry him to the cave, and so with slow, majestic strides he starts off beside them.

Just as they have cautiously approached the gate, and are on the point of passing through it, they hear the sound of running feet rapidly coming nearer, accompanied a moment later by the quick, short breathing of some animal or animals, straining every nerve for some extra exertion.

"Hist!" says Pitsane, "it is the dogs. They run as though the wolves themselves were upon their tracks."

"They have gotten scent of us," says Pierce, "or perhaps they have even heard our voices. There is no estimating the instinct of a dog."

Even as he speaks three large, gaunt dogs of the mastiff species spring through the gate and leap upon them. Two are the dogs belonging to the mission-house; the third, a great, yellow powerful-looking brute with a massive head, is Spoorer ("game-tracker"), Mazika's dog, who as soon as he catches sight of his master nearly goes wild with delight, his puppyish gambols being exceedingly ludicrous for one of his years and habitual dignity.

When without the gate the little party halts for a moment, thinking to catch sounds of other dogs or perhaps to see some of the brutes crouching near. But all is silent upon the hills. With the same instinct with which the dogs of the mission-house and of Mazika have so unerringly found their masters, the others have doubtless got wind of the fleeing Bamangwatos and are even now upon their track.

As they draw near the entrance to the cave Pierce bids his companions wait a few moments until he goes forward to prepare Ellie and Hope for a sight of Mr. Lillington.

He cannot tell how desperately his father has been wounded, he says to them after he has cautiously related the manner in which he has been found. It may be, he tells them, that he has only been given back to them to be taken away again, and that they must be very brave and calm and not excite him by any outcry, as he may regain consciousness at any moment.

Pierce's words have their effect, for, though the hearts of both young girls are nearly breaking with grief, and it is all they can do to keep from crying outright at sight of the silent, blood-stained form upon the litter, they nevertheless heroically restrain their feelings, and set about doing all they can for the loved father and uncle.

Besides a wound upon the head and another near the shoulder, Mr. Lillington has been desperately wounded in the side, as they soon discover. With what knowledge he has obtained through his father's careful instructions, added to the information he has himself acquired through a two years' close reading of surgery, Pierce sets to work, with Cunnyngham's aid, to dress his father's wounds. All this time there is no sign of consciousness from the wounded man and but little sign of life.

When his services are no longer needed in the trying and delicate task of dressing his uncle's wounds, and Ellie and Hope have established themselves close beside Mr. Lillington to watch anxiously for any sign of returning consciousness, Cunnyngham walks apart to talk with Pitsane and Jim, who have stretched themselves upon a couple of skins near the fire in order to snatch what rest they can. Upon a similar skin reposes the massive form of the Zulu, now suffering greatly from his wounds, yet, after the manner of his race, giving little sign.

Pierce has bestowed upon the bandages about his face and head renewed attention, and is now doing for him all that his partially-trained skill can suggest.

"Pitsane," Cunnyngham says as he approaches the Hottentot and the Kaffir, "I know that you and Jim must be already greatly worn out with the events of this night, and what I am about to ask of you may seem very heartless, but it is only the extreme urgency of the case that drives me to it, I assure you. As you know, the position in which we are now placed is one of much danger and difficulty, despite the fact that we are now safely sheltered in the cave. This is well enough, so far as the present is concerned, but we must also think of the future, and not only think of it, but provide for it by taking advantage of such opportunities as are now within our reach. In my uncle's condition he may linger for weeks ere he recovers—if he recover at all," he adds sadly. "During all this time we shall doubtless have to remain in the cave. Should we be released from our confinement, even after a period of a few weeks, there is still the journey across the country to be thought of. For this we are not prepared as we should be, neither are we prepared to linger long within the cave. We must have more supplies, and we must have some tools, additional feed for the oxen, a cow or two, some goats, if we can get hold of them, and by all means the donkeys, and at least two of the best horses. It is now half-past one o'clock. In a little more than four hours it will be daylight. Do you not think that within that time we can have made at least three trips to the mission-station and back? I would not ask it of you, my poor fellows! seeing how tired you are already, did I not recognize the desperate straits of the situation. As you know, the Zulus, believing that they were about to be attacked by a body of horsemen from the Cape, have suddenly fled, leaving their work of destruction incomplete. We know them too well to doubt for a moment that as soon as they discover their mistake they will return to finish their dastardly deed by applying the torch to everything left within the village. Even by dawn their scouts will be out in every direction, and when they learn that the village is deserted they will at once swoop down upon it and leave nothing behind to tell the tale. Therefore what we do must be done quickly—to-night?"

"Pitsane is ready to go wherever the young Eagle says," the Hottentot quickly replies, as, arising from the skin on which he has been lying, he shakes himself as a great dog does on being aroused from slumber. "For the good father and the good father's children Pitsane would gladly give his life if that would help them. Shall he therefore turn back for the sake of a little fatigue? No, no; that is not the way a man would do—that would be as a child. Let the Eagle then tell Pitsane what he wants him to do."

"Jim too, massa," the Kaffir says in his low, guttural tones—"Jim ready to do what him can. Him mo' sleepy dan tired, but him soon git ober dat."

"Then come along, my brave fellows, and we will go to work.—No, no, Pierce, you must not think of going. You have done enough for to-night." This last is to his cousin, who, having overheard a part of the conversation, is now insisting that he too shall be allowed to go and help all he can. "You must stay here and keep watch with the girls. Your father may need your attention at any moment."

"And now," Cunnyngham says, as, having reached the top of the gorge by the wall of banian trees, they stop for a moment to listen and to recover their breath, "Pitsane, you go to the stables for the donkeys and the horses. Get both my sister's and cousin's donkeys, and the three that are my uncle's. Select two of the best horses. Stay! get three. Be sure that one is Khiva, the horse that Captain Murray gave my uncle. Ride Khiva, and lead one of my uncle's donkeys. Chumah, Susi and the others will follow. You will, of course, have to return to the cave by way of the main entrance of the village. Go cautiously, and it is unnecessary to tell you to look well about you. When you have reached the cave turn the horses and donkeys in with the oxen in the upper part of the gorge, and be sure the barricade is secure, for should any of them get out they would be likely to stray back to the village, and we would then have our work for nothing. When you have done this return here to the wall of banian trees, where I will await you.—And you, Jim, go to the cattle-pen, select five of the best milkers with young calves, eight or ten head of beeves, twice as many sheep and as many goats as you can get together, with two or three of the nannies and their young families. Turn all the others loose, so that the poor creatures may not suffer the tortures of fire when those bloodthirsty savages return to apply the torch.—And you, Pitsane, do the same for the horses and the donkeys.—Both of you see the rest of the cattle well out of the village and toward the pasture-grounds ere you take out your droves.—Pen the cattle, Jim, in the upper end of the gorge, as I have told Pitsane to do with the horses and donkeys. Return here, as I have also told him to do, and I will tell you what next."

Cunnyngham has made ten or twelve trips from the mission-house to the top of the gorge, each time well laden with supplies, when Pitsane joins him. A half hour later Jim also returns, each of them with a favorable report.

It is now a quarter to four o'clock, and Cunnyngham, recognizing that what is further done must be done quickly, instructs the two to convey the supplies he has placed near the top of the gorge down into the cañon and some little distance along it, to where he designates a thicket of thorn, behind which they are to conceal the articles. In about an hour's time this is finished, when the little party starts off for a last trip to the mission-house. A few faint streaks of red are already beginning to stain the eastern sky, while here and there about the village the crow of an awakening cock is heard.

"There isn't a moment to lose," Cunnyngham says with anxious glances toward the fast-reddening sky. "Go to the hen-house, Jim, and get a dozen hens and a couple of roosters. Tie their feet together with these strings, so that you can carry them well.— You, Pitsane, come with me."

As Cunnyngham enters the little side room, or kind of pantry, where many of the household stores are kept, something soft rubs against him. The next moment he catches the sound made by the gentle purring of a cat. Holding the lantern so that the rays fall downward, he sees that it is his cousin Henrietta's cat, "Pussy Tea-kettle." Near by is an open basket in which are five fat sleeping kittens.

"Poor pussy!" says Cunnyngham, "it is awful to think of your being left behind to be burnt up in the house; and not only you, but your helpless little family. No, no, it shall not be if I can help it; I will take you and the kittens out."

But as he does so and deposits the basket under one of the trees in the garden, Madame Pussy deliberately picks up one of the soft, purring balls and starts with it back to the house.

"Evidently this will not do," Cunnyngham says to himself in much perplexity. "The poor foolish pussy seems determined to have herself and family cremated? Yes, I will do it," he exclaims aloud as a sudden thought seems to strike him. "Henrietta will be so glad! And," he goes on after another pause, "while I am in this kind of business I will make somebody else happy also." As he says these words he picks up a box in which there is a small magic-lantern with some views that belongs to Marvin, and hands it to Pitsane. "And still another some one," he continues, as from the sitting-room he takes several photographs and a half dozen or so of the choicest books.

A few moments later, as he goes on through the orchard in the direction of the path leading down into the gorge, there is borne aloft on his shoulder, in addition to the books and pictures under his arm, the small basket in which the fat kittens are snugly reposing, while Madame Pussy Tea-kettle, seemingly well assured as to the journey upon which her offspring are bound, as well as of the good intentions of their conductor, trots contentedly along at his side.

As Cunnyngham, Pitsane and Jim meet at the top of the gorge and prepare for the descent the light in the eastern sky has so far increased that even remote objects are now plainly visible. They therefore make their way as quickly as safety and their burdens will allow down the somewhat precipitous path, and it is with a feeling of deep thankfulness that a few moments later they find themselves enclosed in the deep gray shadows at the bottom of the gorge.

Assuring himself that the remainder of the supplies are well hidden within the dense growth of the thorn coppice, Cunnyngham leads the way to the cave, still with the basket of kittens safe upon his shoulder and Madame Pussy Tea-kettle close at his heels. The rays of the rising sun are just gilding with light the tops of the trees along the summit of the gorge as the entrance to the cave is reached.

CHAPTER IX.

"The Lord is the Maker of them all."

SO thoroughly worn out are the occupants of the cave with the events of the night and morning —for three of them, as we have seen, have toiled on until well into the morning—that it is late in the afternoon of the day following the night of the massacre at the mission-station ere they arouse themselves from the deep slumber into which they have fallen. Ellie, Hope and Pierce have taken it by turns to watch beside Mr. Lillington, but have finally all three succumbed to the heavy sleep that has crept upon them. Even the grim Zulu, at first restless from the pain of his wound, has at last slept soundly.

In Mr. Lillington there is little if any change. He still lies in the same unconscious condition, moaning feebly at times and never once opening his eyes. The children are unremitting in their ministrations, and when Ellie, out of her great desire to do everything that will help her dear father, has tried bathing his face in water in which ammonia has been dropped, and holding a bottle of the strong fluid to his nostrils, she is much encouraged to note a very decided change in him—a change, she hopes, for the better. A faint color begins to steal into his white face, and he occasionally makes a few restless movements with his hands and arms. In the mean time, Mamochisane, assisted by the Kaffir Jim and superintended by Hope, has prepared a meal that is both breakfast and dinner. Despite their sad and anxious hearts, they all do full justice to it. Even Mazika is persuaded to eat something. The children are especially ravenous, and, fearing they may make themselves sick, Ellie has at length cautioned them to desist. Chitane, Spoorer and the other dogs come in for their share, and eat like famished wolves—all except the former, who seems so overcome by his master's condition that, after picking a few bones in a lifeless sort of way, he returns at once to the couch upon which Mr. Lillington is lying and takes up his old place beside the pillow.

The delight of Henrietta on finding her cherished Pussy Tea-kettle safe, with all her little family, is so demonstrative and genuine that Cunnyngham feels well repaid.

As soon as the meal is over Cunnyngham proposes to Pitsane and Jim that they go and see after the supplies they have hidden in the thorn coppice.

They pick their way cautiously, taking care to shelter themselves as much as possible behind the tangled growth of bushes and vines along the edge of the gorge, for by this time they feel assured the

Zulus either must have returned to the village or are keeping watch upon it. Before they have proceeded halfway, the mingled sounds of many hoarse shouts and of various outcries coming to their ears, they stop suddenly and shelter themselves behind some stunted but thick-growing acacia-bushes. Ere they have decided whether to go on or to return to the cave they catch sight of numerous thick clouds of smoke blowing over the gorge.

"It is the Zulus," says Cunnyngham, "and the Boers too, I doubt not. They have returned, and have set fire to the village. I think we had better go back and wait for the darkness ere we attempt to remove the supplies."

When the inmates of the cave are told what is happening at the mission-station, they sit with paling cheeks and beating hearts, not knowing but that at almost any moment they may be tracked and their hiding-place discovered. But as the afternoon wears on and the night approaches, they gather about the entrance to the cave and watch with varied emotions the great red glare in the sky that is made by the burning mission-station. Directly there comes to them a scent both sickening and overpowering, which, they recognize with a shudder, arises from burning flesh. Then they know that it is the kotla with its human contents.

The reflection from the burning buildings lights up all the sky overhead and falls with such intensity upon the trees along the edges of the gorge that every trunk and limb stands out with distinctness. Ellie thinks with an aching heart of the result of so many years of hard, patient labor even now being lapped up as so much tinder by the merciless flames, and thanks God that in his blissful unconsciousness her father knows nothing of it.

So long does the light from the burning station continue to be reflected into the gorge that it is not until the following night that the supplies are removed from the thorn coppice to the cave. Ere leaving with the last load Pitsane and Cunnyngham cautiously make their way to the top of the gorge and peer over it in the direction of the station. All is a heap of smouldering ruins, with here and there a red tongue of flame shooting up from some substance that is long in burning. Nowhere is there a sign of life; all is desolate and deserted.

"The Zulus are gone," says Cunnyngham in a low voice—"gone after wreaking their mean revenge like the fiends they are." Then as he struggles bravely with the tears that are beginning to rise, "Good-bye, old Lepelole! good-bye, dear place! One can scarcely dare hope ever to look upon your like in these wilds again. But as sure as a just God reigneth, he will not long let your blackened ruins and the charred bones of your massacred people cry to him for vengeance."

The fifth day following the night upon which he

has been borne to the cave there is a decided evidence of returning consciousness in Mr. Lillington. On the morning of the sixth day he opens his eyes with a look of recognition upon the face of Ellie, who is bending the nearest to him.

"Do you know me, dear father?" she asks, quietly, struggling bravely with herself so as not to excite him.

He gives an answering movement of his eyelids and smiles faintly upon her. In three days more he is able to converse, though but for a few moments at a time, and then only in barely audible tones. By the end of another week he is a little stronger and can talk with his family for longer periods and altogether intelligibly. He can even sit up propped by rolls of skins and by the pillows. But he is in great pain all the while, and the ugly wound in his side has altogether refused to yield to treatment. Even his own skill fails to suggest anything further to do.

The knowledge comes to him soon that he is in a most critical condition, and then that the end cannot be very far off. How he dreads to make this known to the patient, loving hearts that have watched beside him for the past two weeks! But it must be done. They must be prepared, else will the shock be too great when it does come. Besides, there are many things about which he must talk to them. The question of the future even now presents itself. It must be met and answered.

In the uncontrollable bursts of grief following upon his painful revelation it is long ere he can get them to listen calmly to the plans for their future that have revolved through his mind while he has been lying upon the couch of skins and apparently with his eyes closed in quiet slumber.

"Be strong, my children," he entreats them—"be strong and faint not, and God will surely give the grace to sustain you through this affliction. Put your trust in him, and so shall you, like the sparrow pursued from house-top to house-top, find at last a resting-place—yea, even in the bosom of the Most High. 'As thy days so shall thy strength be.' Oh rely upon this! God himself has *promised* it, and he *never* forgets his promises. And now let us talk about what it is best for you to do after I am no longer with you to advise and direct."

He closes his eyes and remains quiet for a few moments. In a little while he speaks again:

"I know of nothing better to suggest than that you try to reach the village of Sechele, fifteen days' journey due south from this. Once with him, I feel confident he will do all he can to help you on to the Cape."

"The words of the good father are well meant," says Pitsane at this juncture and in his native language, "and he gives to his children the counsel he thinks is best and most wise. But since the good father has lain here sick unto death from the wounds received from the spears of the Zulu dogs, many things have come to pass of which my father knoweth naught. Even now all the paths that lead to Sechele's, as well as those that bend toward the Cape, are watched by the Matabele wolves and the Zulu vultures. They know that my father's children have escaped and are somewhere within the forests, and that sooner or later they will seek to make their way to the good Sechele. Everywhere between here and Sechele's and the Cape they swarm like the vultures that circle about the dead carcasses of the beasts. Would my father send his children to be eaten of these dogs and devoured of these wolves?"

"I had not thought of that," Mr. Lillington murmurs faintly, his face working with emotion. "O my Father, the way seems dark, exceedingly dark. Show me the light. Have pity upon these helpless ones and guide them from this wilderness."

In a few moments he speaks again, this time in calm tones: "What are the chances, Pitsane, to get through to Kingone or Quilamane on the east coast?"

"No better, my father; even worse. Here is Mazika, who will tell you that even to attempt to pass through the country of Mosilikatse would be like rushing into the fangs of the most deadly of all the Matabele wolves. He and his would devour without mercy."

"Pitsane has spoken, my father," the Zulu adds

in his deep musical language, "and the words of Pitsane are wise. On the one hand are the hungry Boer dogs and the fierce Zulu wolves, and on the other Mosilikatse, the treacherous chief with the cruel heart and the bloody hand."

"Then God help you, my poor children!" the missionary cries in his despair. "I know not what to advise."

"If the good father will listen, Pitsane will tell him of a way whereby his children may escape the clutches of the Matabele wolves. It is a long and tedious way, and there are many dangers, but Pitsane believes that it is now the only one left to the father's children."

"And that way, Pitsane?" Mr. Lillington questions eagerly.

"The way that leads to the Chobe River and to the Makololo—the old brave Makololo, the people of the wise and good Sebituane and the friend of the great Livingstone."

"But the Makololo have met with many reverses since Livingstone was last among them, especially since the death of their young chief, Sekeletu. Numerous tribes have made inroads among them and reduced their once proud power."

"But nevertheless, my father, there are many of these people still left upon the banks of the Chobe and along the broad current of the Leambye. They would gladly welcome the children of the good father, the story of whose kind, brave work among their brothers, the Bamangwatos, has long ago traveled to them. Ay, and they will do more than welcome them: they will help them on down to the coast, where the great ships wait to bear them to their own country."

"But the Chobe lies in a north-westerly direction from this, and to reach it, it will be necessary to pass through a portion at least of the dread Matabele territory."

"Not so, my father. By going straight from here in an easterly direction to the Kalahari, into it some miles and then turning due north, there will then be no danger from the Matabele wolves. Of all ways this is the only one left to the children of my father, and though it is so long and so full of dangers, and there are so many hardships to be met with on every hand, yet Pitsane believes there is no other by which they could go with a chance to escape with their lives. It is the very last direction in which the wolves will expect to find my father's children, for they would as soon think of guarding the way to the great skies above as the paths that lead to the Kalahari."

"But the Kalahari itself," exclaims Mr. Lillington, "that dread place of blistering sands, parched vegetation and of torturing thirst! They will assuredly perish if they make any such an attempt as that."

"No, my father, *no!* They may perhaps suffer, and suffer much, but they will not die. The great

God whom my father serves will not permit it. Men with white skins have crossed the Kalahari before without perishing—yea, and women too; and what they have done so may others do, even the tender children of my father. Near the desert lives Shobo, the great Bushman guide who twice went across with the mighty Livingstone. Fear not; he will see your children safe through all the dangers."

"There seems no other way," Mr. Lillington says after a moment of deep and painful thought—"no other way, my children, except for you to try and reach the Makololo. Once with them, they can undoubtedly help you to the coast, and will do so, I feel assured, if they can. But it is a long and dangerous journey any way we look upon it, filled too with such hardships that it is terrible to think of these delicate girls as facing, and of the tender as enduring. But God is good, and his loving-kindness is ever about those who put their trust in him. Do you think you are prepared with sufficient supplies to make the start?" he turns to question of Cunnyngham.

"Oh yes, uncle; we are far better prepared than many who have attempted similar journeys. We have everything that is absolutely necessary—a strong, commodious wagon, plenty of the best salted oxen, horses, cows, sheep, fowls, at least two months' provisions, firearms and tools of various kinds."

"You have shown activity as well as wisdom in your preparations," his uncle says commendingly.—

"And Mazika and Pitsane and Jim," turning his eyes entreatingly toward their black faces and speaking in tones that are tremulous with some deep emotion—"my good, brave fellows, you will not desert my children?"

"Nebber, massa!" Jim says, speaking first and for all the others, for well he knows their feelings on the subject. His broken English is very deep and impressive as he continues: "De good farder's chillern nebber know what 'tis to be 'serted long as Jim an' 'Sane an' 'Zika hab bref in deir body. Dey go wid 'em ter de ens' o' de yearth fus'; dey spill ebber drop o' deir blood for 'em."

"The Kaffir has spoken," Mazika says in his liquid, rounded Zulu, "and his words are as the words of truth. While Mazika has one drop of blood to give he will give it for his father's children."

"As the lioness protects her cubs," says Pitsane in his guttural though not altogether unmusical Hottentot, "and the rhinoceros cow her calf, so will Pitsane lay down his life for the children of the good father, the true, brave man who has taught him that all men are equal in the sight of the great God whom he serves."

"God bless you, each and every one!" Mr. Lillington says fervently. "Oh, may the words you have spoken stand as an everlasting monument to the better and nobler impulses of your race! God made us all, Mazika, Pitsane, Jim; the same hand that fashioned the white skin to cover my face made also the black one that covers yours. He is the Father of us all. The great and universal language he teaches us is love: 'Thou shalt love thy neighbor as thyself.' Again he says, 'Greater love hath no man than this, that a man lay down his life for his friends.' And this is just what you propose to do, my brave, true fellows. For me and mine you are ready to die. Oh, the God of heaven and earth, the Maker alike of the white man and the black, the great and universal Father, bless you for ever and bring you at least to know the fullness of his glory in his home beyond the stars!"

The next day Mr. Lillington grew very restless. Fever set in, and in three days more he was wildly tossing in delirium. All that loving and gentle ones could do was done for him. Day and night they watched him untiringly; hour after hour they were beside him holding the cooling draught to his lips or fanning his fevered brow. With aching hearts and tearful eyes they watched the slow but sure advance of that Shadow that falls alike upon the hearts of the young and of the old—that draws with stern impartiality in ghastly outlines its hideous form upon the ice-gorges of the polar seas and the glaring sand-heaps of the tropic deserts—the Shadow against which even the world's Edens are powerless and the Happy Valleys not free from entrance.

On the morning of the twenty-third day since

they had been inmates of the cave, and following upon a night of comparative quiet, Mr. Lillington at length opened his eyes with a gleam of consciousness in their depths.

"Bury me," he said faintly, "in the little cemetery on the hill beside my dear wife and the loved ones who have gone before."

A few moments he closed his eyes, then opened them again with one long, last loving look upon all the tearful faces grouped about him.

"O God of the fatherless," he murmured, his weak lips moving in prayer, "be a Father to these my helpless ones. Oh bless them, kind God—bless each and every one of them. O Guardian of the helpless, O Protector of the oppressed, O Rock of refuge for those in trouble, be thou near. Comfort and help, for Jesus' sake!"

At sunrise he was dead, and the wails of his stricken children told how truly desolate he had left them.

Pitsane and Jim procured from the forest, where many weeks before they had been sawn, the boards with which Cunnyngham's own hands made the coffin in which his uncle's body was placed.

At nightfall of the following day Pitsane and Jim were sent to dig the grave within the little cemetery on the hill. Thither a few hours later the body was carried by Cunnyngham, Mazika, Pitsane and Jim, Pierce alone of his children following as mourner, for the others, especially the girls, have become so exhausted by their grief as to be utterly unable to make the trip.

Cunnyngham's voice was shaken by a storm of emotion as he attempted to repeat above the open grave into which the coffin had been lowered the beautiful and comforting words of the fourteenth chapter of Revelation :

"'Blessed are the dead which die in the Lord from henceforth : yea, saith the Spirit, that they may rest from their labors; and their works do follow them.'"

As the first clods were falling upon the coffin-lid the attention of the group about the grave was attracted by the sound of pattering footsteps. It was the poodle Chitane, who had followed them from the cave, and who, as soon as he caught sight of the open grave, took up his stand near it, whining piteously. When it was filled it was all they could do to induce him to leave it. Indeed, he did not do so, even at the last, of his own accord, Pierce having to lift him up and bear him away in his arms.

For many days following upon Mr. Lillington's death and burial the occupants of the cave seemed too deeply stricken with grief to think of aught else or to begin any preparation whatever for their long and dangerous journey across the plains. Even Mazika, Pitsane and Jim seemed to have lost all interest and to be immersed in the common sorrow. The grim Zulu, the grateful Hottentot and the faithful Kaffir had all loved the kindly, generous man who had looked upon them, not as slaves and dogs, as the Boers had done, but as men and brothers.

But hearts cannot long remain so cast down and grief-stricken. Youth is naturally strong and buoyant, and a week after Mr. Lillington's death active preparations for the start across the plains were begun. Mazika had almost entirely recovered from his wounds by this time—though the one upon his cheek had left a terrible scar—and was thus enabled to give them much valuable aid.

An incident has in the mean time occurred which has made an addition to the little party by no less a personage than old Kamati, the blacksmith. Happening to go one evening on a scouting-expedition to gain, if possible, some knowledge of the movements of the Boers and Zulus, Pitsane has stumbled upon a half-starved creature hidden away in the rocks of the basalt cliffs. He is greatly surprised to find in this emaciated object the once fleshy and vigorous blacksmith. Kamati has escaped in the confusion attendant upon the stampede of the buffaloes, but in the excitement has gotten lost from his people. Ever since he has lain hidden in the rocks, fearing to venture out by day lest he shall be seen by the dreaded Boers and Zulus. At night he has procured what meagre food he has so far subsisted upon—roots, berries and a quantity of half-burnt corn obtained from one of the partially-consumed ruins of the village.

It makes the tears spring to Ellie's and Hope's sympathetic eyes to see the ravenous manner in which the poor fellow devours every article of food that is set before him.

Under Kamati's direction an anvil, a bellows and some coal are now obtained from a little cellar beneath a mound in the rear of his hut, where they have escaped destruction in the general conflagration of the station. This seems a special dispensation of Providence to the trusting little band in the cave, all the more so since, from long standing, many parts of the iron-work of the wagon have become loosened and need attention.

With the aid of Kamati and Pitsane, Cunnyngham sets about a complete overhauling of the wagon and the getting of it into the best possible condition for hard usage.

The wagon is almost new, having been used very little, and only for one considerable trip, that from the Cape to the mission-station. It is about fourteen feet long by six wide, and, though solidly built, is yet unusually light and easy-moving for its size. Over the top of the wagon is stretched a high canvas cover or "tilt," a protection against sun and rain. On either side of the vehicle is fastened an additional canvas sheet with falling sides, so arranged that the whole can be stretched out and pegged to the ground, when, lo! there are two as nice tents as one would need to have. The bottom of the wagon is ingeniously fitted with various boxes and lockers. In these the ammunition and the stock of provisions are to be placed, and in others, which are water-tight and made somewhat in the shape of casks, is a supply of water preparatory to passing over arid desert wastes. These boxes and lockers are so arranged as to make a level surface upon which blankets and other articles for forming a bed can be spread. To the sides of the wagon above this are fitted numerous smaller boxes for miscellaneous stores; brackets or racks for the holding of the rifles, guns and other firearms; also receptacles for the carpenter's and blacksmith's tools.

To draw this wagon there is a team of twenty large, strong Bechuana oxen, four of them having afterward been added to the sixteen first carried to the cave. Sixteen is the usual team, but Mr. Lillington has been careful to provide four extra ones, so as to guard against casualties. These oxen are what is known as "well-salted;" that is, they have worked over many parts of South Africa, been exposed to all sorts of hardships, and thus become proof, moderately speaking, against many things to which the fresher animals would easily succumb.

Their arrangements being now perfected and everything having been put in first-class order for the journey, the trusting little band that is thus fearlessly going forth to face many of the worst dangers of savage Africa agrees that the start shall be made on the following Monday evening at sundown. By journeying at night they will avoid much of the danger of being discovered by any prowling band of Zulus or Boers, and, as it will be much cooler, it will be less trying, not only upon themselves, but upon the cattle. Afterward, when they are farther upon their route and have grown accustomed to the heat of the sun, they can divide the time between the day and the night.

The goal they desire to make during the first night is a certain pool or spring in the now dried-up bed of a river-course eighteen or twenty miles away, where, in the dense jungles of mimosa that surround it and sheltered by the overhanging cliffs, they hope to remain safely hidden through the next day.

CHAPTER X.

"He will be our Guide even unto death."

UPON the following Monday evening, a full half hour before the sun had set, everything is in readiness for the start. The wagon stands before the entrance to the cave with the oxen yoked to it. About the barricade that has served to make a secure pasturage-ground of the upper end of the cañon Jim has collected the cattle preparatory to driving them out. Two of the horses stand ready saddled and bridled, while a third has simply a bridle and blanket, another saddle having been unprocurable.

About the mouth of the cave the little group is gathered, for ere they start forth upon the long and dangerous journey across the savage wilderness they assemble to ask help and protection of Him who guards even the bird's flight.

In a deep and earnest voice Pierce reads the beautiful and comforting words of the ninety-first Psalm. Then they fall upon their knees and clasp their hands while Cunnyngham prays aloud to God for strength and help to pass safely through the many terrible dangers they are about to face.

Starting Out for the Journey.

Page 151.

When prayer is ended they take their way each to the appointed place he or she is to occupy in the caravan, and the march is begun.

In front rides Cunnyngham on one of his uncle's horses, and at his side the grim and faithful Zulu mounted upon another, the one that has no saddle. It has been hard work to get Mazika to mount the horse. Long has he protested that Mazika is no child that he should be carried by the swift beast with the slender legs. But as Mazika's wounds still get angry at times, strong persuasion is brought to bear upon him to induce him to spare himself as much as possible; and he finally mounts the horse, though still against his inclinations. He is riding in Zulu fashion, with his knees pressed close against the sides of the horse and his feet stuck out almost at right angles. Behind Cunnyngham and Mazika come the cattle, driven by Jim—five cows with their calves, the extra oxen, a half dozen beeves, a dozen head of sheep, and as many goats. Jim has the privilege of riding one of the donkeys.

Following close upon Jim and his cattle is the great wagon with the yoke of sixteen strong, splendid oxen attached. At their head, as leader, walks Pitsane, while old Kamati is upon the driver's seat. It is understood that they are to change about in the leading and driving. Cunnyngham, Pierce, and even Mazika, are also to have their turn handling the span, while Jim too is to be relieved at intervals of his care of the cattle.

In the wagon are Ellie, Hope, Henrietta, Marvin, Baby Louise and Mamochisane. There, too, snugly ensconced in one corner set apart for their especial use, is Madame Pussy Tea-kettle with her little family, the latter in one month having grown to quite a respectable size. At Henrietta's feet, upon a skin rug, is the poodle Chitane, now somewhat recovered from the state of dejection into which he has been thrown by his master's death.

Beside the wagon rides Pierce, mounted upon his father's favorite horse, Khiva, named for a famous African king, and which has been the gift of Captain Murray. About his heels frolic the dogs that have come to them at the gates of the mission-station, now sleek and well fed. Mazika's great yellow dog, Spoorer, as though scorning the injudicious gambols of the younger ones, walks with dignified tread beside the horse upon which his master sits. Fastened to the pommel of Pierce's saddle are the reins of the halters by which two of his uncle's donkeys are tethered, Chumah and Susi following of their own free will.

Among the other appointments of the wagon, there has been fitted to the top of the body on either side a stout plank about nine or ten inches wide and running the whole length, each of which is so fastened by hinges that it can be put down or up at pleasure, thus serving as a protection against the spears, arrows, or even bullets, of the enemy in case of an ambuscade. On a platform at the rear of the wagon are secured two large coops, or rather cages. In one of these are the fowls that have been secured from the mission-station, while into the other, at regular periods, are put first the young calves and then the kids, so as to relieve them in part of the trying fatigues of the journey.

On starting out from the cave the little caravan carries with it what is a full two months' supply of provisions. Of such articles as flour, Indian cornmeal and the grain wherewith to make other meal when this is exhausted there is a much larger supply. In addition to flour, meal and corn, the commissariat contains such articles as coffee, tea, sugar, crackers, a small quantity of pickles and preserves, a dozen or two of lemons and limes, some cheeses made of the curds of goats' milk, bacon, even one or two home-cured hams, and a somewhat large supply of "biltong," or dried game-flesh.

Among the miscellaneous stores are candles, soap, tar, tallow, matches, nails, spare bits of canvas and ropes and many other useful things too tedious to mention. There are, also, Mr. Lillington's medicine-case, with a stock of medicines additional to what that contains, a sextant and compass, a small but powerful telescope, a case of surgical instruments, various blacksmith and carpenter tools, including the anvil and bellows and a small grindstone on which to sharpen the axes and hatchets.

With the personal effects of Ellie and Hope are carefully packed sewing articles of various descriptions, such as needles, thread, scissors, while Pierce has many small chemical apparatuses and arsenical and other preparations for preserving natural-history specimens, he being especially fond of chemistry and natural history. Marvin's store consists of a collection of numerous fish-hooks and lines, a kite with a gorgeous tail, to which he has clung to the last, a wonderful rubber ball, a spinning-top that goes to sleep beautifully—all presents his dear dead father has obtained for him from the Cape, at great trouble—and his beloved magic-lantern and views, the last the gift of Captain Murray.

Among the stores intended partly for barter and partly for presents to the different savage chiefs, especially to those with whom they may have trouble in getting across their country, are glass beads of various colors and sizes, gilt and copper rings, pocket-knives, gayly-painted tin cups, iron spoons, and a bolt or so of calico and baize which their father has kept for bartering purposes at the mission-station. They have also a very good supply of ammunition, several guns and rifles and two revolvers.

As the little caravan defiles out of the gorge near the main entrance to the station the sun has set and the moon has already risen. With tearful eyes and sad hearts Ellie and Hope look upon the blackened ruins of what has been the only home they have known for years. As rude as have been its appointments, as wild as have been its surroundings, it has nevertheless held many things that have been most sweet and pleasant. Now like wanderers they must go out across the great wilderness that stretches between them and the only other home they have on earth.

When opposite the little cemetery upon the hill a pause is made that the eyes of these desolate children may look once more—nay, for the last time—upon the mounds that cover all of the earthly part of that about which have been bound the purest and the strongest cords that have held them to life. As they go out across the great wide desert how often will their hearts turn back with a sick and dreary longing to the one dear and sacred spot nestled like a bit of God's own acre in the midst of the silent and desolate stretches of this African valley! A short distance beyond the mission-station the little caravan turns somewhat suddenly and sharply to the left and makes its way over a rude wooden bridge that at this point spans the river. As the rise of a hill on the other side is reached, involuntarily they turn for a last look upon the mission-station.

The few fleecy clouds that have been at play about the moon have now gone scurrying off, and the strong, clear light falls full upon everything, even upon the line of low reeds along the river's course. Against the southern sky the beautiful stars of this hemisphere, far more beautiful here than elsewhere, glitter like gems above the towering crests of the distant mountains that stand out in such bold relief. But there is no boldness, no glare, in the moonlight, which seems to throw a mantle of peace about those who gaze upon it, as it also throws a mantle of silver over everything upon which it rests. In another moment they have descended the hill, and Lepelole, with all its joys and sorrows, its days of pleasure and of pain, its life of rare delights and of bitter heartaches, is left behind for ever.

Slowly but steadily they keep on their way. Every hour there is a short stop of at least ten minutes to allow the less hardy of the cattle to rest. Careful watch is kept in every direction in order to guard against any sudden surprise on the part of hostile man or savage beast. But beyond the occasional skulking form of a hyena or a wolf no danger threatens: God seems, indeed, to have them in the hollow of his hand.

For the first three or four miles after leaving the mission-station they pass over a country that is comparatively level; then it begins to rise gradually to the foot of a line of mountains that lies directly across their course. The ascent, though rough and broken in many places, is neither very steep nor extremely difficult, owing to the winding nature of the track they follow. They find the descent of the range a little more difficult than the ascent has been. More than once the path grows so rugged that great care and caution are necessary in order to get the oxen and wagon safely along.

All night they travel, and then, just as the whole of the eastern sky is breaking into one glorious mass of light, they reach the bed of a dry water-course some five or six miles from the foot of the last ridge down which they have toiled. Here Mazika, who has so far acted as guide on account of being more familiar with the country in this direction than any other member of the party, says they are to "outspan;" in other words, to unyoke the oxen and prepare to encamp.

They follow the track of the water-course for perhaps two hundred and fifty or three hundred yards. Here somewhat suddenly, after having passed around a thick coppice of low-growing acacias, they come upon a pool, or rather a spring, of most excellent water that is sheltered by an overhanging ledge of rock. They are now in one of the wildest portions of the river-bed. On either side the bank towers many feet above them, covered with a tangled growth of bush and vine and interspersed here and there with clumps of swaying, feathery ferns and tall, rank-growing reeds.

The spring itself is about two feet deep, and gushes with much freedom from the very heart of the earth. Around it, as though to give it a cooler and still more inviting appearance, are clumps of tall ferns and dewy grasses and the fragile stems and creepers of many delicate ice-plants.

At this inviting spot they hope to remain securely sheltered during the day, as well as to obtain the sleep and rest so necessary to fit them to endure the fatigues of the coming night's travel. The oxen are outspanned, watered and turned to graze upon the luscious grasses that grow in such rich abundance all along the river's bed. The other cattle and the horses and donkeys are also treated in the same manner, after one or two of them have first been tethered in order to prevent them from straying. The fowls too are watered and given grain to eat. Then a sheep is killed, and while Kaffir Jim milks the cows, Ellie, Hope and Mamochisane see to the getting of breakfast. And a most palatable meal it is when ready, consisting of lamb nicely roasted, biscuits, eggs, coffee for the older ones and rich sweet milk for the younger.

When all are satisfied, even the dogs and Madame Tea-kettle and her little family, Mazika carefully puts out the fire, fearing that the smoke may attract attention. That is, he puts it all out with the exception of one large chunk, which he husbands with a view to saving matches, securely wrapping it in the ashes. Then the arrangement having been entered into for Cunnyngham, Pierce, Mazika, Pitsane, Kamati and Jim to take turns about in keeping watch, they all, with the exception of the one who is to go on guard-duty first, lie down to the much-needed rest. Even the children and old Mamochisane, despite the fact that they have slept much and well during the journey of the previous night, nevertheless feel themselves so overcome by the common drowsiness that prevails as to soon fall into a slumber quite as deep and sound as the others. Ere lying down they have agreed that they will have but one more meal for this day, and that well toward evening.

The sun is just two hours high when Mazika, who has been the last on duty, awakens them with the intimation that it is time they were making preparations for the evening's meal and the night's travel.

While the meal is in preparation Cunnyngham coaxes Ellie and Hope to go with him and Mazika to the summit of a small wood-crowned hill near by, where they desire to make some observations of the surrounding country by means of the telescope. The hill is only a few hundred yards directly to the right of the camping-place, but as they have to go back along the bed of the stream to the point at which they have entered it, it is altogether the walk of a half mile or more.

It is more a mound than a hill, and of that peculiar cup-shape so common in Africa. It has an altitude of only about seventy-five or a hundred feet; but as much of the country round about is rather level, and the other hills in the vicinity are of less eminence, they have a very good view.

Suddenly, Cunnyngham, who has the telescope adjusted to his eye and is pointing it first in one direction and then another, gives a quick little cry and almost lets the instrument fall from his hand.

"What is the matter?" asks Hope hurriedly.

"There, Mazika! take the glass," Cunnyngham says, hastily placing it in his hand. "Quick, old fellow!" he says again to Mazika, "and bring it to bear upon that clump of acacias out yonder, and tell me what you see."

"Zulus!" is the one terrible word that falls from Mazika's lips, as, being familiar with the use of the glass, he has adjusted it to the proper focus.

"'Zulus'!" repeats Ellie, feeling that in spite of her every effort she must cry out in this sudden terror that has come upon her. "Oh, surely not, Mazika! Look again! You must be mistaken."

As to Hope, at the first sound of that dreadful word she has leaned heavily, pale and speechless, against the tree near which she has been standing. The tree, but a mere sapling, begins to bend under her weight.

"Mazika is not mistaken, missy. It is Zulus —Zulu dogs, full a score in number and with shining assegais ready for battle."

"And are they coming this way, Mazika?"

"Straight as the arrow flies, missy."

"About how far away are they?" this last to Cunnyngham, who has again taken the glass.

"Only about a mile and a half, I should judge, but perhaps a little more," his lips striving in vain to speak the words steadily.

"Then may God help us, for we are surely lost!"

"Say not so, child of the good father," exclaims Mazika, falling into his old rounded, musical Zulu. "The hand of Mazika is strong, his heart as the heart of the black rhinoceros that fears naught, and his mighty battle-axe, the great Balala, is thirsty for battle. Before Balala's awful blow many warriors have kissed the dust, and many more will yet kiss it ere Mazika himself goes down. Fear not, child of the good man with the warm hand and the brave heart; a score of warriors are as but the chaff before the wind to the hand of Mazika, but as the grass the tongues of fire lick up to the kiss of the mighty Balala!"

"Oh, Mazika," Ellie entreats, "do not talk so extravagantly. You are a brave man, I know, and you are strong, as you say, but what are even *your* strength and *your* bravery against a score of bloodthirsty savages armed with their deadly assegais? Oh quick! tell us what to do!"

"There is nothing," says Cunnyngham, answering ere the Zulu can speak, "except to return to the camp and prepare to make what defence we can. I, for one, propose to sell my life and that of those dear to me at as great a cost as possible.—What say you, Mazika?"

"The words of my white brother are brave; they are the words of a man and warrior. Many Matabele dogs shall kiss the earth this night ere

Mazika sleeps with his face turned to the land of his fathers."*

"Oh, this is dreadful to think of!" cries Hope piteously at this moment.—"O dear God!" clasping her hands and falling upon her knees, "hear us —hear us now as we pray to thee! Help us! save us! for unless you do, we are all lost."

It is surely in answer to this impassioned prayer that just at this moment Cunnyngham, who has been again looking through the glass, cries excitedly as he drops it:

"Oh look! look, all of you! for you can see it plainly now without the glass. But be careful to keep within the shadow of the trees."

They all obey this hastily-given injunction, and as they raise their eyes to glance in the direction in which he is pointing more than one heart almost ceases to beat, so great is the anxiety that now takes possession of them.

The Zulus have come out from the shelter of the woods, have crossed the sandy strip, and are now bearing straight toward them across the grassy plain. But even as the watchers under the trees gaze upon them with almost pulseless hearts and bated breath, there happens something that causes the blood to rush back again in its normal condition and every faculty to experience a great reaction.

* It is the custom of the Zulus, when buried away from home, to be sepultured with their faces turned in the direction of Zulu-land.

The Zulus come straight on with heads erect and their terrible assegais catching and reflecting the rays of the now fast setting sun. But suddenly across their path, as though frightened from their covert by the approach of the dread enemy, there bounds a large herd of "klip-springers," or mountain gazelles, a beautiful species of the antelope tribe. With wild yells, the faint echoes of which are borne to the watchers even at this distance, the Zulus spring to the chase, some brandishing their assegais, others making ready their bows and arrows.

"They are gone!" says Mazika—"gone upon the track of the swift-bounding deer that will lead them a chase long after the sun's setting ere they are caught. Another way now will the Zulu go, another place will know his camp for to-night. The children of the good father are safe."

"That was certainly a miraculous escape," says Cunnyngham, still white and with his hands trembling in spite of himself.

"It was God's mercy," says Ellie reverently. "Did you not hear Hope's prayer?"

When they return to the camp and tell the others what has happened, there are many expressions of deep gratitude at the miraculous escape, and most fervent is the prayer of thankfulness to God for all his mercies that is offered up at the beginning of the evening meal.

"'Surely I know it shall be well with those who

fear God,'" reads Pierce impressively from his father's well-worn Bible, and Ellie's voice has a stronger and fuller ring as it leads the evening hymn, despite the fact that they have to sing in somewhat subdued tones in order to guard against detection.

By six o'clock they have "inspanned" and are ready for the start, which Mazika tells them must be early in order to reach by eleven o'clock a certain spot some fourteen miles distant.

Their way for many miles yet must lie along the course of the river-bed. Thus, as its banks are very high and deep, and in many places shut in by all manner of dense-growing shrubbery, it will be extremely difficult as well as dangerous to attempt to travel after the moon has gone down. There will be not only the peril to be apprehended from lurking wild beasts, but also the danger of either losing their way or of being dashed to pieces against some of the precipitous ledges with which the gorge is lined. As the moon sets at a little after eleven, it is most important that they shall have reached their next camping-place by that time.

It is a tortuous and trying journey along the river-course, even with the friendly moonlight to aid them, but beyond a thrilling adventure with a leopard, nothing further occurs to disturb them. This creature, which seems very bloodthirsty and determined, suddenly springs at the throat of the horse Mazika is leading, just as they have entered one of the wildest portions of the gorge. It misses it, however, and lands in front of the horse upon which Pierce is mounted. The animal rears wildly, and but for the youth's firm seat in the saddle would surely unhorse him. As the crouching beast turns for a second spring, this time upon the Kaffir, Jim, who has sprung forward to catch the bridle of Pierce's plunging horse, a mighty swing of Mazika's great axe lays it dead across their path.

"Dis here mighty bad plan 'bout trabblin' at night," philosophizes Jim as, quiet and order having once more been restored, they proceed on their way. "Fus' t'ing you know lion wid him great blazin' eye gwine ter come; den what happen, I wonder? But what wid de sharp eyes o' dem sneakin' Zulu watchin' ter spy us out troo de day, it eben wors' dan de beasts."

"There is very little danger of meeting a lion in this section, I have heard Mazika say," Cunnyngham here reassures him. "He says there isn't water enough to suit His Lordship. When we get farther on, about the 'vleys' and big pools, then we may look out."

At a few minutes after eleven o'clock, just as the moon is setting, they reach their second camping-place. Here Mazika decides to keep a fire burning through the remainder of the night as a precaution against the attacks of numerous panthers, wild-cats, jackals and such troublesome and dangerous beasts, the howls and cries of which are already beginning to sound unpleasantly near.

The next night's march is a repetition of the preceding one, with the exception of the adventure with the leopard, which in this instance is substituted by a most dangerous encounter with a ferocious pack of ravenous jackals, out of which they come at last with safety, but with the loss of two of their sheep and one of the goats, which are killed and carried off by these bloodthirsty creatures.

That night, which is the third since their starting out, they camp at a spot, still along the bed of the dried river-course, a little more than fifty miles in a slightly north-westerly direction from the mission-station. They are now well out of the usual range of the Zulus and Boers, but there is still great danger, Mazika tells them, to be apprehended from one or two tribes that are great allies of the former, although on most hostile terms with the Boers, who have treated them shamefully; hence they have declared uncompromising war upon all the whites.

CHAPTER XI.

"He shall give his angels charge concerning thee."

THE spot that has been selected as their third camping-place is even more wildly picturesque than that at which they first stopped.

The rocky walls of the gorge, however, are not so precipitous nor so high. Indeed, there are many places at which it is quite easy to climb them, even to the top, where an unbroken view of the country may be had in more than one direction. In the distance stretches the long line of mountains over which our travelers have passed in their first night's journey. Farther beyond, bolder and more towering crags rear themselves against the horizon. These last are more than fifty miles away, yet so dry and clear is the atmosphere that in this wonderful climate objects at even a much greater distance have been known to be visible.

Although the spot at which the little caravan has now halted until the following night is not so well shut in as those of their previous camping-places, it is nevertheless one in which they can with some precaution lie securely hidden. There is on every side a luxuriant tangle of trailing vines, lush grasses and bending ferns, with thick coppices of acacia. A little beyond the camping-place the bed of the river runs almost on a level with the surrounding country, forming a most convenient outlet.

Here, a little while after the breakfast-hour, appears Mazika on his way to reconnoitre for the purpose of discovering if the country in front of them is sufficiently clear of danger to allow of their proceeding on their way. They are now, he had said to them, about eight miles from a village the chief of which is a great ally of Mosilikatse. As the way before them lies within less than a mile of this village, it will be quite dangerous to attempt the journey until the outlook for a safe passage is known to be favorable. Therefore the brave Zulu is determined to satisfy himself as to this matter, and, although it is daylight and he will run a great risk in thus exposing himself, he nevertheless sets determinedly forth. Ere leaving he cautions the party not to quit the ravine for any space of time, to build no fires until toward night and to tether the cattle so that they will not stray.

It is a long and trying day to all, for, the ravine being so closely shut in, the heat is at times almost unbearable. Even Henrietta, with all her irrepressible spirits, seems for once to have lost the better part of her energy and light-heartedness. Nevertheless, she determines to take up again the Catechism she had begun teaching Jim at the station, and which has been sadly interfered with by the painful and exciting events of the past weeks. Jim comes readily in response to the notice she gives him, the broad smile that displays his great white teeth showing how eager he is to resume the rôle of pupil to so charming a little instructress.

"Jim, who made you?" questions Miss Henrietta, coming at once to the point.

"De great Man in de sky, missy."

"And what is his name, Jim?"

"Him name God, missy."

"Of what did he make you, Jim?"

"Out'n de black mud, missy."

"Oh no, Jim; he made you of the dust of the ground."

"Mus' er been mighty black dus', missy."

"And for what did he make you?"

"Ter 'tend de cattle en' min' Miss Ellie."

"Oh no, he didn't, Jim. He made you for something far better than that—for his own glory."

"What dat, missy?"

For a moment Henrietta is puzzled. It is indeed a hard question for a little girl to answer. But after a few moments of earnest thought she determines to do the best she can.

"When God made man, Jim," she says at length, speaking very slowly and impressively, "he made him in his own image; and because he had made him in his own image God was very proud of him and wanted him to feel how good it was to be made in the Creator's image. He hoped, too, that when man saw how glorious was the image in which he had been made, he would do everything he could to honor it; that is, that he would do nothing vile or sinful, nothing that would make God sorry that he had given him his own likeness, but, on the other hand, would do all he could to make himself more like God, good and pure and true, so that God, seeing how beautiful was the work he had made, would take glory in it."

"Any dere a black God, missy?"

"Oh no, Jim; there is but the one God—pure and white and radiant."

"Den him nebber mek Jim, missy," with mournful conviction.

"Oh yes, he did, Jim; he made us all, you as well as me."

"But you said, missy, 'im mek um all in 'im own picter, en' dat 'im pure and white. Now, poor Jim, 'im so black!"

"Oh, it does not matter about your skin, Jim. It is in your heart where the true likeness of God is placed. If your heart is pure, then you may know that God is there."

Here Ellie calls Henrietta, and the lesson is ended, for this time at least.

About three o'clock in the afternoon Mazika returns. The signs are favorable, he tells them, for a safe passage around the hostile village, though the utmost caution will be required. This evening a great feast is to be given in honor of some exploit of the chief, Mondokoro, to which many Zulus have been invited. Doubtless the Zulus they have seen on that evening at their first camping-place have been on their way thither. At ten o'clock will occur the great war-dance, and if they can manage to reach the neighborhood of the village while this is taking place it will be about the safest opportunity of getting by unobserved.

The start is arranged for seven o'clock, and it is their determination to put at least twenty miles between the hostile village and their next stopping-place. To accomplish this it will be necessary to travel not only all night, but well into the next day, as the route over which they will have to pass, with the exception of some five or six miles, will lead for the most part over level tracts, many of them treeless, and others, again, only thinly verdured; and as Mazika is altogether familiar with the route, there will be little danger, he assures them, of their losing the track in the dark after the moon has set. If there was, there would be the light of the stars to guide them.

As they are preparing their evening meal a very exciting thing happens.

Just as they are all gathered near the fire, where a pot of goat's meat is boiling, their attention is suddenly attracted by the heavy crash and subsequent trampling of some large animal that has evidently leaped from some little height into the gorge, and is now running up it toward their camp.

"To that ledge of rock at the side of the gorge, quick, all of you!" Cunnyngham cries, and hurries them thither not a moment too soon.

The next instant there is the piercing cry of "Borele! borele!" (the black rhinoceros! the black rhinoceros!) from Kamati, followed immediately thereafter by the appearance in the cleared spot that forms their camping-place of a full-grown black rhinoceros charging at headlong speed. The first thing it encounters is the rear end of the wagon turned slightly sideways across the line of its course. With one thrust of its deadly horn it dashes the chicken-coop to splinters, kills three of the fowls, and sends the others flying in terror to the shelter of the thorn-coppices. From the wagon the great beast charges full tilt upon the fire where the pot is boiling, overturns it and scatters the burning brands in every direction.

"Aim for the shoulder!" Cunnyngham cries to Pierce, who fortunately has his rifle in his hand at the time of the infuriated animal's entrance of the camp.

He obeys, but the excitement of the moment has rendered his hand unsteady, and instead of striking the monster brute in the shoulder the ball enters a portion of the spine. But it is a most fortunate shot, and made not a moment too soon. In another instant the maddened beast would have charged full upon the trembling group crouched within the shadow of the overhanging rock. But as Pierce's bullet penetrates the spine, it has the effect of partially paralyzing it, so that for an instant it stands perfectly motionless. The next moment Pierce has taken aim upon the huge exposed shoulder and fired the second time. It is a splendid shot, for the ball, ploughing its way through the thick fold of skin, pierces the heart and brings the animal with one wild plunge to the ground.

The slain rhinoceros is a huge beast, and proves, after careful examination, to be in unusually good order for one of his kind. Some steaks are therefore cut from the tenderest part and thrown upon the coals to broil, in place of the stew of goat's meat the infuriated animal has so wantonly destroyed.

A most pathetic little incident happens as the carcass of the huge beast is dragged away. Under one of his great feet is found a mangled and shapeless mass of soft fur that, as they gaze upon it, they recognize as all that is left of poor little Kitten Lightfoot, one of the most headstrong and disobedient of Madame Tea-kettle's somewhat willful family. Instead of remaining to play with his little brothers and sisters on the skin rug over by the great rock, where Henrietta has placed them, and where Madame Tea-kettle herself stays to keep close watch over her somewhat unmanageable little family, Kitten Lightfoot, puffed up with a sense of his own importance and of his mother's old-fogyish ways, has wandered off in search of adventures; and this has been his end!

"Poor little Kitten!" says Henrietta, sobbing

over his shapeless remains, "you were very naughty, I know, and gave your poor mamma heaps of trouble, but I can't help feeling sorry for you. If all of us who are ugly and naughty, and don't every time do as we are told to do, were to be taken off because of our naughtiness, there would be awfully few of us left.— Marvin," she continues, "let us bury Kitten, and let us write something over his grave that will warn all the little children-beasts how very, very sinful it is to be disobedient to their parents."

"But they couldn't read it," says Marvin sturdily.

"Well, maybe they'll somehow *know*. At any rate, I'd feel better if I did it, somehow as if I'd 'tended to a warning I'd been asked to make."

So the tiny grave is dug and the remains of the poor little disobedient Kitten laid therein, carefully enveloped in one of Cunnyngham's well-worn handkerchiefs, which he cheerfully contributes for the occasion. When the tiny mound is raised this epitaph is placed at the head thereof, carefully printed in Pierce's best hand:

To the Memory
OF
KITTEN LIGHTFOOT,
Son of Mrs. Pussy Tea-kettle Grey
(Widow of Thomas Grey),
WHO WAS WALKED ON BY THE BIG RHINOCEROS,
April 17, 188-,
FOR RUNNING AWAY FROM HIS MOTHER.
Children, obey your parents.

In a short while, by means of some strips of plank they have fortunately brought with them, another chicken-coop is constructed. The fowls are soon coaxed back to the clearing by means of a generous sprinkling of grain thrown to them by Ellie and Hope, and, as they shortly go to roost on some low bushes near by, they are finally caught and returned to the coop with but little trouble.

This accident delays them somewhat, and it is not until nearly eight o'clock that the start is made.

By following closely and carefully the many cautious directions of Mazika they are enabled at last to get safely around the hostile village, but they catch an idea of just how critical is the situation from the various sounds that from time to time are borne to them from the centre of the village, where the leaping, howling savages are holding high carnival.

As they reach a point about half a mile beyond the village Pierce rides back to where Pitsane has lingered to help Jim bring up a few head of straggling cattle, and to make sure that there is no sign of discovery or pursuit.

"Pitsane," Pierce says as soon as Jim starts to the front with his stray cattle, "I am fairly devoured with curiosity to return and see the sights that are going on in that village. Mazika tells me that as soon as Mondokoro's people are through, the Zulus present are going to engage in the genuine old Zulu war-dance. Do you not think we might manage to creep up near enough to see without being seen?"

Pitsane shakes his head doubtfully:

"Pitsane thinks not. There would be many risks, and Pitsane would never forgive himself did he not warn the son of the good father of the great danger."

"But if we are cautious we can surely creep through the woods without being detected. We can fasten our horses in that clump of trees there and make our way to the village on foot. The savages will be so taken up with their dancing and feasting that they will not think of anything else. We'll take care to keep within the shelter of the brushwood. Come, Pitsane, let us risk it. We can easily overtake the others in an hour's time. Come, teach me your trick of gliding along noiselessly. I believe you Hottentots could make your way over creaking floors without giving forth a single sound."

Thus importuned, Pitsane at last consents, but still against his better judgment.

Tying their horses securely within the thicket Pierce has pointed out, they cautiously make their way in the direction of the village. Between this thicket and the stretch of woods that encloses the town of Mondokoro there is an open space of waving grass, with here and there a single scrubby mimosa or a tussock of thorns and thistles. If they should be discovered while crossing this, there would be little chance for concealment. They, however reach the shelter of the woods on the other side without detection. Here Pitsane pauses and places his finger upon his lips as a sign for perfect silence. Then throwing his body forward he begins to advance through the matted underbrush with a half-creeping, half-gliding movement that is absolutely noiseless. Pierce endeavors to imitate him, and finally succeeds very well, though he fully realizes that even with years of careful practice he will never acquire the perfection of soundless movement that seems to be a very part of the gliding Hottentot.

Ere they have advanced more than two hundred and fifty or three hundred yards they catch sight of the glow of the fires burning within the open space in the centre of the village. Five minutes more, and they can see clearly the outlines of the dome-shaped huts straggling in somewhat irregular lines across the clearing. A little nearer still, and now they can plainly distinguish many moving forms and catch snatches of noisy shouts and of excited conversation. Creeping to the edge of the clearing and cautiously concealing themselves behind a tangled mass of undergrowth, and within the shadow of a tall tree that towers many feet above them, they are now enabled to see and hear much of what is passing within the village.

The first dance seems to have been over for some little time, and the Zulus are now preparing for the great feature of the night's revelry. There are a hundred or more of them, all totally nude and with their gleaming black bodies smeared from head to foot with a horrid mixture of grease and red clay. In the glow of the fire they look more like demons than men, and as Pierce glances at them a shudder passes over him. To add still further to their horrible appearance, they are throwing their faces into all sorts of contortions and gesticulating wildly with their arms.

A loud beating noise upon some rude, drum-like instrument now summons them to the dance, when they quickly place themselves in a circle. The drum now ceases to beat and the dance begins, with a slow movement to a sort of humming noise that is made by a group of women who have stationed themselves in the rear. The men now begin to stamp and keep time with their feet until the excitement, gradually increasing, culminates finally in a simultaneous spring, accompanied by a series of most blood-curdling shouts. This seems to urge the now thoroughly possessed actors to a most unnatural frenzy, during which they throw their bodies about in the most terrible abandon and their already hideous faces into such horrible contortions as strike a sick fear to the heart of Pierce, and make him wish from the bottom of his heart that he had not been so foolhardy as to venture into such danger. For just how great a danger is this into which his curiosity and rash impetuousness have led him he sees now plainly enough. The picture of these howling, leaping savages going through all these horrible contortions is indeed sufficient to produce in even the strongest mind the most appalling sensations. The dusky glare of the fire, too, blazing in front of the dancing warriors during their wild and unearthly evolutions, added to the flaming torches which many of them have snatched from the burning heaps and are now whirling wildly around their heads, gives an additional degree of awful effect to the terrible scene. At length, nature having thoroughly exhausted itself, the savages begin one by one to drop out of the ring and to fall along the ground, where they lie nearly motionless. Finally, the movements of those who are left grow slower and slower, though every now and then there is a convulsive effort on the part of some one of them to throw the body into wilder contortions than any yet essayed. Suddenly there is a loud tap of the drum-like instrument, similar to that with which the dance has begun, at sound of which the strained evolutions of the remaining warriors instantly cease. They are at once surrounded by a great company of the villagers, men, women and children, who crowd about them to offer congratulations upon the wonderful power displayed by them in holding out so long. This lasts for some minutes, during which those warriors who have fallen out before the dance ended also come forward to compliment their more successful companions, which is done with very good grace considering their own defeat.

Just as the savages are on the point of breaking up to take their way to various parts of the village, Pierce gives Pitsane the signal for their own departure. But, unfortunately, at this moment, in turning around, the youth's foot treads upon a dry twig, which at once breaks asunder, giving forth a sharp, snapping sound. In an instant several of the heads of the savages who are the nearest to them are thrown back and turned in the direction whence the sound has issued. Pierce's heart begins to beat violently, for he fears that all is now lost. And it does, in truth, seem so, especially as some half dozen of the savages now start up, evidently as though with the intention of making toward the spot where the Hottentot and youth are now crouching in momentary terror of being discovered. In a few seconds more all would indeed be over with them but for a timely diversion that now occurs.

The sound of the snapping twig has fallen upon other ears besides those of the savages, and evidently with a note of alarm. Near where Pierce and Pitsane have been crouching two hyenas, one of them but little more than half grown, have taken up their stand, waiting for the savages to disperse, so that they may feast upon the bones of the various animals that have been slaughtered and eaten during the evening. At sound of the snapping twig the younger has been considerably startled, and just as the savages have started up to make their way to the spot where Pierce and Pitsane are crouching, the animal, with one frightened bound, springs into the midst of the clearing directly in front of them. With a loud shout one of the men impales the terror-stricken animal upon the point of his spear. Apparently satisfied that the breaking twig has been caused by the hyena, the savages, after a short consultation, return to the circle of light produced by the blazing fires, thus enabling the Hottentot and the youth to steal cautiously away from their dangerous hiding-place.

"That was a close run, Pitsane," Pierce says at length, as some ten or fifteen minutes later they reach in safety the thicket where their horses are fastened. "I tell you what, old fellow," he continues, when, having mounted, they ride slowly and cautiously away for fear of the sound of their horses' hoofs attracting attention, "curiosity when not properly directed is a bad thing. Here, for the mere sake of seeing how those ugly Zulus looked when engaged in that great war-dance of theirs, I imperiled not only my own life, but that of another."

CHAPTER XII.

"How manifold are thy works!"

PIERCE and Pitsane have not proceeded more than two miles on their way when they catch sight of a figure riding rapidly toward them across the open plain. It proves to be Cunnyngham, who, having grown alarmed at their protracted absence, has returned in search of them.

Pierce feels more deeply than ever the inexcusableness of his conduct when he learns how much his sister and cousin have been distressed in regard to his disappearance, and then and there forms a firm resolve never to be guilty of so thoughtless and so rash an act again.

The little caravan is overtaken some six miles beyond the village. The moon has now gone down and there is only the light of the stars to guide them. But this seems to be sufficient for Mazika, for not once does he lead them astray from the course, even conducting them safely over an outlying ridge of the mountains over which they passed during their first night's travel. Here the path has to be cleared by the use of axes.

While crossing this range they have at the hour

of midnight the rare delight of hearing rich, liquid bird-notes in a roundelay as sweet and pure as ever issued from the throat of feathered songster. In delighted surprise the weary travelers pause to listen, each liquid note falling with a sweet and indescribable effect upon their hearts and seeming to make suddenly glad all the dreary way.

"That is assuredly the 'little shepherd,'" says Cunnyngham as he rides near the wagon where Ellie and Hope are sitting. "I have often read accounts of travelers who spoke of this bird, and of the inspiring effects its glad, beautiful notes had upon them, coming thus unexpectedly in the dead of night."

"'The little shepherd'?" repeats Ellie, interrogatively. "Why is it called that?"

"It was said to have been so named by some of the native farmers and herders because of its familiarity in approaching them while tending their sheep, as well as from the affection it is said to display for these woolly animals. It is a very gentle and harmless bird, and I dare say if we could gain a sight of this brave little fellow, who sings so cheerily in the midst of this darkness and desolation, he would show little, if any, disposition to fly away from us."

They travel steadily all night, only stopping at short intervals to rest the tired cattle, and once for about an hour to give them water from the casks in the wagon.

By eight o'clock the following morning they have

put fully sixteen miles between them and the hostile village, Mazika tells them, but they lack a good six miles' journey yet of reaching the spot where they are to halt. A snack of biscuit and biltong (dried game-flesh) is eaten as they go along, washed down with water from the casks, which they find a little warm and unpalatable from its standing since the preceding night. But despite this drawback they drink it gratefully, thinking how much worse it might be if they had none at all.

The sun has now grown very warm, almost unbearably so whenever a strip of woods is left and they come out upon an open plain. More and more frequent now grow these plains or treeless tracts. The country, too, has undergone quite a change. It is much less rugged, and the forest growths are not so deep in their verdure. Instead of the widespreading banian, there are now more pines and palms, with many clumps of a tree that resembles the wild olive.

Here, too, in great abundance grows the camelthorn or acacia-giraffe, called by the Dutch "kameel-dorn," and so named because of the fondness shown for it by the camelopard. It is also the tree, Pierce tells Ellie and Hope, that gave Dr. Livingstone the belief that it was the same as that of which the ark of the covenant and the frame of the tabernacle were made.

"And is it really so?" Hope asks.

"I do not know, but I think it is. Dr. Livingstone fully believed it, and gave many proofs to sustain his belief. One is that its wood answers accurately the description of it given in sacred history, and the other is that the tree is found where the Israelites were at the time that the ark and tabernacle were built?"

"But I thought they were made of shittim-wood?" Ellie says.

"So they were, sister, and I suppose that is the name by which the camel-thorn was known at that day and in that place. The tabernacle, as we know, was fitted up in the wilderness, or, more definitely speaking, the desert of Arabia. As no other tree from which timber of any size or durability could have been obtained grows there except the acacia, and as the acacia-giraffe is one of the most abundant of this species, there is then full evidence that it is the tree alluded to as the shittim. Dr. Livingstone proved by careful observation, as well as by experiment in various ways, that the wood of the camel-thorn is imperishable, while that usually pointed out as the shittim-wood not only soon decays, but lacks beauty."

Again and again as they pass on their way they come in sight of numerous antelopes, either peacefully feeding or scampering away at their approach. Indeed, the whole face of the country seems richly stocked with these graceful and beautiful animals. But for the peculiar character of their horns many of them might be taken for deer.

As they are passing a slightly elevated mound a short distance to the right of the track they are following, they catch a momentary glimpse of a large fine gemsbok standing alone, while below him on the plain a number of his fellows are grazing.

Another animal of the antelope species of which they have a very good view as it gallops off across the plain in front of them is the nyl-ghau or white-footed antelope. It is one of the most peculiar they have yet seen, seeming to partake of the nature of both the antelope and the ox. It is most majestic in its carriage and bright in its coloring, the predominant hue being a steely blue that fairly glitters as the back of the glossy animal catches the rays of the sun. Intermingled with the blue are several white patches here and there. From the throat and shoulders hangs a dense bunch of hair. It is the largest of any of the antelopes they have yet seen, being over four feet from the ground at the shoulders.

"It is unusual to see a fellow of that species out here in the daytime," remarks Pierce. "But I suppose hunger drove him from his covert. According to travelers who are familiar with his habits, he is said to do most of his feeding at night."

"Well, he does look like a coward galloping away from us as he is doing now," observes Hope.

"But on the contrary, cousin, he is very courageous, constantly being known to attack even the leopard and tiger, although he is very well aware of the fact that these great enemies of his usually get the better of him. It is only shyness that is the matter with him now. He has doubtless never seen such a sight before on these plains as our imposing little caravan presents."

The most curious of all the interesting animals of which they have a sight is the harness deer. As Marvin catches a glimpse of it bounding off before them he suddenly calls out to Pierce:

"Oh, brother, do look at that goat with a saddle on his back!"

They all have a hearty laugh at this; but indeed the illusion is almost perfect, and it is no wonder the little fellow is deceived thereby. The peculiar marks upon the body of this strange animal make him look at a distance exactly as if he had not only a saddle, but also a set of harness, fastened to his back.

Of birds there seems no end. The strips of forest through which they pass are fairly alive with them, and the trills of delicious melody as they sing their morning roundelays fill hearts and ears with gladness. There is a magnificent species of the hoopoe, almost entirely of a deep rich purple color. There are also pigeons innumerable, but these are generally seen only in pairs, running along the ground picking up insects and seeds from the grass.

They come upon many nests of various kinds

of birds, some of them altogether different from any they have ever seen. One of these nests is like a horn in shape, suspended with the point downward. Its greatest diameter is about three inches, gradually diminishing toward the base. It has for some time been abandoned, and as Pitsane detaches it from its resting-place between two branches of a mimosa tree and brings it to them, all bend over it with many exclamations of curiosity and wonder.

Another remarkable nest is one fully two and a half yards in circumference and more than a yard in length. It seems to have been the home of several birds instead of one, all of them quite small, and, judging by a poor dead inmate, to have been birds somewhat resembling the goldfinch. At the bottom of this nest there are as many as seventeen holes or entrance-places, and near the centre and top at least as many more. This strange nest is among the upper branches of a thick shrub-like tree, and as he rides up near it Pierce can easily reach it with his extended hand. As he is on the point of bringing it down for the others to have a view, something flies suddenly and awkwardly forth, almost into his face, and the next moment with a clumsy beat of wings a horned owl alights upon a limb, or rather falls in a blind sort of way to a limb below.

A mile or more farther on Hope suddenly rises to her feet in the wagon, so great is her excitement at what she has discovered, while she exclaims hurriedly,

"Oh, do you see that great basket hanging up near the top of that tree! Who *could* have put it there, I wonder?"

"It is not a basket, cousin," says Cunnyngham, laughing; "it is a bird's nest."

"A bird's nest?" incredulously.

"Yes, a bird's nest, or rather the nest of many birds. If I mistake not, that is the former home of a company of the sociable grosbeaks, who have now doubtless gone to seek another neighborhood where bugs, berries and seeds are more numerous. At any rate, it seems so from here. But let us stop, and I will send Pitsane to get the nest. If it is really what I think it is, it will be well worth an examination."

It proves indeed, as Cunnyngham has said, "well worth an examination," for never have they seen anything more curious and wonderful in bird-architecture.

While suspended from the tree it has had the basket-like appearance that has deceived Hope, but now that it is removed, and they have a closer view, it bears more resemblance to a hogshead than to anything else. It is fully three yards in circumference, and is composed of a strong coarse straw regularly thatched, the straw having been so ingeniously woven that all the ends point downward, thus avoiding the possibility of the rain entering.

"There is wonderful instinct for you!" says Cunnyngham admiringly. "Who will say now that birds haven't a rare amount of intelligence? To think these little fellows have so much sense as to build their abode after this ingenious fashion!"

By half-past ten o'clock the little caravan reaches a small strip of woods surrounded on three sides by a plain covered by tall waving grasses and gemmed with myriads of brilliantly variegated wild flowers. On the fourth side it leads away into a much denser forest, near the edge of which are heaped up many wild and picturesque-looking rocks. In the midst of these there is a deep "vley," or pool, where, Mazika tells them, many animals come to drink. This, he says, is to be their camping-place, and here the tired animals are at once outspanned, and here also the fatigued travelers seek the inviting shade of the trees with deep thankfulness that the long, hot ride is at length at an end.

CHAPTER XIII.

"Lo, I am with you alway."

IT is now Friday, and they are fully eighty-five miles from their starting-point, and about half the distance to the Kalahari desert. As the spot at which they have now halted affords many attractions as a camping-place, and as the poor tired animals seem much worn out with their recent hard trip, it is determined, after some consultation, to remain here until the following Monday morning, deciding to make the start then by the break of day, in order to get through, ere night falls, the dense strip of forest that lies between them and the open plains beyond. Through this forest, Mazika tells them, they will have to cut fully two-thirds of their way, and, although it is not more than twelve miles to the plain on the other side where he hopes to make their next camping-place, it will take them all day with their best efforts to accomplish the passage.

In the mean time, it is decided, considering the somewhat unprotected position of the camp and the nearness of dangerous wild beasts, to erect a barricade of some kind. After they have refreshed themselves by a hearty meal and a few hours of sleep, they all set cheerfully to work upon it, even Ellie, Hope, old Mamochisane and the children doing what they can to help. By sundown they have formed of poles and of scrubby thorn-bushes an enclosure about fifty or sixty feet square, into which, at nightfall, the cattle are all driven, and where, the wagon having already been placed, they prepare to lie down to sleep, feeling almost as secure as soldiers in a fort. But that this security is not so real as it seems is proved by a thrilling experience that takes place ere the night is passed.

About eleven o'clock Cunnyngham, who is on guard, begins to have his ears greeted by all sorts of hideous noises—hoarse growls, harsh yells and deep, piercing cries. Nearly all of these proceed from the neighborhood of the pool among the rocks.

"It seems as though there is a whole menagerie of wild beasts let loose to-night," Cunnyngham comments to himself, not without many cold shivers and various other unpleasant little sensations, it must be confessed. "Well, all I hope is they will not any of them take it into their heads to treat us to an attack."

In an hour or so the noises gradually decrease, and beyond catching a glimpse every now and then of a blazing pair of eyes unpleasantly near, nothing else occurs just at that time to disturb the youth's somewhat trying watch.

Suddenly, just as he is congratulating himself upon the entire cessation of all the hideous noises that have made such unpleasant music for his ear, he is startled by a low, deep growl close at hand. The next moment a huge body comes flying through the air and lands full among the sleeping cattle. In an instant they start up completely terrified and uttering piercing, piteous cries or deep bellowings of fright.

By this time the whole camp is aroused, and the girls, with old Mamochisane, are on the point of springing from the wagon when Cunnyngham calls loudly to them, "Stay where you are! A lion! a lion!"

In the mean time the lion has seized one of the calves, while the dogs, now thoroughly aroused, are leaping about in every direction with a perfect charivari of piercing barks and threatening growls, though they make no movement to attack the dread beast, seeming to know only too well what will be their fate if they do so. Pierce, Mazika, Pitsane and Jim have now gathered about Cunnyngham, all armed, and all watching with fascinated eyes the great yellow brute that, having despatched the poor, struggling calf, is now standing over the body with blazing eyes and threatening growls. They are afraid to fire for fear of wounding, perhaps killing, some of the cattle, many of which are now tearing wildly about the enclosure as though they had gone mad, as they doubtless have for the moment, poor creatures! Several of the oxen have already escaped by literally tearing through the weaker portions of the barricade.

Directly, as Mazika and Pitsane have both advanced to seek some chance to deal the growling brute a deathblow, the one with his spear and the other with his axe, the lion seizes the body of the calf and gives a sudden spring forward, as though to get off with his prey. In an instant Pitsane makes a lunge at him with the sharp point of his spear. It pierces the animal to the depth of several inches, but instead of inflicting a mortal wound only serves to arouse the beast to fury. With a horrible growl he drops the calf and springs toward Pitsane. It is well for the Hottentot that, like so many of his race, he is endowed with a wonderful agility, else would this beyond a doubt prove his last moment on earth. Seeing the intention of the brute, Pitsane, with a quick spring to one side, dodges him, but not sufficiently quick to avoid the stroke of one of his great paws, the sharp claws of which sink to some depth in the flesh of his right shoulder, most painfully lacerating it. The lion turns for the second spring, and this time would doubtless put an end to poor Pitsane but for the powerful and well-directed blow of Mazika's great axe, which, striking directly between the eyes, quite crushes the brute's skull and stretches him in death-agony upon the ground.

It is a young lion, but full grown and of unusual

size, and all feel thankful as they gather about it and realize what might possibly have happened but for the well-directed blow of Mazika's axe. They do not wonder at him for the love and pride he bestows upon his great "Balala," as he calls it, for it surely is a wonderful, and in his hands a most deadly, weapon.

It is now almost daylight, and as nearly all of them have been more or less shaken up by the attack of the lion, they decide not to return to bed. So they set about replenishing the fire, and in a little while the cooking of breakfast.

While this is going on Pierce dresses Pitsane's wounded shoulder, which, though very painful, is not dangerously hurt. Mazika in the mean time has skinned the lion, and is now busy pegging the skin out and rubbing salt and grease upon it preparatory to hanging it in the sun to dry. It will make a fine rug, he declares, for the little ladybird, as he calls Louise.

The ease with which the lion has come flying over the palisade has been a matter of much speculation to them, but the next morning the mystery is fully cleared away. Near one side they discover a small ledge of rock which in the building of the barricade has been overlooked. Crouched upon this ledge, and almost on a level with the top of the thorn fortifications, the lion has found it no difficult feat to spring downward into the midst of the little camp.

The next day the line of thorn fence is moved farther away from the rocks, and also strengthened in many places. The cattle that have made their escape during the stampede of the previous night are recovered.

The morning following the lion adventure, which is Saturday, Ellie, as soon as breakfast is over, gets out her sewing and repairs to the shade of a thick-foliaged tree just without the enclosure. There is much that calls for the attention of her busy and careful fingers, for during the week of rough traveling just passed many rents have appeared, not only in the boys' clothing, but also in her own and Hope's.

While Ellie sews, Hope, who is sitting near, occupies herself in jotting down in a small blank-book the more striking events of their week's journey. This finished, she next, with Ellie's help, makes careful estimate of their resources.

"If the boys can kill some game now and then," says Ellie at length, "I think, Hope, we can manage capitally until we get to the Makololo. Our flour and meal will last even longer than that, with careful husbanding."

"But suppose something should happen, Ellie? What if we did not procure the right kind of a guide to go with us across the Kalahari, and so should get out of the track, and be many more days than we calculate upon in getting to the Makololo, —what then?"

"Then we must trust in God," says Ellie firmly.

That day at dinner an excitement occurs. As they are gathering about the cloth under the trees upon which the dinner is spread, the very startling discovery is made that Marvin is missing. Just as Cunyngham and Pierce have both started up to go in search of him, the poodle, Chitane, makes his appearance, coming hastily from without the palisade. As he catches sight of Ellie he springs toward her and takes a portion of her dress between his teeth. The next moment he begins to pull her with all his strength toward the opening in the barricade.

"There is something wrong with Marvin," she cries suddenly and with much excitement. "Do you not see the dog, how he is trying to lead me?—Gently, Chitane! brave fellow! I am coming.—Oh, what can it be?—There! run ahead; we are all waiting to follow."

At this the dog, as though he understood every word, lets go her dress and springs through the opening in the thorn fence. The next moment they are all, with the exception of Kamati and Jim, who have been left to guard the dinner, close upon his track. Even Mamochisane is there with the little Louise clasped closely in her arms.

About two hundred yards to the right of the entrance there is a small coppice of "wacht-een-bigte," or "stop-a-while thorn," as the Dutch call it. Toward the coppice the dog now makes his way as fast his fat little legs will carry him. As they draw near it faint cries and exclamations reach them. On Ellie's calling "Marvin! Marvin!" a much louder cry is borne to them, but the words, if there are any, are indistinguishable.

"He is there," she cries, her excitement deepening. "That was his voice, but, oh, what *can* be the matter?"

On rounding the side of the coppice that is farthest away from the opening in the palisades, they come suddenly upon poor Marvin caught hard and fast by the fish-hook-like prongs of the "wacht-een-bigte;" that is, they see a portion of him, and take it for granted that the rest is there; which it is, though in a considerably "worsted" condition, as he himself afterward expresses it. He has crawled in on hands and knees for a short distance, and then risen erect, or tried to do so, in order to procure the body of a poor little bird whose life has been pierced out by sudden and swift contact with the sharp thorns. He is making brave efforts to extricate himself, pulling first one way and then another, not angrily or impatiently, Ellie notices with pleasure even at that moment, but slowly and steadily. It is all useless, however; the more he pulls, the more hopelessly entangled he becomes. He might as well seek to free himself from the grasp of a giant. It is not only "wait a while" with him, poor little fellow! but it has evidently proved wait a *long* while, to judge by the exhausted and dilapidated condition in which he now appears.

"Oh, sister! oh, brother! oh, cousin!" he cries, appealing pathetically to Ellie, Pierce and Cunnyngham in turn, "*can't* you help me out of this? I know that I ought to have stopped to think before I came in here, but that doesn't make the thorns hurt any the less. It's just like a lot of horrid old fish-hooks, only worse: the harder I pull, the tighter I get fastened.—Do something for me, Pierce, can't you?—Oh, there is dear, good Mazika!" his face clearing instantly as he catches sight of the tall form of the Zulu. "I know," confidently, "that *he* will get me out, if anybody can."

"Bring axes," Mazika says to Pitsane, and with these two brief words prepares for action.

It is a delicate and difficult task, even with the aid of the sharp axes, to clear a way into the dense thorn-jungle, for the bushes are thickly matted together and the spines or prickles are long and sharp, some of them being full four inches in length, with points as piercing as a steel needle. But the patient and determined Zulu and Hottentot toil on unremittingly, although their hands and other portions of their flesh are repeatedly lacerated. At length they have come so close to the imprisoned boy that working with the axes is no longer safe. Now comes the hardest part of all, as hands and knives have to take the place of axes. But finally Marvin is borne safely to his sister's side, though much the worse for his hour's imprisonment among the "wacht-een-bigte" thorns.

"Oh, Ellie, I thought I never was going to get out," he cries as he throws himself down across her lap. "Those old sharp fellows held me so tight that even Mazika's knife had a hard time to get them to let me go. Wasn't it funny about Chitane, though?" he continues after a moment's pause, and smiling through his tears. "He wouldn't come anywhere about the thorns, though I did my best to coax him to go in with me when I went after the bird; but he wouldn't budge a step. He just sat off there on his little old squatty legs and kept looking at me. I do believe, sister, he knew just what these thorns would do."

"I dare say he did. Do you know, my little brother, what you have just admitted?"

He gazes up at her quickly, much mystified at first; then as her meaning dawns upon him blushes until even his deepest patch of freckles is hidden.

"That Chitane has more sense than I have," he says at length, dropping his eyes. "Oh, sister, I am so ashamed of it, but I must admit that it is so. I went into the thorn-bushes without stopping to think, while Chitane, who is only a dog, wouldn't go even when I coaxed him, for he saw well enough it wouldn't be for his good. Oh, Ellie, I promise you I will stop to think hereafter before I go anywhere or do anything about which there is the least doubt. I just won't be outdone by a dog, now see if I do."

"See that you *do* take the lesson to heart, little brother," Ellie says gravely, "though it *has* been learned from a dog. In the great world to which you are going, if God spares your life to reach it, there are many things even worse than the 'wacht-een-bigte' thorns. The 'stop-a-whiles' tore your clothes and pierced your flesh, it is true, and held you so fast that it took both Mazika and Pitsane to free you. But there are thorns even sharper and more determined than these—thorns which, when once you are in their grasp, hold you so firmly that a giant's strong arm can scarcely release you. There is one thorn that we call bad habits and another that we call bad company. Think of Chitane and the example he has set you, dog though he is, and when you come anywhere near these thorns turn resolutely away or pass determinedly around on the other side."

It is quite a sober and thoughtful face that Marvin carries with him back to the camp, and there is gladness in Ellie's heart at these unmistakable signs of the depth to which the lesson has sunk. But he is a most distressing-looking little object in other ways, and it takes an hour or two of her most careful and patient work to make him once more presentable. The poodle Chitane comes in also for his share of attention, but in a different way. He is cuddled and fondled and called a brave, good fellow so many times over that, but for the fact of his being one of the soberest and most sensible of dogs, he would surely have his head quite turned.

That afternoon Pierce, who is quite skillful with the gun, kills a number of francolin, or wild quail, which prove a most acceptable addition to their evening meal.

That same afternoon Cunnyngham and Mazika, who are also on the hunt for game, witness a most terrific battle between a giraffe and a pack of hungry lions. It is truly a terrible sight, and causes even Mazika to turn his face away for a time. The poor giraffe is almost completely devoured ere the gluttonous lions make off at last with low, satisfied growls.

When Kamati and Jim hear of it, they hasten at once to the spot and secure the bones, which being full of marrow are considered a great dainty by them. Pierce and Mazika at length succeed in killing a young and fat cow-eland, which furnishes abundant fresh meat for the next two days.

In the mean time, Mazika has made for Ellie and Hope a goblet each from the horn of the black rhinoceros Pierce had killed at their third camping-place. These goblets are most ingeniously contrived, and beautifully finished and polished. Both the girls prize them very highly.

"I have heard," says Pierce, "that a vessel of this kind made of the rhinoceros's horn has the power of detecting any poison that may be in the liquid that is poured into it. Is this true, Mazika?"

"The words are true. If that which is the least poisonous be put into the cup of rhinoceroshorn, then will the liquid bubble up till it bubbles over. If it be a very great poison, a poison that makes death, then will the horn split so," throwing his hands widely apart.

That night the roars of many wild beasts and the snorts and cries of others disturb their sleep, while those who are on watch are treated to many thrilling and magnificent sights of the various kings of the jungle. But, thanks to a merciful Providence, none of them show any disposition to molest the little camp, and morning finds everything in safety.

That day is the Sabbath, and never have they seen a more beautiful one. A shower has fallen during the night, and when the sun comes up it shines upon a world of diamonds. They are everywhere. The leaves of the trees are glittering with them and the tall stems of grass look like blades of Damascus steel set with flashing gems. The air is delightfully fresh and cool and laden with the perfume of many sweet growing things. Even the cattle seem to rejoice as they lift up their voices in deep, loud bellowings. The horses, too, neigh gladly. Of all the dumb brutes, only the one poor cow who has lost her calf by the raid of the lion seems sad and dejected, giving vent every now and then to low moans and piteous cries of distress. As soon as morning prayers and the breakfast that follows are over, they have Sunday-school, and Henrietta resumes once more her pleasing task of teaching Jim the Catechism. Mamochisane forms the second member of this class; Hope takes Kamati and Pitsane; while Mazika is left solely to Ellie, greatly to his delight. She finds him both a docile and an intelligent pupil, yet there are some things she cannot make him see clearly, even with her best efforts, among them the beautiful plan of the resurrection. Poor Mazika! he has so long dwelt amid the darkness that now that the light is sent, it for the time almost blinds his eyes with its radiance.

"Where do you suppose we go when we die, Mazika?" Ellie asks him as he has taken his seat attentively at her side.

"The good father told me, missy, that the spirit, that is the talking and thinking part of me, goes to the heaven where the great man, God, dwells. The other, the body, the house in which the spirit lives, goes into the ground. Even that is to rise again. But Mazika cannot see how this is to be true. The dead die," he continues solemnly; "they are no more; they become as nothing. They are as the beast that cannot move when the hunter's knife has laid it low. If the body once goes to the dust, how can it be found again? When Mazika burns a log of wood, there is only the ashes; he cannot find the log; it is gone. There is not even the shape of the log. When the bird is killed the singing part goes; it never comes back again. The bird has no more voice; its song is finished. Now, when the talking part of man gets away, how can it be brought back again?"

"God is a great God, Mazika," the young girl answers earnestly, "and his works are even more wonderful than we know. He put the stars and the moon and the sun in the sky; he makes the lightnings flash and the thunders roar; he sends the rain to water the earth; he causes the trees and the flowers and the grass upon the plains to grow; but, more wonderful than all, he fashioned Mazika's body and mine, and he put into them breath, which is life itself. Then if he can do all this from nothing, do you not think he can put the life back again when once he has taken it away? See! here is an egg. If I break it, Mazika knows that only a watery and yellow substance will come forth. But suppose I put it under the wings of a fowl? Then Mazika also knows that it will bring forth a living thing. It is God's hand that has done it, the same hand that has placed in our nostrils the breath that is life. Mazika too has seen the seeds planted in the ground —tiny seeds, some of them no larger than the point of this pin I hold—seed so light that a breath may blow them away. But in a little while up shoots the glad green blade, and how soon it grows into the strong brave stalk that bears the food for Mazika and for me! The Lord Christ Jesus himself died and his body was placed in the ground, but after three days he arose again and ascended into heaven. So also shall our bodies arise at that great day, brought forth by the same hand that brings the buried seed as a fresh green shoot from its bed of earth. Let Mazika trust Christ, and he will one day know just how it is the talking part may be brought back to the body again when once it has been carried away, and also how the body itself, a shapeless mass of dust, may be given its living semblance."

After Sunday-school they hold church-services, when Cunnyngham, at Ellie's suggestion, reads the fifteenth chapter of First Corinthians and explains as clearly as he can the signification of Christ's death and resurrection. Ellie then, in her own sweet and earnest way, relates the story of the Saviour's crucifixion and burial as narrated by the evangelists. Her heart is cheered to note the absorbed attention with which the dusky portion of her audience regards her from the beginning until the close.

The greater part of the day is spent in an entire cessation from work of every kind. Not even a fire is lighted to get either supper or dinner, cold meals being eaten instead. It is truly a day of rest. At the evening's service the departure of the Israelites into the wilderness is read by Pierce, and many incidents of various portions of their journey narrated.

CHAPTER XIV.

"He sendeth the springs into the valleys."

AT least an hour before daylight on the following morning the little camp is astir. By sunrise everything is in readiness for the start, and a few moments later, just as the great orb of day comes up bright and glorious, the head of the little caravan is put in motion and the journey is resumed.

Now comes the most trying time of any since they have left the mission-station, for the march to-day is through the dense forest, where for fully two-thirds of the way the road has to be cut out with knives and axes. The trees are not only close together and of dense foliage, but they are so entwined with numerous tough climbers that at some spots it is difficult to get through even by aid of the axes. One of these climbers proves especially difficult to deal with.

"If we are to accept Darwin's theory that even the vegetable kingdom gives evidences of possessing instinct," says Pierce, "then I should say the instinct of this toughened old customer is to do all the mischief he can."

This proves the worst climber of all, as well as

the densest and most difficult part of the forest, and they are fully two hours cutting their way through a space of not more than the third of a mile. Other climbers they meet with, but none so terrible as this which they nickname "The Dragon's (not the dragoon's) Sword."

As Pierce is tugging with all his might at one of these unmanageable creepers that has twisted itself high up amid the boughs of a tall but somewhat slender tree, a funny thing happens. Making an extra effort, Pierce gives a tremendous pull, when all at once the top of the tree snaps off. The sudden relaxation of the tension against which he has been pulling sends Pierce flying heels over head into a dense mass of shrubbery. At the same moment a small black body shoots downward from the dismantled top of the tree and falls some little distance beyond him upon an uncovered portion of ground.

"A monkey! a monkey!" cries Marvin's excited voice. "Oh, brother, do look at the monkey!"

And a monkey indeed it proves to be, a young monkey about half grown. It is quite stunned by the force of the fall, and when, after a few moments, it revives and attempts to make off, it seems unable to do so through some injury to its back.

"Oh, do let us keep it," urges Henrietta. "What a grand pet it will make! I never did have a monkey for a pet, though I've always wanted one. Oh, brother, do give it to me here in the wagon."

"Let her have it," Ellie returns in answer to

Pierce's look of inquiry. "It would be cruel to leave the poor thing here to suffer."

"But do you think it will ever get well?" questions Henrietta with the tears in her eyes, for, having a very tender and sympathetic heart, she is already much attached to the poor little suffering creature.

"Oh, I hope so. I can't see that any of the bones of the back are broken. It is only bruised, perhaps."

Much comforted, Henrietta proceeds to do everything she can devise for the relief of this new pet.

As they toil and struggle on through the tangled labyrinths of the forest, they are more than once filled with the apprehension that they may yet, in spite of their exertions, be forced to spend the night in it. The thought is far from a pleasant one. Indeed, it is most harrowing, for well they know how extremely dangerous at night are the buffaloes, elephants and other large animals, fresh traces of which they see all around them.

The sun is almost down when the edge of the dense belt of wood is reached and they come out upon an open plain or flat, the surface of which is quite sandy and heaped here and there with piles of fantastically-shaped rocks. For a short distance beyond the forest there are many very luxuriantly-growing acacias, with now and then a lofty candelabra-shaped euphorbia and various clumps of an evergreen tree resembling the cedar. But soon these give place to numerous tamarisk coppices and low-growing stretches of the hardy karroo-bush. There are, too, numerous isolated aloes, stunted and dwarfish, about which grow dense tangles of thorns.

The sun has now declined and everywhere is a dense gray gloom. It throws its shadows all about them; it creeps even into their hearts, filling them with an oppressed and dreary feeling. In comparison with the dense green wood through which they have recently come, freshened by its bits of moss and peeping wild flowers, it is like exchanging a scene of vigorous childhood for the inert chill of old age. The only living thing they see is a solitary vulture, which, startled from its feast upon the decaying carcass of a jackal, spreads its broad gray wings and sweeps over them with a rushing sound.

Despite their hard work and the steady vim with which they have pushed their way onward, they have come only about ten miles from their last camping-place, Mazika tells them, and must go at least two miles farther before they will reach a place at which it will be safe to camp without having first erected a barricade. As they are nearly exhausted with their day's experience in the woods, this last is not to be thought of.

The camping-place is at length reached, a kind of hollow shut in by precipitous masses of rock. There is, however, an opening at one side through which the wagon and cattle may be driven. It is an excellent place in which to pass the night secure from the attacks of wild beasts, but it has one serious drawback: there is no water. Against this, however, Mazika has guarded by having had the casks filled at their last stopping-place. There is still a sufficient supply left, although they have had to draw very freely upon it while coming through the woods.

From this point Pitsane, who knows more of the country now than Mazika, takes the lead.

By daylight they are off, and ere the sun has risen have made two miles across the plain.

The "flat" now proves to be several successions of valleys, separated from each other by ridges of sand in some places, and by sharp upheavals of rocks in others. There is, of course, little vegetation, and such as there is is quite unattractive. Occasionally, while passing along the more sterile parts of these desert-like tracks, they come upon precipitous upheavals of black basaltic rocks.

These hills crossed, they enter upon a country that consists mainly of large patches of trap-covered tufa, having little soil or vegetation except tufts of grass and wait-a-bit thorns in the midst of extensive sandy stretches.

The heat is now intense, and the hot glare of the sun upon the white sand makes their heads ache intolerably. Cunnyngham and Pierce are finally driven to seek the shelter of the covered wagon, where the two girls, Ellie and Hope, and the children lie almost gasping for breath. Mazika, Pitsane, Kamati, Jim and Mamochisane stand it much better, but the poor cattle and the horses and donkeys are suffering greatly. It is therefore with a feeling of deep relief that about eleven o'clock they reach a small grove of low-growing tamarisk trees. By this time they are not only suffering intensely from the heat, but also from thirst, the supply of water having given out some distance back. The cattle too are bellowing piteously. As the travelers can see no sign of water in any direction, their spirits begin to sink, until a word or two from Pitsane reassures them. There is water near, he says confidently.

In a little while he has discovered two or three sand-wells, which have apparently been dug by some wandering tribe. These wells exhibit much perseverance and skill in their construction, being from ten to twenty feet deep and from twelve to fifteen in diameter. As they are partially filled with sand, and no water is anywhere visible, Ellie and Hope are not the only ones who wonder whence the precious fluid is to come. In a little while Pitsane, who has darted off to a clump of tall-growing reeds, returns with several of them about a half inch in diameter and from fifteen to twenty feet long. These he carefully presses down into the sand at the bottom of one of the wells, and with a confident air bids Ellie, Hope and the others drink. They at once obey, and find that they can get quite a refreshing draught of the fluid by drawing it up through the reed by mouthfuls. But there are still the poor dumb brutes, who cannot quench their thirst in this way. Taking a spade, Pitsane descends to the bottom of one of the wells by means of a rope, the other end of which is tied about a tree and the length gradually let off by Jim and Kamati. When Pitsane has reached the bottom the rope is unfastened from about his body, when he gives the signal for it to be drawn up again. This is soon done, when a bucket is attached to it and let down into the well. Pitsane now begins to dig into the sand at the bottom of the well and to send it up when dug by means of the bucket. In a little while, to the great joy of the thirst-tortured cattle, the water begins to come instead of the sand and gravel. It takes two hours of hard work to reach the precious fluid and to get the horses and cattle all watered; but through the entire time Pitsane, Kamati and Jim hold out bravely.

As the sun gets higher and hotter they are thankful for the shelter of even these small shrub-like trees, among which they now remain. A most amusing incident, though in some respects quite a thrilling one, occurs as they are encamped at this place.

On leaving Lepelole there has been one thing to which Kaffir Jim has clung most persistently in spite of every difficulty. This is the long tin horn with which he has been wont to summon the Lepelole population to their meals and to prayers. He has come upon it that night when they have visited the kotla in search of Mr. Lillington, and amid all the terrors and distress of that time he has safely kept his precious horn. At times it has served as a gentle goad to the lagging energies of the cattle; again its shrill notes have summoned them when astray. Even when he lies down to sleep the precious horn is clasped closely in Jim's hands.

On this occasion he has thrown himself down upon a skin rug, which he has fastened about him as a protection against the unpleasant maraudings of various ants, flies and other troublesome insects. Head, body and limbs are all enclosed in the rug, only an opening large enough to breathe through being left, while under his arm is securely tucked the tin horn.

Suddenly, just as the little camp is in the midst of its deepest sleep, it is violently aroused by a series of piercing yells that seem to come from some little distance outside. Their horror is great when they behold a huge lion trotting off as fast as he can with the skin rug between his teeth, and poor Jim securely wrapped in its folds.

There is a simultaneous spring for the guns on the part of Cunnyngham, Pierce and Pitsane, while Mazika grasps his great axe. But suddenly, even as they have sprung forward in pursuit, a long, loud, ear-splitting blast wakes all the silent echoes. It must prove deafening indeed to the lion, since the terrible instrument from which it comes is thrust right up against his head. Instantly dropping his burden, the lion gallops off, roaring with fright. Quite unhurt, Jim wriggles from the rug and makes his way back to the camp as fast as his long, slim black legs can carry him.

They remain at this place until seven o'clock in the evening, when, to avoid the heat, they have decided to journey to their next stopping-place during the night. This is to be in the neighborhood of a series of fountains, near the first of which, Pitsane tells them, there is a small tribe of Bamangwato who have fled hither from their former village near the boundary-line of the Matabele territory in order to escape the raids of the fierce and cruel Mosilikatse.

Accordingly, at seven o'clock they are off, and at sunrise the next morning have reached in safety the fountain known as the "Fountain of the Rising Sun" because of its standing upon a prominence where it catches and reflects in a thousand different lights and with all the prismatic hues of the rainbow the rays of the sun as it comes peeping up over the eastern hills.

A little farther on they come upon the village of the Bamangwato. They find both the chief, Nakomi, and his people exceedingly friendly, especially when they find that they have come from Lepelole. It is only a little while after they have made their camp that the chief and several of the head-men and women of his tribe pay them a visit, bringing with them, by way of a friendly offering, a sweet kind of gum very pleasant to the taste, some curds of goat's milk, a few ostrich eggs and a brace of fine wild guinea-fowls. In return the Bamangwato are presented with some beads, some copper rings, two or three yards of cloth, together with a pocket-knife and a large red handkerchief for the chief.

Late in the afternoon, after our travelers have enjoyed a very refreshing sleep of several hours, the chief and the people return and give them a very pressing invitation to spend the night in the village. This they soon decide to do, especially as they are quite anxious to learn all they can of the country beyond.

These Bamangwatos, they soon discover, have large flocks of sheep and goats, which they keep at various spots along a desert-like expanse some little distance beyond the fertile stretch about the fountain.

While here, the Caucasian portion of the little caravan is inducted for the first time into the mysteries of making ostrich-egg omelet. The manner of making the omelet is this: At one end of the egg a small opening is made and into it is put a seasoning of salt and pepper. The egg is then well shaken, so as thoroughly to mix the white, the yolk and the ingredients. After this a hole is dug in hot ashes, where it is placed until completely cooked.

When ready it is a very palatable dish for three or four persons, since one of the eggs of this great bird contains as much as two dozen of those of the common fowl.

They find Nakomi's people well versed in many of the native industrial arts. The women prove to be great mat-makers. These mats are woven of various flags, reeds, and even of a species of bulrush that grows quite luxuriantly in the neighborhood of the fountain. Earthen pots and other vessels are also manufactured by the Bamangwato. These are made solely of the mould obtained from various ant-hills. In addition to the earthen vessels they manufacture various vessels of wood, some of them most ingeniously shaped.

Ellie and Hope have two plates, two bowls and a pot and a jar of earthenware presented to them by the kindly Bamangwato, and they find them afterward most useful.

CHAPTER XV.

"My God shall supply all your need."

AT sunrise the next morning, having bidden adieu to the chief Nakomi and his people, the little caravan is again on its way. Their route leads them now over a succession of sandy, yet in many places quite fertile, plains, richly covered with tall grasses and fine brushwood. Near the middle of the afternoon, when eyes and head are aching with the intolerable glare of the sun, they come in sight of a long blue line stretching off toward the horizon.

"A lake! a lake!" cries Pierce delightedly, while Marvin and Henrietta clap their hands in joyful anticipation.

Pitsane, however, only shakes his head in anything but an encouraging way.

A mile farther, and their beautiful lake turns out to be nothing but a large hollow, in the rainy season doubtless filled with water, but now quite dry and covered with innumerable saline incrustations. These, catching the light from the sun, have reflected it again in the deep blue line the young people have seen and mistaken for a pretty sheet of water.

That night they encamp near the borders of the largest of all the series of wonderful fountains by which this section of country is marked. It is called "Elephant Fountain," probably more on account of its size than from any association with that animal, since very few elephants are found in the neighborhood.

Near this fountain they find a tribe of Bechuanas who have been living here for a number of years, having been driven from their former village northwest of the Transvaal by the persecutions of the Boers. They are a very intelligent people for savages, strong and fine-looking, and partially civilized in many of their ways. Their mode of dress, too, is much above that of the ordinary savage, though many of the women still cling to the old custom of wearing copper rings about their wrists and ankles.

Their chief, Mokatchani, is a well-informed savage of perhaps sixty years of age. When a young man he had been attached to the mission-station of Kuruman, and had there heard both Moffat and Livingstone preach. For the latter he has a special veneration, while among his proudest possessions is a small Bible in the Sichuana language which Livingstone himself has presented to him. Upon the fly-leaf is written in the great missionary's own hand:

MOKATCHANI,

Sekomi's tribe of the Bakwains,
Bechuana-land, Dec., 18—,
From his friend
D. Livingstone.

"All the ends of the earth shall see the salvation of our God."

The chief speaks the pure Sichuana language; therefore it is no difficult matter for them to converse with him. It is a very soft and easy-flowing language, and when well spoken is quite melodious.

They are greatly entertained by Mokatchani's talk. There is about him, too, a fund of dry humor that is irresistible. His theory of the order of creation is both amusing and striking. Says Mokatchani:

"Since we believe that one Being created all men, then we must also believe that he improved upon his work as he went along. First he tried his hand on the Bushmen, but he didn't like them, because they were so ugly and their language was like that of the frogs. Then he tried the Hottentots, but their mouths were so great they couldn't talk without qua-quaing like the night-heron; so they didn't please him either. He then exercised all his power and skill and made the Bechuanas, which was a great improvement; and at last he made the white people, which were best of all; and," concludes the flattering old chief, looking very meaningly at the Cau-

Pitsane and the Buffalo.   Page 225.

casian portion of his audience, "then he was so very well pleased indeed that he has never made anything since."

A pressing invitation is given by the chief and his people that they remain with them a day or two. This they finally decide to do, especially as the meat department of their commissariat has run rather low, and the chief tells them that this is a capital part of the country for game. So they arrange to remain until Monday morning.

It is now Friday. That same afternoon Pitsane quite distinguishes himself by killing unaided a fine large buffalo. They have been both amused and interested when he has prepared himself for the hunt, for, finding the old ties and inclinations far too strong for him to resist, Pitsane has arrayed himself in the full Hottentot fashion, even to the bow and arrow and the spear. It is only at the last moment that Pierce can induce him to carry a rifle, suggesting that it will surely prove a far safer weapon in the midst of danger than either his bow or spear.

When the remainder of the little hunting-party, which has been separated for a time from Pitsane, comes upon him rather suddenly, they find him sitting upon the haunches of a freshly-slain buffalo and chanting to himself one of the battle-songs of his people.

Our young travelers find much to increase their wonder and interest in the great "Elephant Fountain." Among other things there is a large cavern, the entrance to which they can plainly see above the line of water.

The more Pierce gazes upon the entrance to the mysterious cavern, the more it excites his interest and curiosity, until finally he is quite overcome with the desire to explore it. He is a most expert swimmer and diver, and he feels assured that the only difficulty will be in getting up from the water. But this, he decides, can be overcome by help of Pitsane, Jim and a supply of ropes. He decides that he will say nothing to Cunnyngham, for fear he will try to dissuade him from the attempt, Cunnyngham being of a more cautious nature than Pierce.

That afternoon, which is Saturday, while the others, well sheltered from the sun by the trees of the village, are having a most enjoyable nap, Pierce steals away accompanied by the faithful Pitsane and Jim, who carry as many pieces of stout rope as they have been able to get together. Reaching the side of the fountain, he at once divests himself of his clothing and fastens the rope about his body. Creeping as near to the edge of the water as he can, he plunges boldly in. It is very cold—so cold, in fact, that for a few moments his teeth chatter. But in a little while he grows used to it, and with vigorous strokes sets out for the entrance of the cavern. It is a great deal wider than it appears to be from the cliffs, and he has no trouble in entering it.

He is much struck by the beautiful transparency of the water all about the cavern's mouth. However, on closer inspection he does not pronounce it a cavern, but a tunnel—a tunnel that has every appearance of having been cut by the hand of man. He is sorry when his length of rope comes to an end and he can go no farther. He is almost tempted to undo the knot about his armpits, fasten the rope to a projecting ledge and go on without it. But good sense and cool judgment finally prevail, and, scrambling out of the water upon an overhanging shelf, he prepares to rest for a few moments ere setting forth on his return. He is now several feet into the passage. Only a dim gray light like that of twilight prevails, yet he can see some feet farther on. But beyond this all is an impenetrable blackness. He is much struck by the sparkling appearance of the water beneath him. It seems to reflect the light of a thousand scintillating substances. The roof is also covered with another formation—a very curious formation, in truth, and one that attracts his curiosity to such an extent that he begins to climb up nearer to it by means of various projecting ledges, so as to satisfy himself as to what it is. When within reaching distance he discovers that the dark, pendent, ball-like formations dotted here and there over the surface of the roof are made by the bodies of innumerable bats and owls. To his astonishment, they are all dead, all firmly fastened to their clinging places, and all as well preserved as mummies.

He is on the point of descending again to the water when two great eyes of light very near together attract his attention. He wonders what they can be. Surely not the eyes of some beast, since it would be next to impossible for one to be here. Creeping nearer, he finds two brilliant pebble-like stones firmly imbedded in the earth—so firmly, in fact, that they for a long time resist his efforts to dislodge them.

"Suppose they should be diamonds!" he cries with a beating heart as he finally holds them in his hand. Then after a moment's pause, "Oh, pshaw! it *couldn't* be true: it would be too much like the Arabian Nights. However, this may be the workings of some ancient diamond-mine, abandoned on account of the workmen coming suddenly upon a spring of water that overflowed everything."

Placing the shining stones in his mouth, he enters the water again and swims back to the point at which he left Pitsane and Jim. Here, clinging to the rope with both hands so as to prevent it from cutting his body, he is safely hauled up to the rocks above.

Ellie and Cunnyngham have quite a scolding for him when they learn of his adventure, but are filled with wonder at his description of the mysterious passage, as well as at the sight of the sparkling stones. They agree with him in his supposition that the fountain is but the water-filled shaft of an abandoned diamond-mine.

"They are assuredly diamonds!" Cunnyngham exclaims in some excitement in reference to the stones, "and doubtless of much value. If they *are*, it is truly a most fortunate find, for I have often wondered how, in case we reached the coast in safety, where we were to procure the means of defraying the expenses of our passage to America. My uncle gave me all the money he had, but it is nothing like enough. He said when he gave it to me that God would surely provide the remainder."

Miss Henrietta especially is nearly wild with delight at sight of the flashing stones. Scarce knowing their real value, she teases Pierce to let her have one of them for the centre-piece of a wonderful collar she has recently fashioned out of red cloth and black beads for her pet the monkey. But Pierce assures her that his treasures are far too valuable to be entrusted to the keeping of a mischievous little ape, who would as soon swallow them as not.

The little creature has now almost entirely recovered from its hurts, and is able to walk, though apparently still with some pain. Despite Pierce's implied predictions, it proves in many respects quite docile, and has already learned to follow Henrietta about like a dog. However, at times it displays toward the others a very naughty disposition, which Pierce emphatically declares ought to be switched out of it. But so long as her pet is sick and suffering the little lady will hear to no such forcible means of correction.

Henrietta has named her pet Murray, in honor of the kindly and genial captain they all remember so gratefully. The full name is "Captain John Murray Lillington," but on Ellie's suggesting, with visible amusement, that the real Captain Murray might not relish the idea of having his name so closely associated with so ugly and so unpromising a pet, Henrietta compromises the matter by calling him "Captain John," then "Captain Jock," finally decapitating it permanently into "Jock."

The chief, Mokatchani, and Marvin in a little while grow to be the fastest of friends. To the great delight of the usually grave and dignified savage, the lad brings forth his wonderful spinning-top and rubber ball. It is interesting to watch the expression of the chief's face as the top, seemingly instinct with life, flies from the boy's hand and describes its graceful circles upon the ground, and it is indeed most amusing to note the comic changes the same face undergoes as, flat upon the ground, Mokatchani lies with his ear bent down to listen to what it says before it quite goes to sleep.

"Him talk, him say many heap o' t'ings," he declares in his broken English, "but him all one long, sing-song, hum-hum word. Him say, 'Zoo-o-o-o-o-zoo, how you do-o-o-oo-doo?' an' me say, 'Velly well, me t'ank you; de samey to you.'"

The ball too comes in for its share of interest. "Him hab one little birdie inside o' him to make him fly so straight up to'rd de sky," declares the chief oracularly.

On parting with his young friend, Mokatchani, greatly to Marvin's delight, presents him with a parakeet, a wide-awake, saucy fellow a friend of the chief has brought all the way from the forests about the Zouga. It has already learned to talk, and can repeat many words and sentences both in Sichuana and in broken English.

Not to be outdone by Miss Henrietta in the way of a select choice of a name for his pet, Marvin has called it "Colonel," finally diminishing it to "Colo."

On Sunday, Cunnyngham, at the chief's request, holds religious services among the people. Youth though he is, he is very earnest and impressive. Ellie's sweet singing, too, seems to make a most pleasing impression upon the dusky hearers.

CHAPTER XVI.

"They that dwell in the wilderness shall bow before Him."

THEY are off the following Monday morning at daylight, followed by the best wishes of the chief and his people, as well as by many regrets, for even in this short time they have succeeded by their cordial, fearless manners in completely winning more than one heart among the tribe.

After leaving the Bechuana camp some half dozen miles behind, their way for the most part lies across dry and sandy plains, destitute of even a suggestion of water and having very little vegetation.

It is well for our travelers that they take old Mokatchani's advice and carry a full day and night's supply of water, otherwise they would suffer greatly from thirst. As it is, they suffer enough from the heat of the sun, and the poor tortured animals, on being stopped near noon for two or three hours' rest, seek even the scanty shade of some low-growing karroo-bushes with neighs and bellowings of the deepest enjoyment.

They follow as closely as they can the route mapped out for them by Mokatchani, and that afternoon, a little past sundown, reach, as he has told them they would be likely to do, a village of Namaquas who have fled hither all the way across the dread Kalahari in order to escape the persecutions of some neighboring chief.

The Namaquas prove very friendly, especially so when Pitsane comes forward to act as spokesman. Being of the same race and speaking nearly the same language, it is not at all difficult for them to understand each other, and in a little while every preparation is made to receive the travelers into the village. A huge bonfire is at once built within the palisades, the chief and head-men don their best attire, while word is now sent to the little caravan that it may enter by the large entrance-way of the village and will be made welcome.

As soon as Cunnyngham and Pierce dismount, they, together with Mazika, Pitsane, Kamati and Jim, are led within the circle that has been formed by the warriors of the village around the fire. A short distance within the circle and about halfway between it and the fire are the chief, Topnaar, and several of his principal men. The chief is a little old wizened man with a monkeyish face covered with as many wrinkles as the too-rapidly dried outer hull of a walnut is apt to be. Dirt has so accumulated upon his person as to make his skin almost indistinguishable, while, as though it were not sufficiently disguised, it is smeared with a thick coat of red ochre and grease. In imitation of the costume of the half-civilized Bechuanas, with whom he has had much friendly intercourse, he is attired in a baggy pair of trousers made of roughly-dressed jackal-skins. He has no shirt, however, and no shoes or stockings. Over the upper part of his body he wears a kind of cloak made of the skins of goats with the hair on. It is fastened about the neck and thrown back over the shoulders, leaving the shrunken, hairy chest completely bare. About his wrists and ankles are attached bands of iron with pendent copper beads, while his head is adorned with a little round skin-cap in which is stuck a dilapidated ostrich-feather.

The men are attired very much after the same fashion as the chief, save that not many of them wear trousers, but instead the skin of some animal fastened about the waist and falling to the knees. Their heads, too, with the exception of those of a few of the more prominent members of the tribe, are destitute of any covering. The women wear short skirts of skin, some few of cloth, while nearly all of them have the upper portion of the body covered with a kind of bodice made from thousands of little rounded pieces of ostrich egg-shells strung on strings. The married women are distinguished from the single by having their hair raised high above their heads and dressed in the shape of a helmet.

As Cunnyngham, Pierce and the others enter the circle the chief motions them to a seat upon some skins that have been placed near him on the ground. A large dish of butter is now produced, from which the chief begins to smear his face and chest and those of the principal men who are grouped about him. This accomplished, he picks up the dish and advances toward Cunnyngham and Pierce.

"Oh my!" the latter exclaims quickly and a little nervously, it must be confessed, "what *can* he be about to do? Surely not to smear our faces with that horrid stuff after he has fairly washed his own in it and the faces and chests of those other horrid dirty fellows?"

But this is exactly what the chief *is* about to do, as both Pierce and Cunnyngham soon discover, greatly to their consternation and disgust.

"Quick, Pitsane!" Pierce calls out. "Quick! there's a good fellow, and invent some excuse for us—anything to keep that dirty stuff from being smeared over us."

"If the great chief of the Namaquas will listen to the words of his black brother, he will tell him how the white chiefs are much pleased with the friendliness of his greeting, and how their hearts are made glad that Topnaar has gone so far as to provide the dish of butter, which they recognize is the highest welcome he could give them. But in their own country the white brothers have a better way than this of welcoming the stranger whom they wish to receive as a friend; it is by shaking the hand. Therefore, if the chief will now permit it, the white chiefs will return his friendly greetings after the manner of their own country."

Greatly pleased by the prospect of being greeted as the white brothers greet, Topnaar forgets all the anger and chagrin he might otherwise have felt at the rejection of his precious bowl of butter. Therefore he at once settles back into his former place, assumes great dignity and awaits the advances that have been suggested. A little later, when not only his hand but those of many of the head-men have been grasped and heartily shaken by the young strangers, Topnaar's little old wizened face is one broad smile of delight.

In the mean time, the women of the village have taken charge of Ellie, Hope, Henrietta, Mamochisane and the baby, and are treating them as kindly and as hospitably as it is in their power to do. There are many things about the new-comers that arouse the deepest curiosity and wonder. In the first place, they are the first females of the white race they have ever seen. One or two white travelers have at different times visited their village, both at its present location and at the former. But they have all been rough, thick-bearded men, no more like these delicate, fair-skinned girls, with their smooth faces and long soft hair, than if they were not of the same race. No wonder these simple savages look upon them as creatures of an altogether different world. But as much as Ellie's and Hope's hair calls for their wonder and admiration, it is nothing like the feelings with which they examine the long golden curls of the little Louise. They cluster about her and grasp the beautiful strands in their hands, twist them over their fingers and lay them against their faces, until the poor little one, growing at length thoroughly frightened by so many strange countenances bent near her, cries to her sister to take her away, and, running to Ellie, hides her face in the skirt of her dress. Seeing the fear displayed by the little one, the women are much distressed, for in spite of their ugly faces their hearts are kind, and to produce this effect upon the child has been very far from their intention. They are therefore much relieved when, after a great deal of coaxing on Ellie's part, Louise is finally induced to hold her head up, and, after throwing a kiss at them, to say very sweetly,

"I t'ank oo ver' much for t'inking my hair so pooty. Oo is ver' nice, an' me lub oo. Da-da!"

With the last meaningless, but in baby language quite expressive, exclamation she throws them another kiss and drops them a most charming little courtesy.

She does not speak the words plainly, nor would they understand them if she did, but the look in the sweet baby eyes, the cunning movement of the tiny hand from the lips toward them and back to the lips again, the demure bob of the golden head, are quite sufficient. They understand these if they understand nothing else.

Learning how dreary and desolate and utterly devoid of shade is the track over which they will have to pass during the morrow, and receiving from the chief the assurance that if they will wait until the following night he will, for a small consideration, send two of his men with them as guides, they decide to tarry until the time specified. That evening they sleep most soundly with the protection of the village about them, a part of the company in the wagon as usual, and the others upon blankets under shelter of the canvas stretched out from each side of the wagon. The bed of those on the ground is made much softer by the addition of several armfuls of dried rushes tendered them by the hospitable Namaquas.

The next day they have ample opportunity of looking about the village and of studying much of the dispositions and habits of the Namaquas. These people display much skill in the manufacture of baskets, stools and a rude kind of chair, though very few of them sit upon these chairs after they are manufactured. Oftener than anything else the chairs are found hanging from the tops of their huts by way of ornament. Two of the baskets and one of the stools are presented to our little party, and afterward prove of much service.

The Namaquas are also, like so many of the savage tribes, strong believers in sorcery, and have at their village various "kaiaobs," or witch-doctors, both male and female. These "kaiaobs" are firmly believed to possess the power of making rain, of restoring the sick to health, of discovering the cause of a person's death and of performing many miracles.

While our young people are at the village an incident that is most revolting—to them, at least—occurs.

One of the chief's wives being taken suddenly ill, a "kaiaob" is at once called in. In this instance it is a woman, and as on her way to the hut she passes by the wagon where our young travelers are assembled, they think they have never seen a face more repulsive. She has not long passed them when the sounds of quite a hubbub within the hut attract their attention. Very soon Pitsane, who has by some chance been within hearing-distance, returns to tell them that the witch-doctor has declared that a great "toros," a mythical kind of serpent, has fired an arrow into the woman's back, and further asserts that unless a couple of goats are forthwith killed and the combined hearts of the two placed upon the wound the woman will die.

"That is just a trick of the wily old witch-doctor to get the flesh of the goats for herself," concludes Pitsane with confidence. "She will apply the hearts of the goats to the woman's back, but the rest of the flesh she will apply to herself."

The words are hardly spoken when two men pass by on their way to the chief's cattle-pen, where some of these animals are always kept in case of an emergency, as at the present. A little later they return with the two slain goats.

The Namaquas have a superstition in regard to the hare which, as soon as they have heard it from the chief, impresses our young people very much. One expression in it especially seems so akin to a certain passage of the Bible that they wonder whence these people could have obtained it.

"Once upon a time," begins the chief, "the moon called the hare and bade him convey to man the following message: 'As I die and am born again, so you shall die and be again alive.' The hare hastened to obey, but instead of saying, 'As I die and am born again,' he said, 'As I die and am *not* born again.' On his return the moon inquired what words he had conveyed to mankind, and on being informed the moon indignantly exclaimed, 'What! have you said to man, "As I die and am *not* born again"? If this is true, then *shall* you die and not be again alive.' With this she hurled a stick at the hare with such force as to split open his lips, which is the cause of his queer-looking mouth to this day."

On account of this legend the flesh of the hare is not eaten by the Namaquas, for they firmly believe that if they do so they will at once die. Old Topnaar further adds: "We are still so enraged with the hare for bringing us such a message from the moon, that we will not let him live near us, but when we find one we send him on and on."

When speaking of the moon Namaquas do not say, as our young people are so used to saying, that it "rises and sets," but that it "dies and is born again."

But the most ridiculous theory they have is one in regard to the rising of the sun.

"The great fiery ball that shines up yonder," says one of the villagers in explanation of the matter to Pierce, "is nothing but a mass of fat on fire. At night it descends into the sea. There it is caught by the chief of a white man's ship, who cuts away a portion of the tallow, and giving the rest a kick, it bounds away, sinks under the waves, goes round below, and then comes up again in the east."

"The sun, moon and stars are all God's work," says Pierce, trying to speak as impressively as he can. "He put them into the sky to give us light by day and guidance by night. They never go out of the sky, but stay there always. It is the earth that moves. When it turns over from the sun, then it is night; when it turns back toward the sun, then it is day."

"The world cannot turn," declares the man, much astonished, "for if it did we should all tumble about and roll off, and the trees would stand on their heads, and the rivers would flow out of their beds."

They are standing near the wagon as they are speaking. Seeing a tin bucket half filled with water standing upon a stool near by, Pierce takes it up and with a swift dextrous movement swings it around and around so that not a drop is spilled.

"Now, why does not the water come out of the bucket?" he questions. "I turn it around and around, I even turn the bucket upside down, and it still stays. So we stay upon the earth without falling off, although it swings around and around. As the movement I give the bucket is just the movement to keep the water within, so the movement the earth has is just such a movement as to keep the objects upon its surface undisturbed.

"I am afraid that was a very far-fetched illustration," Pierce says in confidence to himself a few moments later, "but at the time I couldn't think of anything else that the poor ignorant fellow would be at all likely to comprehend. I wonder what the scientists would say?" he questions with an amused laugh.

As for the poor man, he is so badly frightened by what Pierce has done as not to be capable, at least for a time, of even thinking of what he has said. That the youth should swing the bucket in so violent a manner around and around, and yet not spill the water, is truly a most wonderful thing. In short, he looks upon it as nothing less than magic, and at once runs away as fast as his legs will carry him to tell to his associates how the young white witch-doctor has turned a bucket upside down without any of the water running out, and also how he has said that the world is constantly rolling over, and that the sun is not a ball of fat, and that it never was known to go down into the sea, and ever so much more.

Quite a pathetic, and yet in most respects an

amusing, incident occurs ere our friends leave the Namaqua village.

The moans and piteous bellowings of the poor cow whose calf the lion has destroyed have by this time become so distressing that even the people of the village are touched with pity. Topnaar suggests that a straw calf be made for her, declaring that he has often cured cows of his own in this way. At first the white people are greatly amused by the idea, but finally decide to let it be tried, especially as it can do no harm.

"She will slobber over it as though it were her own," declares the chief confidently. "You will see if she does not."

With these words he sends several of the women to prepare the calf. In a short while they return bearing what our young travelers are surprised to see is really a first-rate imitation of a baby bovine, spots and all. Slipping up behind the cow, they place it near her when her back is toward them. All at once, on turning, she beholds it. A most joyful bellow is the result, followed by a delighted licking of its bogus skin. Indeed, she shows every sign of having recognized the calf as hers, and continues to treat it to a series of most animated caresses, lowing deeply and contentedly to herself all the while.

But suddenly a most amusing thing occurs. On giving it a more demonstrative caress than any that has yet preceded it, her rough tongue comes in contact with a defective portion of the material, when a considerable rent is made in it through which at once protrude numerous wisps of hay and straw. Instantly the animal nature asserts itself over the maternal, for, bending her head downward with a sudden little excited sniff, she proceeds at once to devour most greedily the alluring outlines of her pretended offspring.

When all is over and the bogus calf has entirely disappeared, she seems rather ashamed of herself, but principally on account of her haste and greed. Strange to say, from that time forth she makes no further moan for her lost calf, seeming now to regard its disappearance as quite natural and after the way it should have gone.

That evening, before the preparation for their departure is begun, Cunnyngham, at Ellie's request, holds a public service to which all the village is invited.

CHAPTER XVII.

"They shall be mine, saith the Lord of hosts."

AT sundown they bid adieu to their friends the Namaquas, and, accompanied by the two guides that Topnaar has for a moderate consideration provided, turn their faces bravely in the direction of the Kalahari, that dreaded bugbear of South African travelers.

Topnaar also accompanies them for a short distance on the way, trailing behind him the branch of a tree that is thickly covered with small red berries. This, he declares, is to give them success on the journey and to take them safely beyond any snares that may be set for them.

After gravely shaking hands with them all, even with the children, and begging a few strands from Baby Louise's hair as a charm, he leaves them, and the last sight they have of him he is standing still in the midst of the grassy track over which they have come and waving wildly above his head the branch with the red berries.

It is a glorious night, one of those magnificent tropical moonlight nights that have been so often described by travelers in this hemisphere. With the soft hush of the moonlight over everything the way does not seem either so dreary or so desolate as it would doubtless appear during the day. Occasionally they come upon a clump of stunted acacias or a small thicket of thorn-bushes.

At daylight they outspan near the kraal of a tribe of Bushmen under their chief, Mokonn, about eighteen miles from the Namaqua village.

Our young travelers have heard much of the state of extreme degradation in which these people, the lowest of all the African tribes, live, but they are scarcely prepared for the reality.

The habitations are mere burrows in the earth, giving to the entire place more the appearance of dens of wild animals than the abodes of human beings. The people, too, are such a dirty, miserable, woe-begone-looking set of creatures that it brings tears to Hope's and Ellie's sympathetic eyes to look upon them. They are entirely nude with the exception of a small skin covering that hangs from the waist to within half the distance of the knees.

But for the guides they have brought with them our young travelers would find it extremely difficult to make themselves understood. Even as it is, misunderstandings are constantly occurring—misunderstandings that might sometimes have very unpleasant results but for the merry and fun-loving disposition of the Bushmen. In truth, never have our young friends seen a people so degraded, having no comforts and but a scant portion of the barest necessities, and withal dwelling in such content and cheerfulness, or a people whose dispositions so strongly belie their looks. Their entire worldly possessions consist of a burrow in the ground, a bit of skin to partially hide their nudity, and a few miserable-looking dogs and goats that seem never to have known what it was to partake of a full meal in all their life.

Only the great black ants seem to flourish, and they are here in abundance, giving to our travelers again and again much trouble and annoyance. Just where they get the moisture to work up the mortar for their queer-looking abodes seems a mystery, for on Pierce's asking of Pitsane where water is to be found, he is told that there is none whatever hereabouts.

"No water! Then how do the people live?"

Principally by storing up in the shells of ostrich-eggs during the rainy season a supply of the precious fluid and by burying them in the sand, he is told. Again, they obtain from the tubers of certain plants hidden in the earth a refreshing supply of the life-sustaining fluid. It is also chiefly through these plants that the goats and dogs are kept from dying of absolute thirst. The hiding-place of these plants is discovered by means of a stalk about the size of a crow's quill which runs for some little distance along the top of the ground.

Near the habitation of these Bushmen, Pitsane also tells Pierce, there are a few sand-wells, or rather what are little more than mere "sucking holes." The method of obtaining water from these holes is both singular and repulsive. The supply is generally procured by the women, who gather about the spot with their vessels, which are usually nothing more than ostrich egg-shells with a small hole at one side of them. Thrusting the end of a large reed down through the sand to where the water is, they apply their lips to the other end. The water is then sucked up through the reed into the mouth, whence it is ejected into an ostrich-egg-shell vessel by means of another reed leading from it to them. Sometimes the water is simply squirted from the mouth into the vessels. It seems revolting to write of this, but then there are other methods and ways of these degraded people which are even more repulsive.

The cows belonging to the little caravan seem to attract the attention of Mokoun and his people more than anything else. They crowd about them, talking and gesticulating with all their might, and when Jim, having finished the morning's milking, holds up for their inspection the buckets of rich, foaming milk, they leap into the air and clap their hands vigorously together, then upon their sides and chests, thus displaying extraordinary delight and appreciation at so unusual a sight. They finally fall upon the ground and roll from side to side with their tongues protruding. Ellie and Hope are frightened, thinking the poor creatures have assuredly gone into a fit, but Cunnyngham reassures them by telling them that they are only expressing their great delight at seeing what must appear to them a most magnificent array of cattle for one camp to possess.

"Poor creatures!" says Hope pityingly; "I know they are half starved. Let us give them some of the milk."

"You may do so if you think best," returns Cunnyngham, "but I am afraid it will end in having the whole village around us begging. It will be hard to give to some and not to others, and we have nothing like enough to go around. These poor creatures have so long subsisted upon the roots and berries of the desert and the carcasses of all kinds of animals, that it would be little less than an absolute cruelty to give them a taste of that which might lead them to be less contented with their hard lot. But I will tell you what we will do: we will kill two of the sheep and send them as a present to the chief, with the request that he divide them among his people."

This is accordingly done, and a short while thereafter the sounds given forth by the delighted creatures as they feast upon the meat are like strains of music to the ears of Hope and Ellie. The poor half-starved dogs also come in for a share of the feast in the offal of the slaughtered animals, for

Cunnyngham has taken care to have the carcasses cleaned ere sending them to the chief, well knowing the filthy inclinations of these degraded people.

The wretched dogs excite the sympathy of Ellie and Hope quite as much as their masters have done, and they forthwith proceed to bestow upon them sundry scraps of dried flesh and various odds and ends purloined from the commissary department of the wagon, and others, again, that are more than odds and ends. The dogs are indeed most pitiable-looking objects, little more than skin and bones, with glassy eyes and froth-covered jaws. One of them especially attracts Hope's attention. He is a large dog—large even with his skin clinging close to his bones. His hair, what little there is left, is gray in color with stripes of black. His head is in shape somewhat like a wolf's, only more massive, while his eyes, in spite of the sickly gleam starvation has given them, have a much more intelligent look than those of the rest of his fellows. It makes Hope's heart throb with pity to notice the innumerable marks of stripes and blows upon his poor emaciated frame.

"He must have a very cruel master," she says. "If only I could take both him and his miserable fellows and make fat, happy creatures of them!"

Late in the afternoon of that day, as they are about to begin preparations for their departure, Hope's attention is attracted by a commotion a short distance to the right of where the wagon stands. On turning in that direction she catches sight of the same dog she has been so deeply pitying ravenously devouring a pair of skin shoes that Pitsane has made for Mazika only two or three days before.

Jim has already spied the miserable brute, and is now running toward him hallooing loudly. Pitsane and Kamati have also started hastily in the same direction, but, despite the shouts and the various other demonstrations, the poor starved brute still keeps up his vehement attacks upon the shoes.

Others now catch sight of him, among them a number of Bushmen who have been lingering about the camp in order to see the travelers take their departure. With these is the dog's master, who as soon as he comprehends the situation recognizes, doubtless, that this is a shabby return indeed to make to those who have bestowed so many favors, and forthwith proceeds to impress this fact in the most emphatic manner upon the seemingly ungrateful brute.

When the blows from a great stick in the Bushman's hand first rain down upon the scarred body of the miserable brute, he merely shrugs up his back, opens his jaws and grins in a most ghastly manner. Evidently this is but an every-day occurrence to him. But flesh and blood are flesh and blood after all, and as the blows continue to fall thick and fast he drops the remnant of the shoe he has nearly devoured and crouches before his master howling piteously.

Hope can stand no more. In a moment she is flying over the ground that intervenes between her and the inhumanly belabored brute, and ere any one can surmise her intention has thrown herself between the howling dog and his savage master. So quick is she that she has precipitated herself in front of the dog ere the man is aware of her presence. Thus she receives across one arm the full force of a blow that has been intended for the dog. It makes her sick and giddy, and for the first few seconds she thinks the bone must surely be broken.

As to the Bushman, when he realizes what he has done he is nearly beside himself with terror. Dropping his stick, he stands rooted to the spot with his eyes rolling as though they would quite roll out of his head. Then, recovering himself, he begins to gesticulate wildly, finally falling upon his knees in front of Pierce and Cunnyngham with his hands clasped entreatingly. As for Hope, forgetting for a time the pain of the blow, which has also raised a great angry-looking wheal several inches in length across the soft white flesh of her arm, she is now sobbing over the poor beaten dog with her arms about his neck and murmuring pitying words to him all the while.

"Oh, Hope," Pierce cries as he springs to her side, "what *have* you done? That blow was enough to break your arm. Is it hurt very much, dear?"

"Oh no," she answers quickly, yet somewhat brokenly, "I scarcely feel it."

"That is because you are so much excited. Let go the dog," taking hold of her arms as he speaks and trying gently to disengage them.

"Oh, I cannot; that man will surely kill him if I do. Oh, Pierce, ask him if I may not have the dog. I will give him anything that is reasonable."

Pierce goes forward, and by using Pitsane and one of the Namaqua-men as interpreters, makes known to the Bushman Hope's desire to possess the dog, at the same time asking him to name what he will take for the creature. The man is very much surprised at first, and hesitates a long time, but he finally makes public his willingness to take in exchange for the dog a pocket-knife that Pierce has shown him and the skins of the two sheep recently slaughtered.

"The poor miserable brute is hardly worth so much as that," Pierce comments to himself. "I hope my cousin will have no cause to repent of her bargain."

It is quite evident that on her own part Hope has no such apprehension, at least not at present, for the moment the trade is struck and the dog is hers she starts up joyfully, calling to him to follow.

"I shall call him Smike," says Hope a few minutes later.—"You remember, Ellie, the wretched, half-starved little creature in Dickens's *Nicholas*

Nickleby who was the cruelly outraged hack of all those dreadful Squeers?"

"Yes, dear, and the name *does* seem most appropriate," reaching out her hand as she speaks to pat the dog's great bony head.

Hope has no trouble in getting Smike to fall in behind the wagon as they start off from the Bushman village. Indeed, he has even in this short time so learned the tones of her voice that he will get up at once and follow anywhere she leads.

But the most pathetic picture is that made by Smike's late companions, the dogs of the Bushmen village. In a wildly-staring, curiosity-stricken group they sit upon their lean haunches and watch the departure of the caravan.

CHAPTER XVIII.

."He made and loveth all."

ABOUT midnight, as they are passing near a small oasis-like expanse in the midst of the almost trackless waste over which they have come for the past ten miles, their attention is suddenly attracted by a glare of light that seems to penetrate an opening in a tangle of shrubbery.

"That must be a camp," says Cunnyngham to Pitsane as they are riding together at the head of the little caravan. "Why, who can it be at this place and awake at this hour?"

"If Pitsane mistakes not, it is Bushmen—Bushmen who hunt the ostrich."

On riding in the direction whence the light issues they find it is as Pitsane has surmised. The Bushmen are eight in number, the greater part of them entirely nude. But, strange to say, all of them but two have on queer-looking skin caps, which they seem to think is all the covering necessary and quite ample for the entire body. With the exception of one who seems to be the leader, they are squatted about a small fire on which is placed a strange-looking round vessel that seems to have something boiling within it, doubtless a soup made of the bones of some animal recently slain.

Pierce and Pitsane dismount and approach the camp, and by means of various signs and with what help Pitsane can give, Pierce soon learns that they belong to the same kraal of Bushmen recently passed, and are, as Pitsane has surmised, on an ostrich-hunt. They have already been a week away from the village, and have slain over a score of ostriches, besides gathering a large number of eggs. Pierce makes the Bushmen's hearts quite happy by the purchase of a goodly number of the feathers and eggs.

The sun is quite two hours high and its rays are beating fiercely down upon them ere they reach the kraal of the Bushman, Shobo. The curiosity of our young wanderers concerning this man, whose name has become so well known through its close association with that of Livingstone, is so great that scarcely a day has passed since the journey was begun that they have not thought and talked of their meeting with him.

They find the kraal of these Bushmen in every respect a decided improvement upon that they have left some twenty miles back. The village has some regularity about it, the huts being arranged in rows. About them all there is quite a respectable barricade of thorn-bushes. There are also several small

Coming on a Bushmen's Camp.

herds of goats in good condition, and even a cow or two.

On the inquiry being made for Shobo, they are much shocked to learn that the old chief is very ill—in fact, said by the fetish-man (medicine-man) to be about to go to the other country of which he has so long talked.

At first the fetish-man declares most positively that they cannot see the chief, but on Shobo himself learning of the presence of white people in his village, he at once sends for them. Pierce and Cunnyngham respond to this message.

"Shobo heart him make glad to see one mo' time w'ite brudders," he says in broken English as they approach him, and he motions them to a seat upon a skin rug. "Shobo him plenty got fear him nebber see no mo' w'ite people same as w'ite fetish-man Shobo loved.* W'ite fetish-man done gone way ober big desert; him gone one time, him gone two time, him gone tree time, an' den him nebber come back no mo'. Shobo go wid him one time, Shobo go two time, Shobo go tree time, but Shobo no go wid him when him come back ober desert las' time. Fetish-man him go on down to Cape. Dere he go 'way on big city what moves on water,† an' him nebber come back no mo'. Can w'ite brudders tell Shobo where fetish-man gone?"

"If it is Dr. Livingstone of whom you speak, Shobo," Cunnyngham says in deep, feeling tones,

* Livingstone. † A ship.

"then he has indeed gone away never to return. He is in that world beyond the sky of which he has doubtless told you often."

"Oh yes, him tell Shobo one big heap 'bout great world where mighty chief lib name God. Him tell 'im b'leebe in great Man, den him tek Shobo some day lib wid him. Oh, is fetish-man weally gone where great God stay? Den Shobo him no mo' 'fraid. Him see dere good fetish-man what say all men brudders."

"Then you loved Livingstone very much? he was good to you?" Pierce questions.

"Him one big heap good to po' Shobo, but him yillie heap stern too. Shobo need it. Shobo one time mighty bad man. Him git mad, den him leab go bang 'gainst tree as not; him smash yudder heads dere too if dey in his way. When Shobo go bad, fetish-man jus' look one time at Shobo—look one time hard like him look 'im troo—den Shobo no mo' all ober big smart. Him jus' fall down an' creep 'way. Wish him could die. Den fetish-man him follow Shobo; him say kind word to Shobo. Den Shobo feel mo' yillie still wish him mo' die dan ebber.

"One time Shobo lose way. No water, no water anyw'eres. Country him all dry up. Oxen nearly die; men nearly die. Fetish-man wife look like him all time ready dead. Yillie chillen dem sholy dead, Shobo t'ink. Shobo lose him head like him lose way. Shobo like one 'sleep. Shobo no find water. All dry country, no water ebberways look. Den yudder w'ite mens git mad, say big heap bad words Shobo. Wan' er strak Shobo wid stick; fetish-man no let 'em. Him say, 'Shobo no all bit to blame.' Him feel some mad wid Shobo too, but him no show him mad like yudder mens. Him talk kind to Shobo. Him tell him try to t'ink where water is. But Shobo done lose him head, an' Shobo dat night run off; him 'fraid yudder white men kill him when de day come if he no find water. Him no stop till him git to Mahobe.

"Den fetish-man him git troo de desert; find Shobo heap time later. Shobo t'ink now him sholy be killed. But no; fetish-man him talk kind same's ever to all-bad Shobo. Him tell him mo' 'bout de great sky-man what care for eben all-bad Shobo. Him tell him heap mo'. Him say de kind word ebber day him stay where Shobo was. Him tell him great Man's name God. Him tell him great Man lub Shobo big heap if Shobo just make try do what right; but when Shobo all ober bad an' no sorry him bad, den sky-man no lub him. Den Shobo him t'ink what fetish-man say, an' him all time sorry him big bad ober. Den fetish-man fall down by Shobo; him clasp him han', an' him pray to great Man in sky gib Shobo new heart. Den Shobo him pray too what fetish-man tell him. Den new heart mus' come, 'cause Shobo no mo' feel bad all ober, an' him no mo' long to go bang 'gainst tree. Him like new Shobo all troo an' troo. Him come an' tell him people. Him try let yudders know 'bout great Man what make ober all-bad hearts. Some him people b'leebe, some on'y laugh, but Shobo him no git mad. Him tell 'em 'mong yudder tings dey mus' no longer lib in holes. So Shobo git 'em make houses. Den Shobo git 'em be one heap mo' clean. An' den him git 'em mo' goats an' one, two, tree, fo' cow. Him sho' 'em heap t'ings what people do what try please great Man in sky. Shobo people now mighty heap good to what hab been. Shobo him great lot glad, an' when him see good fetish-man up dere, him too be mighty heap great glad hear what Shobo done."

Ellie and Hope are much struck with Shobo when they see him, while he, on his part, takes greatly to them. Henrietta, too, comes in for her share of the old Bushman's regard, and is never better pleased than when she is allowed to go and read to him from her little pocket Bible, which she does during every day of their stay at the village.

On making inquiries of Shobo, our young travelers are much perplexed and worried to learn that there is at present no one in his village who has sufficient knowledge of the Kalahari to prove a trusty guide across it—that is, in the direction they wish to go. There are many, it is true, who say they know, and who are eager to attach themselves to the little company because of their desire to obtain the liberal amount of pay that is offered. But whenever the matter is referred to the old chief with the name of the applicant, he shakes his head very decidedly. He assuredly ought to know, he says, if any one does, the real difficulties of the undertaking, as well as the great peril that is invited by having a guide who is not expert about finding water. There are many men of his village, he tells them, whom he could trust if only they were here, and again and again he bemoans the absence of his son, Horoye, who, he tells them, knows almost every foot of the desert and would be just the very one to go with them. But Horoye is away at present with fully a dozen of the best and most trusty men of the village. As they are on a trading-expedition, it is not known when they will return.

Finally, just when their despair is at its height, two Bushmen from a neighboring kraal make their appearance at Shobo's. They are armed with their bows and poisoned arrows and are on their way to hunt ostriches. When they hear of the dilemma of the little party, they at once offer their services as guides. They seem very clever fellows, have a straightforward way about them and faces much more intelligent-looking than the average men of their class.

Our young people are inclined to put much confidence in them, but on the subject being broached to Shobo he is quite doubtful as to their ability. They may know the desert very well, he says, but the water, the most important thing of all, will they know what to do about that? It finally ends in Shobo sending for them and questioning them minutely. Our young friends await in much suspense the result of this interview. Late that afternoon Shobo makes his opinion known to them. As it seems so absolutely necessary for them to proceed on their journey, and as it is not known when Horoye and his men will return, he, Shobo, thinks maybe these men will do. They have stood the test of his numerous questionings fairly well, and while they are not so good as Horoye or Shobo himself would be, still they may succeed in getting the little caravan through all right. He, Shobo, would be glad, nay proud, to have the travelers remain with him and his people as long as they care to stay, but if they think it necessary to go on, then the men may be given a trial.

Each one of the traveling-party is for pushing on at once. They have already been at Shobo's village more than a week, and as every day decreases their stock of provisions, there is great danger that if they do not soon proceed on their way the store will be quite exhausted ere the Makololos are reached. It is true they can add to it from time to time by the flesh of such animals as they chance to slay, but still this will not help matters much if once the supply of flour and meal gives out. It will be a most trying diet to live on flesh alone. Shobo comes manfully to their aid in this matter by insisting that they shall take with them a quantity of pumpkins, potatoes and maize his people have recently obtained in trade with a tribe of the Bakalahari. This they finally consent to do on Shobo agreeing to receive the value of these supplies in such articles as compose the currency of the district. He also informs them that there is another tribe of the Bakalahari about ten miles on their route from whom they may very likely obtain additional supplies of pumpkins, potatoes, beans, maize and the like.

The parting with Shobo is very affecting. He has grown much attached to them, while on their part they have formed for the sturdy old Bushman a sincere regard, as well as an honest admiration for his many fine traits of character. Tears are in their eyes as they shake his emaciated hand at parting, while his voice is little more than a sob as he bids them good-bye:

"Shobo see chillen o' white brudder no mo' here, but Shobo meet 'em up sky."

These are almost the last words the old Bushman ever utters, for after they leave him he turns his face toward the wall of his hut, and in two days more is dead.

Our little party is successful in obtaining from the Bakalahari alluded to by Shobo quite a good supply of potatoes, pumpkins, maize, and even a few beans. They now set forth on their journey with light and trusting hearts, despite the many perils that they know lie before them.

For forty miles after leaving the Bakalahari there is an absolutely waterless track, and had they not been prepared for it their suffering would be great. Even as it is, they have to stint the supply of the precious fluid to such an extent that for the first time they catch a most unpleasant foretaste of what the horrors of thirst really are.

At a pleasant spot in the dreary desert they camp for two days. Here, too, they find a very fair supply of water, and here for the first time they catch sight of a drove of ostriches. They are feeding on the plain fully a half mile away, and seem totally unconscious of the presence of the travelers.

As pleasing a sight as these great birds present to the eyes of our young friends, the sight is even more pleasing to those of the Bushmen guides. The latter prepare at once for the slaughter, determined to procure as many feathers as possible.

First they get out their bows and arrows, taking care to dip afresh the points of the latter in the poisonous matter carried along for this purpose. Next out of a bundle they produce two pieces of wood carved so as to represent the head and neck of an ostrich. These the guides fasten to the napes of their necks so that when they stoop forward the contrivances stand upright. They next cover their backs and shoulders with a kind of saddle made of ostrich-feathers, the feet and legs being whitened with a preparation resembling chalk.

Thus equipped, the two Bushmen make their way slowly and cautiously across the plain in the direction of the spot where the ostriches are so quietly feeding. The birds pay very little attention to what they seem to think is only a new addition of their own species.

But in a moment one or two of the ostriches begin to show some little signs of uneasiness. They raise their heads suddenly and glance backward, as though not altogether assured of the friendly intentions of these feathered strangers. But, alas! they are too late, for even in the midst of the act of doing this the two concealed Bushmen lift their bows and twang go their arrows. The birds that are hit begin at once to reel around like drunken men. Directly one falls, while the other, after trying to run a short distance, staggers from side to side, and also falls dead.

The other ostriches seem determined to keep up their reputation for stupidity, for instead of making off at once out of danger, they only gaze curiously at the strange behavior of their companions, and, moving off a space, go on feeding again.

Two more now fall victims to the poisoned arrows of the Bushmen. By this time it seems to penetrate even the stupid heads of the remaining birds that something is wrong, and one of the Bushmen now, by a false movement, getting between them and the wind, their long legs are at once put in motion for flight.

"If those Bushmen get another shot at the birds now, they will have to run much faster than I give them credit for being able to do," exclaims Pierce, greatly interested. "Why, did you ever see anything to equal the way those birds use their legs? I believe they could outrun the swiftest horse. There! they seem to be heading directly toward this spot. Surely they will catch a sight of us in time to turn another way. Look out! here they come! Quick, everybody, and get to the shelter of the wagons. Steady now, and let's give them a shot as they go plunging by."

By this time the great flying birds are almost upon the camping-place. In another moment they have reached it and are plunging through, scattering everything before them. As they clear the camp there sound simultaneously the sharp reports of four rifles, while almost immediately two of the birds fall dead. A third one, they think, must surely be hit, by the track of blood it leaves behind it, though it keeps steadily on. But gradually its pace begins to slacken, until finally about two hundred yards beyond the camp it suddenly reels and falls.

"I never saw anything so stupid," comments Pierce again. "Why didn't they go around us? They must have seen us at the last, and yet they never made even a movement of swerving from their course."

"Ostreedge him one big heap fool bird," says one of the Bushmen in broken English, having by this time reached the camp in his pursuit of the flying birds, and coming up just in time to overhear Pierce's remarks. " When ostreedge all over heap fear, him run all one way. Him butt him brains out 'g'in' en't'ing in 'im paff (path) 'fo' 'im turn out'n de way. When ostreedge once git all ober scared, him shut 'im eye an' run. Him no open 'im eye for en't'ing. One time me see ostreedge go bang slap 'g'inst tree an' mash him head flat, flat as massa hand."

The seven dead ostriches are now brought into camp and the work of securing the feathers begins. Four of them of course belong to the Bushmen, the others to our travelers. Two of the birds are males, the other five females, and all are, with one exception, fully grown. On the lower part of the necks and bodies of the male birds the feathers are of a deep and glossy black, intermingled with a few whitish ones. In the females the general color of the neck-feathers is of a grayish or ashy-brown, fringed with white. But the most beautiful feathers, as also the most valuable, are those upon the wings and tails. These in both the males and females are of a beautiful pure white that calls forth exclamations of admiration, from Ellie and Hope especially, the moment they see them.

From twenty-five to thirty of these feathers are taken from each bird, though only about two-thirds of them prove worthy of preservation. However, those that are discarded Pitsane carefully gathers up. Ellie and Hope wonder what he can be going to do with them. Their speculation is changed to a feeling of delight when a few days later he presents each of them with a very creditable parasol made of the feathers most ingeniously woven together and fastened upon a frame, which while it is somewhat rudely constructed is, nevertheless, very light and serviceable. The young girls are exceedingly proud of their parasols, and find them really very much of a protection while walking about in the sun.

CHAPTER XIX.

"Plenteous in mercy."

TRAVELING now except at night and in the early mornings is impossible, for overhead is a scorching sun and underneath are great stretches of blistering sand that it would be next to madness to attempt to toil over while it is in this condition. Ten or twelve miles a day—or rather a night—is the best they can now accomplish, even with their bravest efforts. At some places they find that the heat during the day has been so great that the grass as they touch it crumbles to dust in their hands.

But the nights are comparatively cool, and during them, at least, they have some relief, although they have to provide against the great danger of taking cold.

They have left the fertile tract where they have encamped for two days nearly three days' journey behind them, and there is still no sign of water. Lucky for them that they have brought a supply from this camping-place. But in three days it is so nearly run out that there is now only a limited supply for the people, and none for the poor dumb toiling brutes whose sufferings it is already heartrending to witness.

Another day, and now the last drop in the cask is exhausted, and people and animals are alike confronted by the fierce tortures of maddening thirst. Now, indeed, do their troubles begin. All else that has gone before seems as a mere trifle. The two older boys and Ellie and Hope bear up bravely, but it is especially trying to the children, who have no such fortitude to sustain them. The pleading of the poor little baby for water is the most agonizing thing they have to endure.

"Oh," exclaims Ellie, clasping her hands passionately together, "I remember how Dr. Livingstone saw his wife and little ones in just such sore straits as this, and how fervently he prayed for strength and help. It seemed at first as if God had indeed deserted them. Yet at last help came. Oh, surely, if we trust him he will hear and send water."

On the night of the fourth day since the supply of water has given out they lay them down, not to sleep, but to await the coming of the morning they long yet tremble to see. And why this strange contradiction? Because their guides have told them that they must have the daylight in which to find water. Of these guides Cunnyngham and Pierce now begin to entertain serious doubts. But perhaps, after all, the men may not be to blame. Such things have happened before, even with the best of guides.

At length the morning dawns, and with its coming the journey is again resumed, for to stay where they are is to perish, while to go forward may also be to perish, but still it is the one hope that is left to them.

On they toil silently and despairingly. The poor tortured oxen do little more than stagger through the great stretches of sand, their parched tongues protruding from their mouths. The horses and cows are suffering even more, and it takes all the efforts of the drivers, themselves in a pitiable condition, to urge them forward. The goats stand it very well, but the last of the sheep have dropped by the way the evening before. At length the poor cow who has lost her calf also succumbs, and then one of the calves of the other cows.

Slowly and painfully the little company creeps onward, hotter and hotter grows the sun, more terrible the thirst. By nine o'clock, in the shade of the wagon, the little thermometer that Ellie carries among her other treasures registers 110°. This heat, added to the already maddening tortures of thirst, renders their condition wellnigh insupportable. To add to the other misery, Hope, Henrietta and the little Louise show unmistakable signs of having been attacked by that dread scourge of African travelers, fever, and now lie moaning in delirium.

About half-past nine o'clock, Pitsane, who is in advance, sees what he at first thinks is a lion crouching behind a line of scrubby bushes that dot the plain some little distance ahead. But on drawing nearer, he is surprised to discover that it is a Bushwoman in a bent position, and evidently trying to creep away without attracting attention.

As soon as she sees that she is discovered she springs up and endeavors to fly beyond Pitsane's grasp. But she is too late, for he has seen that about her body that has lent him renewed strength and agility. Ere she has more than risen from her crouching position he has sprung from his horse and seized her by the shoulder, at the same time giving her to understand that the circle of ostrich-egg-shell vessels fastened about her body is the only thing he desires, for well he knows the precious fluid they contain.

But, evidently, the woman has no intention of yielding these up easily. By this time, the wagon having come up and Pierce and Cunnyngham catching an inkling of the nature of the encounter, the woman is now given a yard or two of bright cloth and a bunch of beads. There is no hesitancy on her part after this. She at once allows the precious contents of her shell vessels to be emptied into one of the casks in the wagon, jabbering all the while in the most abandoned delight over her newly-acquired treasures.

There is no need to describe the excessive joy with which those parched lips drink of the old Bushwoman's precious store. But, alas! their joy is suddenly quenched by the piteous neighings and bellowings of the poor horses and cattle, which, having caught a scent of the water, are now sending forth the most heartrending appeals.

"Oh, this is terrible!" cries Ellie, covering her ears with her hands. "Can *nothing* be done? Oh, I feel as though every drop of that water burns my throat. See! there is half a cask left; take it and at least rinse their mouths."

"But, my dear sister," protests Pierce, "it is too valuable. Think how much more precious our lives are than those of these brutes that have no souls. My own heart aches for them, but we must let reason guide us in this matter."

"If I mistake not," says Cunnyngham, "this woman can tell us where we may find a small supply, at least, of water. Pitsane is of the opinion that her vessels have not been many hours filled."

At first the woman seems very reluctant to disclose where the water may be found. But after many bribes she finally consents to show them where the water is. To their great joy, they learn that it is not more than an hour's journey distant.

Turning almost directly across their present path, they prepare to follow the old Bushwoman. It is a painful and toilsome journey, and again and again it seems as if the exhausted oxen must surely give out ere it is accomplished. But by persistent efforts on the part of their drivers they are urged along, and at about twenty minutes to eleven o'clock come to a staggering halt beside what seems to be a little wilderness of scrubby karroo-bushes and stunted acacias.

Finding an entrance in the seemingly impenetrable thicket, the Bushwoman crawls through, followed by Pitsane, Pierce, Cunnyngham and Mazika. In the centre is a kind of cleared spot, and almost the entire space is a rocky hollow with a heavy accumulation of sand at the bottom.

Approaching the spot, the woman arranges her vessels in a cluster at her right side, and securing a reed about three feet long ties a bunch of grass to one end of it. Then with her hand she scoops out the sand at the bottom of the hollow until an opening is made that admits her arm to the elbow. This completed, she inserts into the opening the end of the reed that is bound about with grass, and proceeds to pack the sand about it until the orifice is completely filled. Everything being now apparently to her satisfaction, she places her mouth over the upper end of the reed, at the same time inserting a straw in the right corner of her mouth. This straw she keeps in direct communication with a small opening in the top of the egg-shell vessel.

As she draws mouthful after mouthful from below, the woman empties it into the vessel at her side by means of the straw, which guides the flow *along the outside,* and not *through the inside* as some might suppose.

At last the Bushwoman has her vessels filled,

and they are free to obtain what supply they can for the poor suffering brutes.

In three hours the torturing agony of each dumb brute is relieved by a cooling draught of the precious fluid. Even the dogs are not forgotten. But that it has taken great fortitude and tact to reach a successful accomplishment through so harrowing an ordeal no one can doubt. Many times it seems as though the frantic cattle must get entirely beyond their control, while it takes all Mazika's powerful strength and agility to guard the opening that leads through the tangled coppice to the pool. At length all is finished, and, thoroughly exhausted, they are glad to eat without the least complaining the supper of bread and dried game-flesh, washed down with pure cold water.

During all this time the old Bushwoman has shown no disposition to take her departure, but hangs about the wagon, taking in everything with the most astonished eyes. They wonder greatly at her lingering now that she has been repeatedly assured that she is free to depart at any time.

"I think she is afraid that we will follow her," says Pierce. "I surmise that she belongs to a small company of her people who have hidden themselves from some enemy. She does not know but that we may be in communication with the foe and thus disclose their hiding-place."

That night, when all are asleep and even Pitsane, who is on guard, is so far overcome by the terrible trials and exhaustions of the last three days as to sink into heavy slumber, the old Bushwoman steals away, whither no one knows. The desert may have swallowed her up, for all the trace she leaves.

As the symptoms of those who have been stricken with the fever grow more alarming on the following day, our weary travelers decide to remain where they are for the next two or three days, or at least until there is a more favorable turn in the condition of the sick. By clearing away some of the thick undergrowth, enough shade is procured to shelter the animals during the fierce heat of the day.

While camping at this spot Cunnyngham and Pierce have some entertaining experiences with a small drove of ostriches, and through them learn many interesting things of this gigantic bird.

Late one afternoon, while making a kind of scouting-tour in a circle of about two miles from camp, they come suddenly upon the parent-birds and a happy family of newly-fledged young ostriches that are concealed by a large sandbank. The moment the birds catch sight of the enemy they take to flight, but not rapidly, because of the not very assured movements of the young fledglings. As it is the first time the two youths have ever seen the newly-hatched ostriches, they at once start in pursuit, determined to catch one or two of them if possible.

Suddenly dismounting, they each seize one of the young birds, and regain their horses ere the male parent can prepare for the attack, which would undoubtedly ensue but for their quick movements. They decide to keep the two young ostriches and see if they cannot tame them.

"At any rate," says Cunnyngham, "I feel that we will have no trouble in finding something with which to feed our two pets. We can give them chaff, barley, maize and an occasional handful of cracked corn."

On being introduced into the coop where the fowls are, the two young ostriches show unmistakable signs of fear, while the fowls, on their part, give vigorous evidence of resenting the intrusion of such uncouth-looking companions. But in a little while all is amicably adjusted, and at the end of two or three days they are living as happily together as though they were of one family.

On the evening of the sixth day after stopping at this camping-place, the condition of the fever patients having grown more favorable, the little caravan is again set in motion.

Another long and dreary waste now stretches before them. Two days and three nights have passed since they left the little fountain in the acacia-thicket, and again, as before that place was reached, there has been one absolutely waterless track, destitute of signs of life, with the exception of now and then a crawling deadly serpent or a great unwieldy bird of prey.

The last drop of water is now exhausted, and

still there is no sign of any more on all this dreary waste. Though sick and despairing at heart, they nevertheless prepare themselves to face with what fortitude they can a repetition of those terrible experiences that have preceded their coming to the little fountain in the thicket.

The morning of the fifth day finds them passing over a parched and desolate stretch with no sign of life anywhere visible, and with a pitiless sun beating down from a glaring firmament. Here, in one of the loneliest and dreariest spots, they come suddenly upon a solitary grave. At the head there is a rude board fashioned in the form of a cross. The board having been smoothed on one side, the following inscription is cut into it in deep, clear letters:

<blockquote>
"T. C.,
Born April 24, 1848.
Died Sept. 19, 187–.
'God be merciful to me a sinner!'"
</blockquote>

"Oh!" says Ellie, wiping the fast-falling tears, "what a lonely spot to die and be buried in! And yet," with a smile that beautifies all her face, "God can be here as well as elsewhere."

CHAPTER XX.

"He will hear their cry."

WHEN they took up the line of march that evening they had been two days without water, and the poor brutes three days. That evening a most uneasy suspicion took possession of Cunnyngham. It was of the Bushmen guides—a doubt as to their knowledge of the locality in which they now found themselves. Again and again Cunnyngham questioned the guides as to the probability of water being found in the vicinity. At first they had seemed truly concerned, and answered these anxious questionings by the assurance that water would surely be come upon before very long; but again, on being pressed in regard to the matter and urged to do their best, they had grown sullen, and finally would scarcely answer at all when addressed.

It was these things that had combined to give Cunnyngham that restless and uneasy feeling of which, with all his efforts, he could not get rid. How well grounded were these fears and anticipations was shown only too forcibly when, the morning having come, the terrible revelation was forced upon them that their guides had deserted during the night. With the direction to Jim and Mazika, who were at that moment at the head of the little company, to go straight forward until directed otherwise, they had walked back toward the rear of the wagon.

That was the last ever seen of them. One thing, however, only too forcibly appeared, and that was, that the absconding guides had taken good care to provide most liberally for themselves at the expense of our young travelers, one of the best guns, an axe, a supply of ammunition, two blankets, some beads and cloth, a quantity of ship's bread and two of the goats being taken off among other things.

Abandoned thus by their treacherous guides, our friends now find themselves in the midst of the wild and almost trackless desert with no knowledge whatever of the course before them, and, to add more acutely to the horrors of the situation, suffering agonies from thirst.

The terrible day draws on toward its close, the evening is approaching, the time at which the march is generally resumed, but there seems literally not strength enough left to the suffering brutes for them to make even the effort to start. The men, too, appear to have lost all their spirit and to be utterly regardless of the consequences of their inaction.

"My God, this is terrible!" cries Cunnyngham. "If we do not move off from this place we will surely die here!—Pitsane, Jim, my good fellows, why do you not yoke the oxen?"

"Hab tried, massa," is the Kaffir's reply, but in a way that is altogether a contrast to his usual animated movements, "but with all de beatin' me only get t'ree ob um to 'im feet."

"Oh, try again, my good fellows, try again! We *must* be on the move. It is—"

But at this moment a voice in agonized supplication falls upon his ears. It is Ellie, who with clasped hands and streaming eyes is beseeching succor of Him who has promised to hear even the ravens when they cry.

"Our Father God," entreats the young girl with burning lips, "hear us now when we cry to thee. Send help, O God, for Jesus' sake! Behold, we are utterly dependent upon thy will; our very breath is in thy hands. O God, behold our suffering and pity us. Oh, it cannot, *cannot* be that thou hast forgotten us, that thine eyes are veiled to our distresses! Remember, O God, thy servant, our father, who out of his love and zeal for thee served thee long and faithfully. Oh, for sake of him, thy faithful servant, hearken now unto the cries of these his children in the hour of their sorest distress. O God, hear! hear! pity, pity, and save! —save for Jesus' sake!"

Utterly exhausted, the young girl falls back upon her pallet in the wagon, and with closed eyes and bated breath lies like one who is dead.

But see! what is this which, even as the last despairing words drop from the tortured lips, begins to outline itself along the distant horizon? A floating bit of cloud no larger than the skirt of an infant's robe. Then another and another come to keep it company, until at last a great mantle thick and murky is spread across the face of the descending sun.

"Rain! rain!" shouts Pierce. "Oh, thank God, it is going to rain!—Pitsane! Kamati! Jim! arouse yourselves, my good fellows, and put the casks to catch the precious fluid. And come, let us take the spades and scoop out hollows to catch some of it for the poor brutes."

There is now no longer any sign of listlessness. The casks are placed so that they can be guarded from any sudden rush toward them on the part of the thirst-maddened brutes, while a firm, hard bottom is made for the hollows the workers soon have scooped out.

These details are barely accomplished and the little camp put in the best shape it can to receive the threatening tempest, when forth from the angry clouds leap livid flames of lightning and deafening peals of thunder roll overhead. Suddenly the very floodgates of heaven seem opened, and forth with a rush and a roar the blinding, impetuous, yet life-giving, torrents descend. They pour upon the parched sands of the desert, that lick them up with greedy tongues, into the recesses of the water-casks, where their noisy fall sounds like the sweetest music to the strained ears that listen, and upon the cattle themselves, cooling their burning coats and soothing the tortures of cracked and swollen tongues. With what bellowings of joy they rise up to meet it, and throw out their heads, and lap it in with their tongues, and roll over and over in the pools it forms beneath them as though they could never get enough!

For nearly two hours the torrents pour, followed near the close by a heavy fall of hail. Then almost as suddenly as it came the force of the tempest abates. In a little while hail and rain have both ceased altogether, and now there is a damp, raw chill in the air, which is quickly followed by an atmosphere of such intense cold that our travelers feel at once that they must by some means procure a fire. There are many damp things to be dried, and others, again, that are soaked through and through; for although the two thick coverings of the wagon have kept everything within the vehicle comparatively dry, yet much of the bedding and many of the belongings of those who sleep in the little drop tents at the side of the wagon have become so wet that it would be dangerous to attempt to sleep on them ere they are dried. But where are they to obtain the fuel for a fire? As far as the eye can reach there is absolutely no sign of vegetation, not even a twig of any kind.

The night has now come on. All around the

desert lies in solitary vastness, nothing but stretch after stretch of desolate sand, with no stir, no warmth, no promise of anything pleasant anywhere visible.

Finding it simply impossible to obtain fuel of any kind on this barren spot, they at first arrive at the conclusion to huddle together as best they can and brave it out till morning. But as the atmosphere grows colder and colder every moment, after a time assuming a degree of temperature that makes their teeth chatter forcibly together and their whole bodies to feel as though the very marrow in their bones is freezing, they unanimously decide to inspan and move on until they come to fuel of some kind.

All hands fall to work with what alacrity they can to prepare for the move. The yoking is accomplished, and the party once more sets out bravely across the desolate plain.

For four hours they struggle courageously onward through the cold and in the face of a biting wind that has now sprung up. Again and again it seems as if they must give up and fall by the way, for, added to the other perils, a great drowsiness has now seized upon almost every member of the party, and it takes their bravest efforts to keep themselves from falling asleep. It is, as they realize only too sensibly, the fatal drowsiness that precedes the last sleep of those overcome by cold.

There has been at first only the light of the stars to guide them, but after a while the moon comes up.

All is as bright now as day, and to their great joy they soon after espy the straggling outlines of a small stretch of scrubby bushes. They succeed in cutting several of the larger, tree-like bushes, and having found also a quantity of dried twigs, they manage to keep up a cheery blaze throughout the night. Not only are chilled bones newly invigorated, but the bed-clothes and other saturated articles are thoroughly dried.

Despite the intense chill of the preceding night, the next day shines out bright and warm. After the morning meal is over and preparations are made for passing the day at this spot, a consultation is entered into respecting their future course. Abandoned as they have been by their treacherous guides in the midst of one of the most cheerless and desolate parts of the inhospitable desert, trying indeed is the prospect that stretches before them.

"I am of the opinion," says Cunnyngham, "that our safest course at present is to try to find some spot where there is water, and where we can also secure some protection against the heat of the sun, and construct a temporary abode. It is now the first of November, and the annual rains, I doubt not, have already set in upon the country below, and we may confidently expect our portion of them here in the desert by the last of the month. If, then, we can find some place where, comparatively sheltered, we may pass the months of the rainy season, we can then resume our journey across the desert with one horror less to confront us, the horror of thirst, for there will be ten pools of water—nay, twenty—then where there is but one now. There will be also the reasonable hope of coming every now and then upon a patch of watermelons, with which liquid fruit I have heard certain parts of the desert abound after the annual rains. In the interval, by means of the compass and through other aids, we can gain some knowledge of our whereabouts and of our future course. We know that the country of the Makololo is almost due north from the Kalahari. Alas! I had hoped we should have reached it at least two weeks ago, but God has disposed otherwise. Besides," he continues, taking up his old line of thought, "if we can establish ourselves at some temporary camping-place, there is the possibility of our abode being chanced upon by some one of the many stray parties of Bushmen who are constantly wandering over the desert."

"Further," says Pierce in a voice of concern, "there is something else that appeals most strongly for the course you suggest. Hope, Henrietta and Louise have been now nearly two weeks sick with the fever, while Ellie, I fear, is also about to take it. Mamochisane, I think, has it already, and this morning I noticed some very unfavorable symptoms in Marvin. If we push on with them to the river-country in this condition, it will be almost certain death for some of them. We still have three axes and seven pairs of good strong arms left. If only we can find any sort of a showing for timber, we can assuredly erect a serviceable shelter."

"But have we sufficient provisions for such a step?" questions Cunnyngham after a moment of sober reflection. "I had not thought of this when I proposed the plan."

"We have some flour and a little meal yet," returns Pierce. "Then there are the maize and some of the pumpkins and a few of the potatoes and beans we obtained from the Bakalahari. And I heard Ellie say only yesterday we had enough dried meat to last us at least two weeks, with double the quantity of ship's biscuit. I doubt not but that we can occasionally kill some game, and there is the chance of finding some spot to plant seed and have a little garden. But come now and let us go and consult with Pitsane and Mazika."

The two sagacious blacks fully concur in the opinion of their young friends, and when they set off from their camping-place at sundown that evening it is with the understood determination to seek a favorable spot for their abode during the next four or five months.

CHAPTER XXII.

"All Thy creatures magnify Thee."

THEY have now a two days' supply of water for themselves and one and a half days' supply for the animals, so that it is with cheerful hearts that they set forth once more across the barren plain.

Just at sunrise the next morning, as they are passing over an unusually inviting grassy stretch, they are much startled by suddenly catching sight of what seems to them the outlines of a village drawn directly across the horizon. With hearts that increase in gratitude every moment they now press forward toward the village. But on coming within hailing distance of it they are greatly surprised to see no sign whatever of human life.

"Well, it *is* queer!" ejaculates Pierce, his face showing plainly all the perplexity he feels.

A light seems suddenly to break upon Cunnyngham, at the same time that an amused little laugh escapes Pitsane, while Mazika nods his head knowingly.

"It is an ant-village," says Cunnyngham joining in Pitsane's laugh. "How silly of us not to have discovered it sooner!"

"Ant-villages fool many travelers far older than my white father's children," says Mazika. "Fool even great Zulu warrior, Dingaan, who one day rushed upon one with his men, flinging right and left the assegai, and thinking he had surely this time caught the enemy asleep."

"I wonder if any of the creatures are inside?" observes Cunnyngham.

"I have a notion to see," declares Pierce, and he knocks off with the butt of his rifle the top of one of the conical-shaped turrets. Immediately a great flat head, followed by an elongated body about the size of an overgrown grain of rice, appears above the opening.

Suddenly it disappears for a few moments, and when it returns again it is followed by several scores of its companions, who come pouring out of the opening.

Directly they begin disappearing and reappearing, and on drawing nearer the curiosity of the beholders is still more excited to see them bringing from the interior a substance resembling clay. It is brought and laid on, mouthful after mouthful, with all the skill and exactness of a practiced mason.

They travel until about ten o'clock that morning, then, finding another belt of scrubby forest-growth, rest within the scant shade it affords until six o'clock in the evening, when the line of march is again resumed.

There is as yet no sign of water, and as the night advances their march is continually disturbed by the roars and cries of various wild animals. But all this they endure with unshaken fortitude until a fierce tiger, suddenly springing directly in their midst, despatches one of the oxen. The tiger is finally killed, but the adventure so excites them that, after a consultation, they decide to stop for the remainder of the night.

Four or five large fires are now kindled, forming a kind of circle with the wagon in the centre. The male members of the little caravan, with the exception of Marvin, take it in turn to watch and to keep up the supply of fuel for the fires.

No accident befalls their camp that night, and by daylight they have breakfasted, inspanned and are ready for the start.

After leaving the little strip of forest behind they enter upon another stretch of treeless plain. But with increasing hope they notice that the grass that covers it is very thick and vigorous. After a consultation they decide to stop here for an hour at least and give the hungry and jaded horses and cattle an opportunity for grazing.

The sun is a little more than an hour high when the march is resumed, and all at once they catch sight of a line of forest directly across their path. The desert is yet all about them, but as they progress it becomes less like a desert and more like a fertile savanna.

A little shout from Pitsane, who is leading the company, attracts the attention of Cunnyngham and Pierce, and on going forward they soon learn that he has suddenly come upon a well-beaten "spoor," or track, that leads in the direction of what they can now see plainly is quite an opening in the forest.

The nearer they draw to the belt of woods the broader and more firmly trampled becomes the spoor. Where it opens into the shrubbery it is quite wide enough easily to admit the oxen and wagon.

They seem now to be gradually descending, while more and more frequently occur upheavals of rock. At length, in the very centre of a basin-like formation, they come somewhat suddenly upon a large, clear pool of water.

"We could not have found a more delightful spot if we had searched the whole country for it," declares Cunnyngham, gazing enthusiastically about him.—"What says Mazika?"

"Mazika too is pleased with everything but one."

"And what is that?"

"Mazika likes not the look of these great tracks about the pool. Many great animals come here to drink—the lion, the tiger and the elephant. Mazika likes not the thought of the abode of the good father's children and of himself being so near the resort of creatures so fierce and so cruel."

About four o'clock this afternoon Cunnyngham and Mazika, who have been out about three hours prospecting, return to camp very much elated at being able to report that they have, about a mile farther on, come upon another pool of water.

The travelers have barely time to reach the recently-discovered pool and make a few preparations for the night when the darkness closes in about them. Not until morning have they the opportunity to judge to any extent what manner of a place is this one which is likely to prove their home for the next five or six months.

The little sheet of water is not more than four feet wide at its greatest width and about a foot and a half deep at its greatest depth. On three sides it is nearly choked with rank-growing rushes, ferns and with a peculiar reddish-colored grass that attracts Cunnyngham's eyes at once.

"Unless I am very much mistaken, this is an almost certain indication of water underneath—at least so Dr. Livingstone generally found it."

This conjecture proves correct, and in three days more, by constant work, they have a steady flow of water that soon fills the deep basin they have excavated to overflowing, and begins to trickle its way down into the gorge.

CHAPTER XXIII.

"The wilderness hath shut them in."

THE spot selected upon which to erect their temporary home is at the summit of a gently-sloping decline. In the rear it is shut in by a natural wall of precipitous rock that towers full forty or fifty feet above it. An examination of this wall on the reverse side reveals the fact that the top of it is totally inaccessible to either man or beast, while from the side next the encampment it can be reached by a series of shelf-like projections that form a kind of natural stairway. They are thus completely protected from an attack in that direction.

Stretching away from the face of this rocky wall is a park-like expanse of straight-stemmed and dark-foliaged timber-trees, with here and there a widespreading *Ficus indica*, the real banian, and clumps of the beautiful white-thorned mimosa. About the "drop-shoots" of the banians many brilliant vines have entwined themselves, the rich coloring of their pendent blossoms gleaming like globes of flame. High into space the majestic branches of an occasional "iron" tree fling themselves, or the silvery outlines of a sycamore are thrown into relief against a picturesque tangle of evergreen thorns. As to the undergrowth, there is not much of it, save now and then a stretch of berry-yielding shrubs, a cluster of wild sage, a clump of dwarf fig-bushes, and an occasional cactus that bears a crimson flower and stands in some places from eight to ten feet high. From many of the branches of the trees, especially from the acacias, spring bright clusters of a parasite resembling the mistletoe, and, like the mistletoe, bearing berries of a waxy texture; only, unlike the mistletoe, the berries are of a rich creamy yellow.

The soft cooing of the doves, the merry trills and pipes of many sweet-singing birds as they flit from tree to tree or peep shyly forth from the quaint and curiously-constructed nests that adorn the boughs, lend a life and charm to the already pleasant scene that render it delightful beyond description to the worn and weary travelers, and give them a feeling of such tranquil happiness and sweet serenity as they have not felt since setting out upon their long and trying journey. After their tortuous wanderings through the desert it is like a glimpse of some other world.

As she is raised up for a sight of it a beautiful smile breaks over Hope's wan face, while with clasped hands she exclaims, "Oh, how good God is to have brought us here! It would not be so hard to die in a place like this."

"Do not talk of dying, dear," remonstrates Ellie,

while unconsciously a shudder passes over her. For the first time a dreadful thought presents itself—a thought that has been called into sudden being as she notes now more plainly than she has ever done before the extreme pallor and emaciation of her cousin's appearance. Suppose that Hope should die, after all? But oh no, no, no! she will not think of it. Surely, surely, God will not be so cruel as *that!* But the next moment at this impotent outcry against the Maker who gave life, and who alone has the right to claim it, the young girl stands aghast, and, clasping her hands tremblingly together, beseeches pardon of Him who is ever ready to grant it to the honestly penitent:

"O God, forgive me, for I knew not what I said. But, O Father, spare her life! Do not take it from us, for oh it is so precious!"

The condition of some of those who have been attacked by the fever has changed very much for the better since their arrival at this pleasant place, while in others, again, there has been no material improvement that can be seen. Henrietta is very much better; in fact, almost well. Ellie and Marvin too, who have had only a slight attack, are now almost recovered, thanks to liberal doses of quinine administered in time. But Hope, Baby Louise and poor old Mamochisane are still very sick. At present Hope's condition gives them more cause for anxiety than either of the others, for with her youth and usual vitality they have expected to see her make a much more vigorous effort to rally from the dread effects of the fever. As it is, however, she seems gradually to have sunk into a state of extreme listlessness and exhaustion from which nothing appears to arouse her.

The condition of little Louise also gives them much cause for alarm, as violent chills have now succeeded the fever, with some symptoms that Pierce fears threaten pneumonia, caused, he feels assured, by the sudden change in the temperature following upon the rain-and-hail-storm that had overtaken them in the desert. Mamochisane too is similarly affected. The brave and persevering young amateur physician is quite sanguine of the ultimate recovery of all, provided they are not subjected to any unusual exposure or sudden change in the weather. Pierce, Cunnyngham, Pitsane and Mazika have all likewise had a touch of the fever, but not enough completely to prostrate any one of them, and from which, by liberal doses of quinine, they have by now entirely recovered.

While awaiting the proper seasoning of the timber for their proposed abode a temporary shelter of poles covered with the branches of trees has been erected, under which the wagon is driven, the whole being protected by a palisade of stones and thorn-bushes, sufficient in its extent to enclose also the cattle at night. At the beginning of the third week everything is in shape for the raising of the framework of the new abode.

Their first step is to mark off on the ground, close under shelter of the stone wall, a circle of about twenty-five feet in diameter. Around the circumference at short intervals are placed stout, flexible poles. Another pole, much stouter and stronger than any of the others, is now erected exactly in the centre of the circle. The tops of the other poles are carefully drawn together and fastened to this, one by one, by means of stout thongs of the quagga's hide. This satisfactorily accomplished, their next step is to bind about this stout framework of poles with the same strong ligatures an encircling line of pliant young saplings at regular intervals from bottom to top.

The frame of their building is now complete, and looks, as Pierce laughingly declares, like nothing so much as a great, overgrown bee-gum. But Cunnyngham tells him that his laughing will soon be changed to admiration when he sees how nice it will appear when finally shaped and covered.

Their next step is to surround the structure with a trench a foot and a half deep, and so constructed that in case of a heavy rain it will drain the water away from the dwelling. As an extra precaution, however, against the entrance of the water a circular wall of stone is built around the lower part of the structure. This wall, which is about four feet in height, is a most creditable piece of workmanship, and to complete it it has been necessary to make two trips with the wagon and oxen to the deserted ant-village some eight or nine miles away. The material of these ant-heaps forms, when sprinkled with water, a strong and adhesive mortar. They secure enough of this mortar to lay also a floor for their cabin, which proves, after it has been thoroughly kneaded and trampled down and allowed to dry, as smooth and solid as though formed of stone.

"I don't think there is any danger now of our suffering from a flooded cabin," declares Cunnyngham enthusiastically as he surveys the work. "I don't believe we shall be troubled even by dampness, especially when we get the roof plastered."

They now begin the covering of the hut. Thick layers of reeds are put on as closely interwoven as possible, and to make the arrangements even more complete our travelers determine to plaster the entire interior. The only openings that have been left are the spaces for a door and three small windows.

Some frames are next constructed for the windows, which they have taken care to leave some seven or eight feet above the ground. Over each of these frames a thin cotton cloth is tightly stretched, which is subsequently smeared with a compound made of beeswax, a little tallow and pure gum arabic from the acacia trees. Outside shutters of plank are constructed to protect these at night, during heavy rains and in case of an attack. The abode is now considered complete, and with thankful and joyful hearts they take possession of it at the end of the fifteenth day since beginning its erection. But, though the dwelling is in itself finished, their arrangements are by no means so, for there are the shelters for the horses and cattle and for the wagon, some kind of a place to do their cooking, and the palisade to enclose and protect the whole.

In ten days more these various details are completed. The horses, cows, oxen, and even the goats, have now quite comfortable quarters, the wagon is under cover and the palisade that encloses the whole is as formidable as large stones and sharp thorn-bushes can make it. The best arrangement they can devise for cooking is between two ledges in the rock-wall, where the ovens and other utensils can be set back into a kind of cavity above which there is an opening for the smoke to penetrate. A shelter made of stout poles and thick reeds gives the cook protection against the weather. This latter duty has had at first, owing to Mamochisane's continued illness and Ellie's and Hope's prostration from the fever, to fall upon Pitsane. But, Ellie having now recovered and Jim's hand having healed, the latter is permanently installed in that capacity with the former to direct and give him such aid as she can.

The outward arrangements finally completed, Pierce and Pitsane set about the interior appointment of the abode, while Cunnyngham, Mazika and Kamati search out and prepare a suitable spot for a garden. Pierce, with Pitsane's aid, first proceeds to partition off into three apartments the interior space of the cabin. Two of these apartments are half circular in shape, the other and larger one is somewhat oval. The two former are intended as sleeping-rooms, the other as a general sitting-room. The partitions separating them run only about half-way up, and are formed of a network of light, slender poles ingeniously covered over with the stiff fronds of various fan-palms fastened into place by means of a strong and durable rush that is rendered quite pliable by being dipped in water. Before the entrance of each apartment is hung a curtain of cloth that can be lifted or dropped at pleasure.

These partitions satisfactorily completed, Pierce's next step is to procure several strong, straight poles. Taking four of these poles, cut to five feet in length, and placing them in an upright position, he proceeds to fasten between them light, strong side-pieces of the same material. With a small auger he next bores holes at regular intervals along the side-pieces, and, this completed, constructs from one to the other a strong elastic network formed of thongs of antelope-hide interlaced. He has now as durable and comfortable a bedstead as any one could desire.

Three of these he constructs—one for Cunnyngham, Marvin and himself, and the other two for the girls' room. As to Mazika, Pitsane, Kamati and Jim, they vastly prefer their pile of skins comfortably arranged in one corner of the youths' apartment; that is, Kamati, Pitsane and Jim sleep there, Mazika choosing to establish himself in the outer apartment and directly across the main entrance, the door of which has to be left open on mild nights in order to secure sufficient ventilation. The windows are also left open at such times. As they have taken care to perforate their door with numberless auger-holes, and have fitted a piece, transom-like, above it, this gives them sufficient ventilation on other occasions. But often and often the weather is so warm as to cause more than one of the male inmates to seek the outside of the cabin, where, throwing a skin rug under the branches, they pass the remainder of the night. Much security is lent them on these occasions by the thought of the stout barricade they have erected around them.

By way of furnishing his and Cunnyngham's bed, Pierce contents himself with numerous soft skins and two good blankets, but for the beds for the girls' room he makes two most comfortable mattresses out of ticks of canvas cloth, stuffed with the soft down obtained from certain large decayed flowering bulbs.

A lounge of olive-wood, with bottom of interlaced antelope-hide and cushions that are also stuffed with the silky fibre obtained from the flower-bulbs, is now constructed for the general sitting-room, and proves a source of much comfort and pleasure to the sick who are convalescing. With hammer, plane and nails a table is next formed with the top made of two wide planks cut from a large "yellow-wood" tree, the sawing, trimming and planing of which have been quite a feat on the part of both Pierce and Pitsane. Two small stands are similarly constructed for the holding of various small articles and for Ellie's sewing material; then four or five stools, and lastly an arm-chair with seat and back upholstered in leopard-skin and arms of beautifully twisted eland-horns, which, taken all together, Pierce considers his *chef d'œuvre*.

With a shelf or two for the books, brackets for the guns picturesquely formed of antelope-horns, and a half dozen or so of tawny leopard, lion and tiger-skins placed like rugs about the apartment, the whole presents a cheerful and homelike picture, all the more so when contrasted with their savage surroundings.

All the sick, with the exception of Mamochisane, are now very much better, Hope especially so. It does not seem to be the fever now that is so much the matter with old Mamochisane as a complication of things that completely baffles Pierce, despite the very creditable knowledge he has of medicine.

CHAPTER XXIV.

"He giveth alike seed-time and harvest."

THREE months have now passed away since the coming of our travelers to this oasis-like spot in the desert. They have had many sore trials, chief among them the loss of all the horses but one, Khiva, the present of Captain Murray to their father, a cow and two of the calves and two of the donkeys, among the latter Hope's faithful and affectionate Chumah. They have all died of that fatal disease known among African farmers as "lung sickness" or "lung fever," brought on by the numerous hardships of their trying journey across the desert, the exposure to the fierce rays of the sun, to the night-airs and dews, and lastly to that terrible rain-and-hail storm with the sudden fall of temperature succeeding it. Only unremitting attention and care in stabling them and the timely administering of certain remedies save the other brutes. As to the oxen, fortunately for our travelers, they have all had this dread sickness, and hence from one attack have secured immunity from another. What is more, they have all been, in the language of the Cape cattle-dealers, "inoculated" against it. This form of inoculation consists in cutting a slit in the tail of the oxen and introducing therein a piece of the diseased lung of an animal that has died from the sickness. The result is that the ox thus inoculated takes the disease in a mild form, which causes a portion of its tail to drop off, and it thus becomes proof against future attack.

Several members of the little party have also suffered from ophthalmia, a disease of the eyes brought on through exposure to the glaring rays of the sun. Fortunately for our travelers, Pierce has had considerable experience with the disease under his father's instructions, so that in each of the present cases he is enabled to bring the patient around all right.

Another trial has also been theirs. The stock of provisions with which they left Lepelole has long since given out, save small quantities of sugar, coffee and tea, a half-can of ship's biscuit and a little jelly; which delicacies Ellie guards with jealous care for those who are sick. As to the others, they have had for the past six weeks to depend almost entirely upon the products of the forest—fruits, nuts, berries and the like—and upon such game as they are able either to slay with the gun or to entrap.

They have at first been put to considerable trouble in finding a spot quite suitable for their garden. But they finally settle upon a kind of valley lying along the river-bed. Four acres are selected, staked out and cleared. In the "patch" beans, peas and other garden vegetables, the cassava, groundnuts, kaffir corn and the like, are successfully sown, and in due season, by proper care and attention, brought to a satisfactory yielding.

One afternoon old Kamati finds a rich store of honey deposited by a colony of wild bees in the clefts of some rocks. He is led to the honey through his attention having at first been attracted by the piercing notes of a honey-bird, which he at length follows, with the result of finding a large and delicious supply of honey—nearly three gallons in all when strained.

The only necessary article they really lack is salt. For some little time after the giving out of the supply with which they have started they are at a complete loss to know what to do. At length Pierce and Pitsane come to the rescue by proposing to go in search of one of the many salt-pans with which the Kalahari is known to abound.

One is at length found some fifteen or sixteen miles north of them, which the discoverers report to have about its margin and for a considerable distance down a solid cake of salt quite two inches in thickness. The wagon and oxen are now sent to convey to the camp cuttings from this saline incrustation. In a few days more, by dint of much patience and care and by various processes of boiling, straining and evaporation, they have an article which, if it is not as white and attractive-looking as the salt known to civilized commerce, is neverless quite equal to it in saline properties.

It is now the middle of February and the rains have set in again, for during the months of December and January there has been a comparatively dry season.

Once or twice during these months our friends have thought quite seriously of abandoning their home in the wilderness and of starting once more upon the arduous journey across the plains. But four things, each one in itself of sufficient moment, have deterred them: the insufficiency of food at their command, the condition of the sick, their knowledge that should they start at this season they would miss the crops of watermelons upon which they have been depending, and lastly that they would in all probability find the water-pools dried off again, for beyond one or two heavy showers the fall of rain up to this time has been comparatively light. They have thus, all things being taken into consideration, returned to their old decision of waiting until the heavier rains of February, March and April have fallen. By that time their crops will be gathered and the sick doubtless sufficiently recovered to travel.

They have now had an ample opportunity of testing the waterproof quality of their abode. The hardness of the rushes and other substances forming the thatch, the closeness of their weft and the coating of plastering underlying all, are such that no drop of rain finds entrance through the roof. The only trouble is at the junction of the rushes and palm mats with the stone wall. Here the rain, running down from the roof, trickles through in a way that is at times most unpleasant. However, this is soon remedied by an outside circle of poles to which the roofing is extended.

Pierce has also added to the general arrangements for Ellie's comfort and convenience in rainy weather a pavement that leads from the door of the abode to the cooking-shed. This pavement, which is of palm-nuts firmly fixed together by an undercoating of mortar, is not only an ingenious piece of work, but quite a pretty one as well. After it has become hardened and been walked on for some time it acquires the smoothness and lustre of polished metal.

More than once they have had a severe storm of wind and rain, accompanied by startling flashes of lightning, in which several trees of the forest have been uprooted or struck by the electrical current. But they are securely protected by the wall of rock that towers like a fortress behind them. Once or twice they have also witnessed from the summit of this rocky wall, which has now grown to be quite a favorite post of outlook with them, the approach of one of those dread sand-storms against which old Shobo has warned them. How thankful they are at this moment that they have this rock and the forest surrounding it for protection! Thankful are they also that the cattle are at the time feeding along the bed of the dried water-course, and not on the plains.

As to the wild animals, they seem to have a premonition of what is coming even before the sand-clouds appear, and rush in terror-stricken groups, some of them with the swiftness of the wind, to the shelter of the woods. In consequence, many of them come dashing right by the enclosure, where a few well-directed shots bring to the earth two large fine bucks, a buffalo and a giraffe.

One of these wild, frightened creatures, a young zebra, unheeding the stone wall that surrounds the camp, dashes against it with such violence as to crush in his skull completely, instantly dying from the effects of the blow. The flesh of this animal, however, is of little value to them, with the exception of one or two portions, on account of a strong, unpleasant flavor; but they preserve the skin, which comes in well for various uses.

The days now speed happily and pleasantly by, despite the fact that they are passed in this lonely and desolate waste far from the haunts of men. The hours of daylight, whether rainy or sunshiny, are taken up with occupation of some kind, either in work about the encampment or in the fields, in the procuring of supplies from forest and plain or in some preparation for the renewal of their journey across the desert. In the evenings, when their frugal supper is over, they gather in the larger apartment, where the time, until ten o'clock, is pleasantly passed in reading, talking, laying plans for the future, and occasionally, for the benefit of the younger ones, in games and pastimes. Sometimes Ellie and Hope, for the entertainment of the others, read aloud from the little stock of books, or Pierce and Cunnyngham relate some interesting incident that has befallen them in a recent trip about the forest or out on the plains, or Mazika or Pitsane is coaxed into the interesting rôle of story-teller.

Sometimes to the pleasant diversions of the evening the two pets, the monkey and the parrot, lend an animated digression by originating some amazing episode, greatly to the edification of their respective owners, each of whom has now come to look upon his or hers as in every way the very smartest and most promising of its kind.

The parrot, Colo, has now learned to talk in very creditable English, greatly to the satisfaction of his young master. But the monkey, Jock, now thoroughly tamed and as hearty and strong as he can well be, proves the source of much more real amusement and interest; for he is an unusually intelligent little animal and has acquired quite a number of tricks. He has, besides, shown himself very valuable in the alertness with which he guards the approach to the abode, having in one or two instances proved a better sentinel even than the dogs. Once he has warned them of the approach of a leopard that has effected an entrance through a weak spot in the palisade. Since that time they have all slept soundly and tranquilly, secure in the belief that Jock will not fail to warn them in time of any threatening danger.

If there is one thing of which Jock is particularly fond, it is to be allowed to go hunting with Pierce, Pitsane and the dogs. Immediately when he can detect any preparations for an expedition of this kind he will show the greatest joy. If allowed to join the party, he evinces his satisfaction and delight by the wildest caperings; if forbidden, he will at once hide himself in some dark corner and mope and sulk, sometimes through an entire day.

One of Jock's favorite pastimes on these expeditions is to climb into the trees and seek for gum and nuts of various kinds, of the former of which he is particularly fond, and over which he works his jaws with all the abandon of a school-girl of the present day with her cakes of taffy-tolu.

Although quite brave in some respects, there are nevertheless two things, in addition to being left alone in the desert, of which Jock stands in great dread. If he but catches sight of a serpent of any kind, he will shake as though with an ague, and, uttering a series of piercing cries, will at once creep as far as possible out of sight. Another great dread that he cherishes is of his own species, for, strange to say, now that he has grown thoroughly domesticated, Jock seems to have entirely forgotten his old haunts and companions. Sometimes, therefore, when he hears the cries of other apes in the woods, although they seem to terrify him considerably, he will yet answer them, for this much of the old instinct seems to have remained. But if, on the other hand, they approach him, he will at once fly, overcome with terror and uttering hideous cries. Never stopping until he has reached the house, he will there creep between the feet of one of the inmates and cower, shaking with fright. It always requires a day or two for him to recover from the shock.

However pleasing he may be otherwise, there is yet one trait in Jock's character that considerably troubles his friends. Jock will steal. Like the majority of his species, he seems to think that anything he may desire is his by right of coming upon it, and sometimes when not coming upon it, but by searching it out. He seems fully to understand the art of unloosing the strings of a basket or other receptacle where something to eat has been stored, especially if it is something of which he is particularly fond. And there is no counting the times that he has stolen milk from the jars and pans after it has been strained and set away. Once or twice both Cunnyngham and Pierce have undertaken to chastise him for these thefts, but beyond keeping out of their sight for a day or two and scowling at them most vigorously when he does come in sight of them or they of him, no effect is produced.

Another depredation of which he is guilty is robbing the hens' nests. At first, when the eggs begin to be missed, Ellie cannot believe that it is really Jock who makes way with them. But on learning of the disappearance of the eggs, Pierce, who has suspicions of his own and some ground for them, as he thinks, determines to institute a watch.

At about nine o'clock in the morning there come, shrill and prolonged, the sounds of the first hen's cackle. Jock, who has been perched in the branches of a mimosa, apparently sound asleep, is now seen suddenly to leap down and start in the direction of the fowl-yard as fast as he can go. Disappearing within the enclosure, he soon reappears with an egg in his mouth, and is making off with it to a secluded corner where he can without molestation enjoy its contents, when just at this moment Pierce appears upon the scene.

"Oh yes, you grand rogue, I have caught you now!" he exclaims as he starts toward him.

The words are scarcely out when Jock suddenly stops, and, assuming a careless position, appears the very picture of injured innocence. His look says as plainly as a look could say, "It surely can't be *me*, now, of whom you are speaking as a rogue?"

The next moment he has placed the egg at Pierce's feet with another look, which again says as plainly as the words could, "*That* is the place to which I intended from the first to bring the egg."

But Pierce isn't at all taken in by this hypocritical performance, although Jock flatters himself that he is. Returning to his watch, Pierce this time waits until Jock has gained his corner, where, coming upon him in the very act of devouring the egg, and a further hypocritical display of innocence being out of the question, the cunning thief is on the spot given such a sound thrashing as he surely deserves.

But this beating, like all the others that have preceded it, having no effect, the eggs continuing to disappear as regularly as ever, and all attempts to shut him away from the nests proving unavailing, Pierce finally decides to resort to the novel expedient of training one of the dogs—a fine English pointer that has been a present from Captain Murray to his father—to keep a watch upon the hens' nests and to bring the eggs to some one at the house as soon as they are laid.

In a few days' time the dog has learned his lesson so well that he scarcely ever fails to come with the egg as soon as the hen has laid it. For the first three or four days Jock stands aside, an amazed spectator of this new arrangement of affairs, and then a most remarkable contest takes place of which no one has even thought, much less expected. Jock now also establishes himself just without the enclosure and close beside the dog, where he lies stretched out, apparently as sound asleep as the dog seems to be; but if any one were noting closely he could see very plainly that his wicked little eyes are far from being closed.

The moment a hen cackles, up spring both animals, when a most exciting race ensues in the direction of the nest. Sometimes the dog reaches it first, and sometimes it is the monkey; but whichever it is, a fierce contest as to who shall have the egg takes place, unless the dog can manage to elude the monkey, which he occasionally does.

Whenever the dog succeeds in gaining the victory he at once runs joyfully to the house with the egg held carefully in his mouth. Nearly always on occasions of this kind Jock, being unable to conceal his chagrin at the defeat, will follow after, grumbling all the way and making threatening grimaces. Sometimes the monkey will keep close beside him until the egg is deposited at the feet or in the lap of some one, when the hypocritical little animal will appear to be greatly delighted at its safe delivery.

If, on the other hand, Jock succeeds in getting the egg, he will at once run with it to the boughs of a neighboring tree or to an elevated perch near at hand, where, having devoured it, he tosses the shell at his adversary as though to make game of him.

Every expedient exhausted without any salutary effect, they have finally to resort to tying Jock during the day, or at least through such a part of it as it takes to secure the eggs.

The other pets, the young ostriches, have by this

time grown so rapidly that our young people are already beginning to entertain serious misgivings as to the feasibility of taking them farther upon their journey. They are now too large to be carried in a coop, and it is not to be expected that they will follow regularly, while to drive them will involve more care and attention than the travelers are capable of giving with the other duties on hand. It is therefore feared that when the caravan starts once more upon its journey the ostriches will have to be turned loose on the plain.

As for the dogs, with but one exception, they have all by this time grown to treat Smike with much friendly consideration and to welcome him to all their gambols and feasts. This single exception, it is needless to add, is Master Chitane, who still holds out as the ugly, stubborn dog in the face of many really humiliating advances on the part of the peaceful and generous Smike. But at last there comes a day, as generally happens in cases of this kind, when the hearty and overwhelming return of good for evil arouses the better side of even this mean little dog-nature.

One morning, when at some little distance away from the camp, Chitane, through some of his high-and-mighty ways, so offends two of the larger dogs that, not having any very great amount of friendly feeling for him to begin with, they forthwith set upon him and give him such a drubbing as he has never known before, and doubtless never will again.

Just as there has been a short lull in the attack, and the dogs are on the point of setting upon Chitane again with a view to completing the lesson, Smike makes his appearance, and at once, without seeming to stop to consider the danger he may himself invite, rushes into the midst of the combatants.

In a little while he has so separated them that he is standing before the beaten and cowed Chitane with his body interposed, so that he completely shelters that of the now thoroughly used-up and frightened poodle.

Recognizing that it is Smike's brave determination to save the life of his former little tormentor even at the risk of his own, and not wishing to injure the courageous fellow for so insignificant a cause as Chitane, the other dogs now withdraw and leave them alone.

Chitane is so badly bruised and bitten that it is with great difficulty he can take even a few steps. Seeing how it is, and not wishing to leave the poor little beggar out upon the plain or to crawl home as best he can in his present condition, Smike forthwith picks him up in his mouth by his long wool and trots off to camp with him. The victory over the surly-tempered little poodle is from this day complete.

But, brave and generous as is this act, Smike becomes the hero of another even braver; and in consideration of the cause in which his life is this time risked he endears himself a hundred times more to all in the camp, who never cease to bless the day that they have brought him from the Bushmen village.

One very hot afternoon, Hope, who by this time has almost entirely recovered, takes a leopard-skin rug and a book to the shade of a mimosa tree in a distant part of the enclosure.

At length, overcome by drowsiness, she falls asleep, and an hour or so later Cunnyngham, who happens to be passing by the spot, is overcome with horror at the sight he sees.

The young girl is lying asleep, one arm under her head, the other thrown some little distance from her, while coiled up between the extended arm and her breast is a huge cobra, or hooded snake, with its venomous head raised ready to strike at her throat. Cunnyngham looks about him for some weapon with which to attack the deadly creature. But another pair of eyes has caught sight of the young girl's peril almost at the same moment that Cunnyngham has discovered it.

As usual when he is about the encampment, Smike has followed Hope, and as she has lain down upon the rug beneath the tree he has stretched himself near at hand. Like Hope, he has been overcome with drowsiness, but now he suddenly awakens, with a quick, somewhat spasmodic dropping apart of his great eyelids, just at the moment that the cobra has darted its head upward from its coils.

In an instant Smike seems to realize the danger, and almost in the same instant has sprung forward to avert it. The snake is in front of him, the back of its head toward him. Just as the venomous fangs are on the point of being buried in the young girl's white throat, Smike's long, sharp teeth have seized the reptile just below the horribly dilating hood with a grasp that I do not believe death itself could make him relax. The next moment he has dashed the snake against a tree with such violence that it never moves again after striking the ground.

That the brave fellow has now paid his debt in full for every kind word, for every gentle pat, for every good meal—of which there have been many —no one will question. Even the ugly bruise that Hope has so long borne for him upon her arm finds its more than eloquent requital in the carcass of the mangled snake from whose deadly fangs his teeth have saved her.

CHAPTER XXV.

"Consecrated, Lord, to thee."

THE middle of March finds our little band in quite a distressed frame of mind. It is now known that old Mamochisane cannot live, while the little Louise, whom they had been thinking for some time previously out of danger, has now taken a relapse and grown alarmingly worse.

The old black woman's many ailments have finally culminated in the only too surely fatal disease—consumption. As it seems to be of the rapid kind, Pierce has told them that her death is now only a question of a few days at best.

At last, about eleven o'clock at night during the first week of April, they are all gathered to witness what with sorrowing hearts they feel is old Mamochisane's last hour on earth.

She is fully conscious, and, though scarcely able to speak above a whisper, yet answers all their questions rationally and in her native tongue, which she seems now to speak with far less difficulty than the broken English she has acquired.

"Are you afraid to die, Mamochisane?" Ellie

questions just a little anxiously as she bends with tear-wet eyes above her.

"No, missie—no more afraid than to go along the broad white path at Lepelole to the great spring where the waters gurgle and where the sun shines all the day through. Once," continues the black woman after a moment's pause, "Mamochisane was all afraid, for then it was everywhere dark—dark as a night when no star shines. But then came the white father and held out his hand to Mamochisane, and he said, 'Mamochisane, do not stumble. Here, take my hand and let me guide you. Do not draw back, do not be afraid; I come not to hurt, but to help you. I am your brother, your brother in Christ Jesus, and the great Father of all, he has sent me.'—Oh, missie, dear good missie!" the old woman cries suddenly, her voice ringing out with a clearness and strength that startles them, "I want to thank you for everything you have done for poor old black Mamochisane. This night would her soul have gone forth among the howling beasts of the great dark wilderness to wander for ever lost, but for my white father and my white father's children. Oh, missie! missie! when Mamochisane thinks of all those who still wander away from the light, the heart of Mamochisane is pierced as the heart the arrow strikes, and her wailings are as the wailings of those who weep for the lost. Oh, missie, who will tell them of the way? who will now hold the light before them, now that the white father is gone, and the white father's children too have turned their faces away from the country of the blacks to seek the country of their white brothers?"

Almost at the same instant Ellie and Cunnyngham raise their heads to glance at each other, while a look, the intense meaning of which it is impossible to mistake, passes between them.

"Comfort yourself, Mamochisane," Ellie says in a soothing voice. "My father's mission was by no means the only one in the country of the blacks, nor even in your section of it. Along the east coast and the west coast, about the great lakes, upon the southern borders, even in the neighborhood of the wild Zambezi, there are planted the standards of many brave soldiers of the cross who have come to tell your people of Him who is mighty to save from the curse of sin."

A happy light breaks over the withered face, while the sunken eyes dilate and glow with the glad reflection:

"Oh, missie, is this true? is this true?"

"It is true, Mamochisane."

"Then, missie, Mamochisane can die with the pang gone from her heart. Oh, bless God! bless God!"

The last words are barely spoken when Cunnyngham, intensely pale, but with a look upon his face that transfigures its every lineament, approaches the bed, and, dropping upon his knees, fixes his eyes steadfastly upon Mamochisane.

"Mamochisane," he says in tones that are barely audible at times through the great emotion that sways him, "if it will comfort you any to know that *I* will be one more to carry the light to those who yet wander in the darkness, then take that comfort with you. If God spares my life to reach the United States—and somehow I do not doubt it—I shall at once offer myself to one of the missionary societies to go in training for the field in Africa.—Here, O God, upon my bended knees and by the side of this ransomed soul that has been given thee as an eloquent witness of what man, even humble man, may do for thee, I consecrate myself to thy work in Africa."

Ere these last sentences are spoken two forms have prostrated themselves beside Cunnyngham, and now, clasping him closely in their arms, Ellie and Hope give vent to the sobs of mingled feelings of sadness and joy that for some moments overcome all efforts at words.

As for Mamochisane, she lies there with glistening eyes and smiling lips, too happy to speak.

Ellie is the first to find her voice:

"Oh, my cousin, you have been rightly named. I can see now the happy light that will come into the face of him whose name you bear when this is told him. In the golden morning of his own young manhood he went bravely and nobly forth at the call of China, and now, following worthily in his footsteps, you have devoted your life to

Africa. Truly that name has been a grand inspiration, leading you ever onward toward all that is noblest and best. Oh, if my father could only have lived to see this day! But do not think," she goes on after a moment's pause, "that you are to be alone in this sacrifice, if sacrifice it can be called. Like you, I see the way clearly now, though it was a hard struggle at first, and, like you, I shall follow unhesitatingly in it. My sex, I know, will debar me from the broader and more useful field into which yours will carry you; but being a woman will make me only the more earnestly desirous of doing a woman's part as only a woman *can* do it. One woman's *full* work for the Master! Oh is it not a hundred—nay, a thousand—times better than the scant and incomplete service of many men! If God wills it that we shall reach the States in safety, I too shall offer myself for the instruction and training necessary to fit me for the work in Africa. To what point they send me matters not, so that it is with you, my cousin, and to the most benighted of all these lost souls that wander in the darkness.—Where there is the most work to be done, where the aching brow and the toiling hands, the blistering feet and the fierce pangs of the fever and the death-dealing darts of savage enemies are but a few of the many discomforts and dangers to be faced and borne in the promotion of thy kingdom, there send me, O Father, and keep me and strengthen me and use me as an humble instrument in thy hands for the accomplishment of thy purposes."

"Oh, Ellie!" Hope exclaims at this moment as, rising, she throws one arm around her cousin's and the other about her brother's neck, drawing them as close to her as she can, "you two have but given voice to all the thoughts that have for so long a time past been crowding within my heart. Many, many times I have wanted to speak them where all could hear, but always my timidity restrained me. Now I say to you in words that well forth from the very depths of my soul: 'I too have chosen, my brother, my cousin. Your cause shall be my cause, your work my work, and wherever that work may lead you there will I follow, and, toiling by your side, will find my sweetest reward in the words of encouragement you each shall give and in the approval of God our Father.'—Oh, Cunnyngham, I have not your zeal nor your strength nor your talent nor your will to wrest success where failure seems imminent; nor your faith and courage, Ellie, to sustain me in the hours of weakness and trial; but what I lack in ability I feel that God will give me in willingness, and cause me yet to be the humble means, through his sustaining grace, of bringing many of these perishing souls to Christ."

"Every word that you three have uttered has found an echo in my heart," says Pierce, who for some time past has been kneeling at his sister's side, and now raises his head to glance bravely from one to the other. "But I fear that you will feel some disappointment when I confess to a conviction that shows me the path of duty not altogether in the direction that it has been shown to you. Yours is to be a mission to sin-sick souls—mine to disease-stricken bodies. I shall offer for the study of medicine, to return, when my course is completed, to any one of these mission-fields in Africa to which those in authority may see fit to send me; but, like you, Ellie, my one hope is that they may send us together or so near together that we may work one with the other."

A wonderful change has now come over Mamochisane. Every word of this conversation has been heard and understood by her. That the children of the white father, the man who has done so much for the spiritual welfare of Mamochisane herself and for so many of her people,—that his children are really, after all, not going away for good, that they will return in a little while only the better equipped for bringing the messages of healing and hope to those sick in soul and body, is happiness enough for Mamochisane. Now, indeed, has the arrow been taken from her heart, with not one pang remaining. No more do her lips send forth wailings for those who wander in the darkness, but all is peace and joy indescribable.

"Missie," says the old black suddenly, turning so as to face Ellie with the full force of her burning eyes, "where is my baby? where is the little one that has so long lain against old Mamochisane's breast?—the little one that my white father's wife placed in Mamochisane's arms when the message came for her to go to the country where the great God dwells, and that the white father himself gave again into Mamochisane's keeping with the words, 'Never leave my little one, Mamochisane. As you have cared for her and watched over her so faithfully for our sakes, now take her and love her and care for her for her own sake.' Oh, missie, many, many times Mamochisane has thought of those words, and again and again has she begged of the great God whom she loves and trusts to make her faithful in the charge."

Carefully and tenderly the little one is brought and laid on the bed with Mamochisane. The pale, pinched face, strangely pathetic now in its look of utter unconsciousness, is turned so that the piercing eyes of the faithful old black woman may rest full upon it. The fair hair sweeps the pillow upon which Mamochisane's head with its cleanly-kept crown of gray-sprinkled fleece lies extended. A glittering strand here and there falls against the heaving breast of the dying black woman or lies like a thread of finely-spun gold across her arm.

For many moments they lie thus, neither moving, the baby's white face upturned, strangely white and deathly still—Mamochisane's black one, alert with all the instincts of life, drooping toward it. Directly those who watch this scene witness that the memory of which never leaves them to their last hour. Not more than ten minutes have gone by since the placing of the little one upon the bed beside Mamochisane, when suddenly the arms of the old black woman are extended, and ere any one can stay the action they raise and clasp the little one against the swelling breast with a quick, convulsive movement, while with a smile that illumines the face as no smile of earth could ever illumine it the lips send forth the glad, exultant cry,

"Mamochisane has *not* left the little one, white father! She is here! she is here!"

A tremor passes along the muscles of the arms; they quiver, then lie motionless, with their burden still clasped closely between them; the light dies out of the eyes, the heavy lids drop across them, but the smile still abides in all its beauty upon the withered face.

When, after some moments of gentle yet persistent effort, the young people release the stiffened clasp of the arms from about the form of the child, they discover the fact—a sad premonition of which has been carried to their hearts with that last ringing cry of Mamochisane's—that both are dead, the faithful black guardian, faithful in death as in life, and the tender innocent charge: the breath of the destroyer of all earthly semblances has claimed each alike, the fragile lily and the scarred and hoary trunk against which it drooped.

And in that same moment that those glad, exultant notes have swelled from the lips of the dying black woman, the two spirits, mingling as the sweet perfume of the opening flowers sometimes mingles with the rushing winds of the night, have been borne upward, upward as the unfettered bird takes its flight, to the waiting ones in the land beyond all shadows. Black soul and white, they have ascended unto Him who has breathed into each the same breath of life, and through whom each is to receive the radiant habiliments of that immortality that is the reward of every soul made spotless through his grace—an immortality born of the glory that shines for ever from the countenance of the living God.

CHAPTER XXVI.

"His hand shall guide them to the end."

AT dawn on the fifth day of May all is in readiness for the renewal of the journey across the plains.

From observations taken as accurately and as carefully as he can with the instruments at hand, Cunnyngham has arrived at the belief that they are not more than a hundred miles from the northern edge of the desert and about one hundred and fifty from the eastern, or, as near as he can calculate, in latitude between 21° and 22° south and longitude 23° and 24° east. Their faithless guides have therefore brought them many miles out of the way, while their own wanderings have greatly increased the distance.

But Cunnyngham has much hope that by means of the sextant and compass, and with the knowledge he possesses of some of the routes gone over by Livingstone and his hunter-friends Cumming, Oswell and Murray, he can yet guide the little band aright in the journey to Linyanti.

He therefore purposes, on leaving the encampment in the wilderness, to pursue a course as nearly due north-east as he can make it, in which direction he hopes, after a journey of two weeks at the longest, to reach the Zouga River at some ford where it has been previously crossed by Livingstone and other travelers. Here, by following the northern bank of the river for some distance, they will doubtless chance upon a village of the Bayeiye, a friendly tribe, from whom a guide may be obtained to conduct them over the best and safest route to Linyanti.

In the mean time, however, there is the probability ere the Zouga is reached of finding on the way a kraal of Bushmen by whose direction the ford can more easily be found.

By a judicious hoarding of their small stores, the result of their agricultural labors and of numerous foraging expeditions through the forest and across the plains, they have, on quitting the encampment in the desert, enough provisions to supply them a month, perhaps as long as five weeks if they can manage to add something to them on the way, which is by no means improbable.

It is with hearts in which many varied feelings struggle for the mastery that they look their last upon a spot where six such eventful months have been passed. Although it has been in the very midst of the savage and inhospitable desert, and although dangers have so constantly beset them on every side, it has nevertheless been as a home to them. The tears fall thick and fast, in spite of their efforts to restrain them, as they close and bar the door upon the hut where so many happy hours have been spent, while choking sobs are added to the tears as they bend for the last time above the mound that contains all of the earthly part of old Mamochisane and of Baby Louise.

Inseparable and devotedly attached in life, in burial they have not divided them, as God has not divided the two spirits at the moment of their happy release. Close together they lie in the same narrow confine of earth, as together they shall arise on the resurrection morn, the black body and the white, to be made partakers with the spirits in the life active, joyous, everlasting, supreme—the eternal life with God.

The grave has been dug under one of the larger mimosa trees within the enclosure, and covered with a raised work of stone, so as to protect it after their departure from the ravages of beasts. Above it the birds sing and about it the winds whisper, while through the leaves of the trees gleaming shafts of sunlight, dropping downward, bring with them faint yet happy suggestions of the greater light that lies beyond.

For the first two days after resuming the journey across the plains their way lies over a sandy tract on which no sign of water appears, despite the rains which have recently fallen. But against this they have guarded by bringing a supply of water with them from the pool at the encampment.

The third day some rain-pools are reached, and again on the fourth and fifth days. On the sixth, seventh and eighth days of the journey they pass through great stretches of watermelons, on which both they and the cattle subsist for the entire three days, finding them a most excellent substitute for the water which they have not.

After leaving these tracts of melons two stages of their journey behind, they enter upon a hard, flat country—as flat as the floor of a modern house. This hardness is accounted for by its having a thin, light top soil lying upon a strata of calcareous tufa. This tract extends as far as the eye can reach, and, despite the thinness of the soil, it yet supports a vegetation of fine, sweet grass upon which the horse, cattle and donkeys revel.

Several mopane and baobab trees are also seen here, some of the latter being of such enormous dimensions that they call forth many exclamations of wonder from our young people. One of them especially is of an almost incredible size. It consists of six large branches and four smaller ones united into one trunk, the dimensions of the latter being, as they find by actual measurement, at three feet from the ground no less than ninety-seven feet six inches in circumference. And yet the trunk is not more than fifteen or sixteen feet in height. The limbs branch to such an extent that Cunyngham feels no hesitancy in declaring that he is confident if the circle that surrounds them could be measured it would be found to contain no less than three hundred and fifty or four hundred feet!

This enormous bulk of branches gives the tree at a distance the appearance of being a whole forest in itself. The lower branches, which are adorned with tufts of leaves, extend from the sides horizontally, and, bending their great weight toward the earth, add still further to the gigantic appearance of the tree. The bark is nearly an inch in thickness, and is of an ash-colored gray, greasy to the touch and also very smooth; the exterior is adorned with a sort of varnish, while the inside is of a brilliant green beautifully speckled with bright red. The wood itself is white and soft and penetrable, so much so that when an axe or other like instrument is struck into it, it is very difficult to release it.

The tree toward which the attention of our young travelers has been attracted in so great a degree is quite hollow, while for several feet up it is denuded of its bark, but despite these ravages it still shows many and most vigorous signs of a wonderful vitality.

"Is it true that baobab trees never die?" questions Hope as they stand gazing upon the battle-scarred monster.

"Oh, I suppose they die *some time*," returns Cunnyngham, "but I believe all naturalists have agreed in considering them the longest-lived of any forest growth, while some even declare that many of the trees now alive and flourishing were in existence at the time of the Flood."

"I cannot believe *that*," says Ellie with much positiveness. "The baobab—or mowana, as the Bechuanas call it—doubtless lives to be many hundred years old, but I feel assured that none of those trees of this species alive at the present day encountered the ravages of the Flood."

"One singular thing about it, at any rate," says Pierce, "is that one rarely finds a dead baobab. Livingstone records that in all his travels he only came upon a single one."

"That is all owing to the wellnigh incredible vitality the tree is known to possess," returns Cunnyngham. "Dr. Livingstone saw several instances in Angola in which the tree continued to grow even after it had been cut down!"

"Why, I never heard of such a thing!" says Hope; "and if any one else but Dr. Livingstone had written that, I am very much afraid I wouldn't have wanted to believe it."

"Is it true that even fire cannot destroy it?" asks Hope again.

"It is true. Neither from within nor from without can fire do the tree irreparable injury."

"Well, how, then, does it ever die?"

"That, my dear sister, is what Marvin and Henrietta would call 'a puzzler.' I suppose it finds its death at last, as all things earthly must find it, in a complete exhaustion of its powers."

A little farther on they come upon a succession of salt-pans, one of them being, they estimate, fully ten miles in breadth. To their surprise, they find near one of these pans a spring of very good water. It is a little brackish, it is true, but not enough so to render it disagreeable.

"The salt-deposits at the bottom of this spring have been removed by human agency, I feel assured," says Pierce, "doubtless by travelers like ourselves; or it may be that we are not far from the habitation of some native tribe, in all probability Bushmen."

Pierce's words have quite a cheerful effect upon the little party, and when they leave the salt-pans behind it is with much hope of soon coming upon a village of some kind.

A few miles farther on they reach a habitation of Bushmen under their chief, Mochotska. They find this people very different in many respects from those of the same family whom they have met on the other side of the desert. While those were of short stature and of a dull-yellow color, most of these are tall, strapping fellows, with strong, powerful limbs, big heads, prominent foreheads and dark, nearly black, complexions.

The chief, however, is an exception, and an oddity, too, in his way. He is rather small of stature, or he seems small in comparison with the tall, powerful frames of most of his people. He has a somewhat large, bullet-shaped head, with a receding forehead, prominent ears, a widespreading nose and keen little black eyes that twinkle like beads on which the sun glints.

One of Mochotska's favorite pastimes is playing on the gorrah, a musical instrument resembling the bow of a violin, though used quite differently, and combining the properties of both a string and a wind instrument. It consists of a slender bow on which is a string made of the carefully dried intestine of some animal of the feline species. To the lower part of the string a flat piece of ostrich quill is attached so as to form part of the length of the string. On being applied to the lips this quill is made to vibrate by strongly inhaling and exhaling the air. The tones that result, while possessing considerable power, are nevertheless so sadly lacking in harmony as to give the impression to the civilized ear of more noise than music. Mochotska, however, judging by the constancy with which he and his instrument keep each other company, seems never to tire of its sounds, but, on the other hand, to enjoy them to the fullest extent.

Mochotska's manner of playing the instrument is—first to seat himself upon a flat rock, with his elbows resting upon his knees. He next puts one forefinger into his ear and the other into his somewhat expansive nostril. His object in this is doubtless to steady the head while in its labor of bringing forth the vigorous sounds with which he keeps up his solo all the way through.

Our young travelers are kindly received by this kraal of Bushmen, who have before had visits from the whites, one or two parties of hunters having stopped with them on their way from the southern country to that about Lake N'gami and the Zambezi River.

For a fair consideration and with Mochotska's aid our young friends are enabled to engage the services of one of the Bushmen as guide to the ford on the Zouga at which they desire to cross. He has also consented, in case they do not succeed in getting one of the Bayeiye, to accompany them all the way to Linyanti.

After remaining two days at the Bushmen village in order to rest themselves and their tired animals, they set forth again upon their journey. It is with very light hearts that they take up this portion of it, for now it seems to them that the worst of their trials, at least until Linyanti is reached, are over. Alas! they are but beginning.

Two days out from the Bushmen village, while crossing a stretch of woods several miles in extent, the cattle are all bitten by that dread pest of African explorers, the tsetse fly. The travelers now realize only too well that the ultimate death of the poor beasts is but a question of time, and while they hope and pray that they may yet reach Linyanti ere any serious consequences take place, still it is with many grave doubts and misgivings that they push forward on their way.

Soon after they have crossed the Zouga they witness the first signs of failing in the oxen that have been bitten. Three of them—two that are leaders and the very best they have—are attacked with staggering and blindness, and in another day have fallen by the way. In three days more two others are dead, the poor horse Khiva and two of the dogs; of the latter, Spoorer, Smike and Chitane alone remaining.

At the end of another three days all the oxen show signs of the fatal visit of the tsetse. Their jaws have begun to swell, their eyes and noses to run, while the poor brutes constantly shiver as though attacked with a sudden ague.

They have now only fourteen of the oxen left, and as this team is insufficient, even when at its best, to draw the huge, lumbering wagon, it is all the poor brutes can now do to stagger along with it, although it has been relieved of everything that could possibly be sacrificed. But even this proves of little avail, for in three days more only nine of the oxen are left, and all of these are in such a condition that they cannot so much as pull the running part of the wagon, with planks across it in place of the frame, which has been removed.

At this point our friends realize that the wagon and all such belongings as cannot be packed upon the backs of the donkeys must be abandoned. As to the poor oxen, their first thought is to kill them, in order to put them out of further suffering, but no one having the heart to undertake this, they are turned loose to fare as best they can. There is plenty of grass upon which they can graze, and water for them to drink, but that the poor brutes will soon be beyond the need of anything of the kind they know only too well.

The condition of our travelers, especially of the feminine portion, is now most distressing, for all have to fare alike in walking. Sometimes, however, the children get a lift upon one of the donkeys, or Ellie and Hope can in the like manner obtain a few miles of rest, but as the poor beasts have usually about all they can carry, the older girls never avail themselves of this means of relief for bruised and swollen feet or stiff and aching limbs as long as it is possible to keep from it. Sometimes, too, the faithful blacks make a litter of boughs, on which they insist on carrying the two young girls and the children for a part of the day at least.

All are now reduced to the single suit of clothing each wears, which in many instances has been brought to a most forlorn condition owing to the innumerable briers and thorny thickets through which several times since setting forth on foot they have had literally to fight their way. Often and often the way leads through woods so dense that every foot of it has to be cleared by the axes before they can make any progress at all. But for the thorns and briers there is no remedy, only the one alternative of pushing their way through them as best they can. As to shoes, not more than half of the party have any covering whatever for their feet, save as they can fasten about them bits of the skins of such animals as they now and then kill.

They manage, however, to secure food enough, such as it is, to keep them from actual starvation, and, though in the midst of such severe deprivations and acute sufferings, they nevertheless keep their hearts aglow with gratitude to God that their condition is no worse than it is. That he will ultimately bring them through it all their faith is as strong now as it has ever been in the sunniest hour of their trust amid the comforts of their old home in the wilderness. Many times now Ellie recognizes the mercy and wisdom of God in taking the little Louise unto himself ere these sorer trials were reached.

At length, after many and varied experiences, none of which it forms a part of our purpose to describe, and after having passed through several villages of natives, some of whom treat them very kindly and others again rather cruelly, and throughout every one of which experiences they are still graciously preserved by the same almighty Power that has taken note of every step of their way since the moment of their setting out, they come to that flat and marshy country that is completely enclosed by the rivers Chobe, Sonta, Mebabe, Tso, and Embara.

Here they find a most distressing state of affairs, for all these rivers having overflown their banks during the recent rains, and the floods having not yet subsided, the whole country as far as the eye can reach is one vast sheet of water. It is true that they are now on the bank of the Sonta, farther away from the worst of the overflowed country or that portion which the rivers named so completely enclose, but still it is bad enough as it is, and for the first few hours after reaching this, which seems an impassable barrier to their further progress, despair reigns supreme.

Doubtless it would not strike them with such overwhelming force were it not that they are completely reduced physically, for previous to reaching this inundated section they have toiled for many hours through a muddy expanse, in many parts of which the water has been ankle deep, with no way of avoiding it. Added to the water, the place is covered with a peculiar serrated grass that at certain angles cuts the flesh like a razor, and by immense walls of reeds, which, as they pass between them, so exclude the air as to produce a feeling of almost unbearable suffocation. Indeed, Hope faints completely away ere she has passed through more than two-thirds of the necessary distance, while Ellie and Henrietta both lose consciousness the moment the open space beyond is reached.

They are now in the most desperate and forlorn straits, for in addition to the terrible state of their clothing, faces, hands, knees and feet are cut and bleeding from the razor-like blades of grass.

On arriving at the inundated portion they are compelled to halt, and to wait until a raft can be constructed of such material as they have at hand. Fortunately, the carpenter's tools have not yet been abandoned.

Near this spot they are also fortunate in finding a deserted village, abandoned by the inhabitants on the approach of the flood, one or two of the huts of which, being at a greater elevation than the others, have escaped the ravages. These not only afford them shelter while awaiting the construction of the raft, but in them they also find a small stock of provisions—some dried game-flesh, a basket or two of cassava, some potatoes and a bag of pressed fruit.

Of the many obstacles met with in the building of the raft, and of the still greater difficulties encountered in the launching of it—the almost impenetrable walls of reeds, the tangled mats of low-growing rushes and the thick masses of papyrus interlaced with convolvulus with which the banks of the river are lined—it is not our purpose to speak. Neither have we the space to detail the many and trying experiences and narrow escapes of our friends in searching for the main channel of the Chobe, by means of which and of the raft, made as stout and serviceable as possible, they hope to reach Linyanti.

At length, after more than a week spent upon

this raft, during which their sufferings from heat and cold in turn, from hunger and from bloodthirsty attacks of huge mosquitoes, gnats, flies and other like pests, and during which time they also have a most thrilling experience with crocodiles and another with hippopotami, in both of which they come near losing their lives, and in which poor Spoorer does lose his life, they arrive at last in sight of the welcome outlines of the Makololo capital.

CONCLUSION.

THE town of Linyanti, capital city of the Makololo tribes, is reached by our young people, after many trying experiences and thrilling adventures, in the early morning of June 17, 187–, just six weeks from the time of setting out from the encampment in the desert. It is situated some miles higher up the river Chobe than the old one first visited by Livingstone in May, 1853. It stands upon a slight elevation that slopes toward the river, and, although the surrounding country is of so level a nature, it is nevertheless possessed of much scenery that is rich and picturesque.

The village is laid out in the form of a long street, at the end of which are clustered the chapel, the school-house, one or two workshops and the late dwellings of the missionaries, Mr. and Mrs.

Helmore, Mr. and Mrs. Mackenzie and Mr. and Mrs. Price, whose wholesale and untimely taking off through that dread scourge, African fever, forms one of the most depressing pages in the history of African missions.

It will be remembered by those familiar with the main incidents of Livingstone's African life that on leaving the Makololo for the east coast, whence he was expected to sail for England, they expressed a desire that a missionary might come and live with them, promising if the desire were granted to remove from the deadly swamps in the midst of which they were then residing to some healthier locality farther up the river. Rev. J. E. Chambliss, in his admirable *Life of Livingstone*, thus sums up the short and tragic history of the mission: "It had seemed very desirable to establish a mission among this people (the Makololo), because of the extent of their dominion, and because at their capital Christian teachers would be in constant intercourse with representatives of numerous tribes. Accordingly, the London Missionary Society, under whose auspices the exploration of their country had been effected, undertook the work of establishing a mission at the town of Linyanti, and appointed Rev. Halloway Helmore, who had been seventeen years a missionary among the Bechuanas, and associated with him Messrs. Mackenzie and Price. These younger men, accompanied by gentle and true-hearted wives, who ventured to hope that they could go where Mrs. Livingstone had gone, left England in June, 1858, and in July landed at the Cape. After many trying experiences the mission-party at last reached the scene of their appointment in February, 1860. In August of the same year, when Dr. Livingstone arrived, there was only the sad story of their efforts and a number of graves. They had come on the ground in the most unfavorable season, and almost from the time of their arrival were the victims of the prevailing fever of the place."

At the time of the arrival of our travelers, in June, 187–, there is no missionary at the village, many who doubtless would have come having been discouraged by the terrible calamity that has put such a complete and untimely ending to the labors of the six brave and zealous spirits. But as the Makololo have a serious intention of again removing their village to some healthier locality, there is strong probability that should they take this step the society will send them another pastor and other teachers, or it may be that some earnest and courageous young soul may be found to volunteer at the call of the Master to face even the dangers of this unhealthy locality. A coming at the proper season, so as to allow time for acclimation ere the fever period approaches, and the timely administering of plentiful doses of quinine, have a telling effect in the fight with the fever demon, as the steady flame of faith and the constant fire of ministerial zeal kept burning in the heart have much to do toward strengthening body as well as soul in the great combat.

In the mean time, however, much good is being done at Linyanti by two native teachers converted and educated through Dr. Livingstone's efforts, and by another brought by Mr. Helmore from Kuruman. These men keep up the good work in school-room and shop, and regularly on the Sabbath and twice during the week hold religious services in the chapel and the kotla.

The Linyanti reached by our travelers in June, 187–, numbers some fifteen hundred souls, quite a decrease from the population of the Linyanti visited by Livingstone in 1853. Then it was a large and populous settlement of between three thousand five hundred and four thousand souls. But the death of the great "lion chief," Sebituane, together with the weak governing powers of his son and successor, Sekeletu, through whom the tribe has been led into numerous hostile encounters with fierce and warlike neighbors and plunged into various disasters, has so reduced this once proud and strong people that much of their former greatness and glory has departed.

But that a measure of energy is still left is fully attested by the neatness, order and thrift visible throughout their capital town. Nearly all the huts, which are tidy and well constructed, have behind them ample gardens that stretch away on one side to the foot of a small wooded hill that has more the appearance of a large artificial mound than anything else, and on the other side to the banks of the river. In these gardens are cultivated maize, millet, pumpkins, onions, parsnips, potatoes, beans, peas and various other vegetables. A few young fruit trees and various banana, cocoanut and other trees are also scattered about.

Each hut has a low doorway in front, protected by a kind of veranda, while about this and extending some feet from the veranda is a circular court enclosed either with rush mats or a wattle hedge. In this court the fires are made for cooking or warming purposes, the food being cooked in fireproof clay pots of native manufacture.

The houses of the head-men, the mayor, court-herald, town-crier and other officials are constructed on a more pretentious plan, having square walls, high roofs and verandas that extend the entire distance of each side. About them are grassy walks, lined with rows of drooping willows, with here and there a palmetto or stiff-fronded palm.

As the raft containing our travelers, reduced through their many and varied disasters and terrible experiences to a state in which death seems far nearer than life, comes suddenly in sight of this cheering and inspiring place, more than one pair of lips give forth a cry of thanksgiving and joy.

The sound of a bell now ringing across the waters adds still further to the inspiration of the scene and to the gladness of their hearts. It is the first sound of anything approaching civilized life that has greeted their ears since that far-away happy time at their own mission-station of Lepelole. It is one of the days on which religious services are held by the native teachers, and the bell-tones that they have heard come from the belfry of the neat stone chapel at the upper end of the village.

The raft having been anchored at a convenient landing-place, they are preparing to disembark, when another sound greets them—a sound that awakens even deeper and more intense feeling than that of the chapel-bell has done. It is the sound of many native voices singing that grand Christian hymn, "Jesus, Lover of my soul," in the well-known Sichuana language.

As the sweet, solemn, pathetic harmony of the many richly swelling voices, joining with such force and fervor in the words of the moving old hymn, float down to them, the tears glisten in more than one pair of eyes, while Ellie and Hope, turning so as to face each other, clasp hands with feelings too deep and too varied for expression.

Ere they have advanced many steps up the slight incline toward the village several of the population, having caught sight of them, are now running forth to meet them.

In a little while, the news of their arrival having been carried to the chapel, they are surrounded, on reaching the foot of the broad street that passes through the village, by a large and fast-increasing assembly, many of the people forcibly gesticulating with their hands, others again asking questions as fast as they can open and shut their mouths, and all overcome by a curiosity none can conceal.

Having singled out the head-man, Mamosale by name, Cunnyngham addresses himself to him, and soon gives him an account of the party, together with the story of their wanderings since setting out from Lepelole, closing with a statement of their present sore straits and needs.

The old head-man proves the very soul of kindness and hospitality, and at the conclusion of Cunnyngham's narrative at once conducts them through the ranks of the congregated villagers, who respectfully make way for them to pass to the huts formerly occupied by the dead missionaries. Here they are at once provided with food, with vessels containing water for bathing purposes and with clothing. As the Makololos dress in what is very much of a civilized fashion, the men wearing fustian jackets and leather trousers and the women petticoats of various patterns, karosses and either fur caps or turbans made of handkerchiefs, there is no great difficulty in finding clothing of a suitable nature for each member of the party.

An hour or so later the old town-crier, Se-Pulenyane, with much state announces throughout the village the arrival of the party.

Mamosale's quick sympathy and ready show of

hospitality are but a foretaste of the warm and hearty welcome that is subsequently shown them on every side by this kindly and generous people. Every hour of their stay they feel increasing gratitude and joy in their hearts, while they do not neglect to return thanks to God for having led them to such a comfortable and hospitable place.

But as much as their hearts are gladdened by the Makololo, their joy is increased tenfold by the news they learn on the following day. A party of hunters from the Cape are now on the river in the vicinity of Linyanti—four white men with an attendant train of more than twoscore servants and bearers. It needs not the names of these white men, which Mamosale afterward calls, to carry to the hearts of our travelers the joyful conviction that they are no other than their old friends Captain Murray and Mr. Cumming, with *their* friends Captains Osgood and Saunders.

A goodly part of the effects of the hunters, including two large canoes and many supplies, are even now at Linyanti awaiting the return of their owners down the river, when the party expect to set off along the Zambezi for the east coast.

In a few days the good news is confirmed beyond a doubt by the arrival at Linyanti of Captain Murray, Mr. Cumming and their friends.

The meeting between the former and our young wanderers can much better be imagined than described. There is so much to be asked and answered on both sides that they sit up the first night of their meeting until nearly day-dawn recounting their many changing and exciting experiences.

There is no further doubt as to the course to be pursued by our young people in reaching the coast. The hunters are fully equipped with canoes, bearers and supplies for making the trip along the Zambezi to Quilamane. Indeed, they have already made it inland, transporting the canoes around the various rapids by means of their sturdy bearers. At Quilamane there is anchored the private yacht of Captain Osgood, waiting to take them to the Cape. From this point it will be an easy matter for our traveling friends to find passage for the States.

Jim will go with them, as it is Cunnyngham's design to have him educated that he may be able to act as a native teacher; Kamati will remain with the Makololos; Pitsane has attached himself to Captain Murray's party; while at a point on the Zambezi, Mazika will seek to make his way to a portion of his old tribe, now established in the mountains to the east of the Banyai country.

It does not form a part of the purpose of the author to describe the events that mark the journey from Linyanti to Quilamane. The task, so far as this volume is concerned, is finished with the recording of the arrival of our young people at the Makololo capital. Suffice it to say, that after many and varied experiences, some of them thrilling in the extreme, and others, again, of not great importance, and after having feasted their eyes to their fullest upon the wonderful Zambezi country, and having had many escapes from fierce and warlike tribes, they arrive at last safely at Quilamane, whence the yacht is taken for Cape Town. At this latter point their kind friends see them aboard a steamer bound for an American port.

Not long since I saw in a newspaper among the names of those accepted by the ———— Missionary Society for the work in Africa that of the Rev. Cunnyngham Blandford, the paper further stating that on the same vessel carrying the Rev. Mr. Blandford to his distant field would go out, as medical assistant, Dr. Pierce Lillington, and as teachers, the Misses Ellie Lillington and Hope Blandford.

Thus have the vows made amid the wilds of the African desert ripened into rich and fragrant fruit.

THE END.

www.ingramcontent.com/pod-product-compliance
Lightning Source LLC
Chambersburg PA
CBHW020320240426

43673CB00039B/874